CAMILLE CRIBARI LINEN

WOLFE *with an E*

An Episodic Journey through an Exceptional Life

— DEDICATION —

TO MY FATHER, WOLFE CRIBARI, one of 11 children of a 20th century family of Italian immigrants.

Born August 6th, 1903 in New York City to parents who had sailed away from Italy in January that same year. An "anchor baby," dad lived in suburban Mount Vernon, N.Y. for 63 years.

An eloquent, exceptional trial lawyer, Wolfe or Avvocato Cribari, is a legend in Westchester County courtrooms half a century after his untimely passing.

Through dad's own words in his well-preserved letters, speeches, recorded conversations, stories and singing voice, I found him again. Several Cribari family members, especially my two sisters, Donna and Carola, happily shared their own dad-memories.

My love of words and stories is a gift from my father. He read or told stories to me every bedtime for my entire childhood. Now I'm telling dad's story, not just for me and my family, but for you who will smile reading this as I did writing it.

This has been an odyssey of love and stories.

I now consider myself a story teller; an homage to my wonderful husband Lou Del Bianco who shares many of dad's artistic, creative talents and his kind, gentle nature. He is also an incredible storyteller.

The value and necessity of storytellers in the world is beautifully described in this prose-poem Scott Christiansen, a cousin on the Ankerson side of my family, sent me years ago as he took on the mission of storytelling for his family.

It inspired me to sit down and write...

Wolfe with an E

Published by Art of English

Picture credits: All photos, documents, letters, telegrams or postcards in this book are either public domain or the Cribari Family Collection, unless otherwise indicated. Some images have been cropped or touched-up for printing purposes, but have not been changed from the originals.

Image quality varies greatly due to the age and quality of the originals. Some will print better than others, and some may look great in the e-book but not as good in print. All were important in telling the story of Wolfe Cribari and were therefore included.

Cover and Book Design by James Woosley (FreeAgentPress.com)

First printed in April 2022.

ISBN: 979-8-9860294-0-5 (paperback)
ISBN: 979-8-9860294-1-2 (e-book)
ISBN: 979-8-9860294-2-9 (hardcover)

VID: 20220827

Practicing an art, no matter how well or badly,
is a way to make your souls grow, for heaven's sake.
Sing in the shower. Dance to the radio.
Write a poem to a friend, even a lousy poem.
Do it as well as you possibly can.
You will get an enormous reward.
You will have created something.

Kurt Vonnegut

They were trying to fit into a culture their
parents never experienced.

Camille Cribari

I'm sure of it. My father said so.

Camille Cribari

— CONTENTS —

INTRODUCTION — THE STORY TELLERS xi
PREFACE — SENTIMENTAL JOURNEY xiii

1 — WOLFE with an "E" 1
2 — DAD'S IMMIGRANT ROOTS 5
3 — NANA'S ADVICE TO CAMILA 7
4 — THE FAMILY LEGEND—NANA WAS RIGHT 11
5 — THE CRIBARI-MANES IMMIGRATION 13
6 — DAD'S FAMIGLIA 17
7 — SCENE ONE: MUSICAL ABOUT THE CRIBARI FAMILY 25
8 — EARLY EDUCATION 29
9 — "AMERICA, I LOVE YOU; YOU'RE LIKE A PAPA TO ME" 31
10 — AN ARTISTIC LEGACY: LOVE OF ACTING, MUSIC, AND THEATER . 39
11 — SCENE TWO: MUSICAL ABOUT THE CRIBARI FAMILY 41
12 — COMMUNITY PLAYERS STAR 45
13 — MRS TOMPKINS - MENTOR, MUSE...MORE? 51
14 — COLUMBIA COLLEGE SPORTS FAN 59
15 — WHAT WOULD YOU LIKE TO BE? SURPRISE! 63
16 — ENTER STAGE RIGHT: CAROLA ANKERSON 65
17 — CAREER CHOICES: THE LAW AND POLITICS 81
18 — SCENE THREE: MUSICAL ABOUT THE CRIBARI FAMILY 85
19 — FIRST CRIMINAL CASE MAKES INTERNATIONAL HEADLINES 91

20 — WOLFE & CAROLA—DIFFERENT WORLDS 99
21 — DISCOVERING ROOTS 103
22 — FAMILY TREES—ROOTS 111
23 — CAROLA AND WOLFE'S FIRST ARTISTIC COLLABORATION........115
24 — A MAN OF MANY WORDS 117
25 — DAD'S HOROSCOPE 1/26/39 121
26 — DECADES OF HOPE, LOSS AND CHANGE 125
27 — BROTHER LOVE 127
28 — THE PATRIARCH: BENIAMINO SALVATORE CRIBARI—
A GREAT AND GALLANT MAN 131
29 — SUGAR CUBES ON THE WINDOW SILL 137
30 — AND A LITTLE CHILD SHALL LEAD THEM 143
31 — DEFENDING PLAYLAND, CRYING AT HIS SUCCESS 145
32 — DADDY'S LITTLE GIRLS 151
33 — PARENTS, SIBLINGS, WIFE & CHILDREN 155
34 — WORLD WAR II ITALIAN-AMERICAN LAWYER 159
35 — "LIVE FOR YOUR COUNTRY" SPEECH 163
36 — STARS AND STRIPES SPOTLIGHTS CASE 167
37 — ON THE HOMEFRONT 169
38 — WAITING IN THE CAR AND OTHER FRUSTRATIONS 171
39 — DAD SETTLES DOWN 173
40 — BUILDING BRIDGES 181
41 — TRADITIONS CRIBARI STYLE 185
42 — DINNER TIME BATTLEGROUND 189
43 — DAD'S IN-LAWS–THE ANKERSONS 191
44 — WAITING FOR HEAVEN 197
45 — SHARING CHILDHOOD MEMORIES 201
46 — CHRISTMAS REVISITED 205
47 — RADIO DAZE...1940's 207
48 — CUTTING RECORDS–DAD'S FORTIES OBSESSION 211
49 — WORLD WAR II AT HOME & ABROAD 215
50 — SINGING PATRIOTIC SONGS OF WORLD WAR II 217

51 — EIGHT OUT OF TEN: CRIBARI FAMILY AT DOLLY'S WEDDING......223
52 — SPORTS ENTHUSIAST & ARDENT FAN......225
53 — WHAT WE DID FOR SUMMER VACATION......235
54 — DAD'S TRIAL SKILLS ATTRACT MEDIA ATTENTION......245
55 — WHEN WE WEREN'T FIGHTING, WE WERE SINGING...... 249
56 — DAD'S AUTOGRAPHS......255
57 — POST WAR PROSPERITY......259
58 — FAMILY VACATION/BUSINESS TRIP TO ITALY SUMMER 1953......263
59 — BACK TO NORMAL......279
60 — "BLESSED ART THOU AMONGST WOMEN" (1930-1966)......283
61 — BREAKING AWAY......287
62 — MARITAL MILESTONES......297
63 — EMPTY NESTERS......307
64 — "THE LAW" THROUGH DAD'S EYES...... 311
65 — MEDICAL & LEGAL PROFESSIONALS CLASH IN COURT......317
66 — PROFOUND LOSSES, HEARTENING GAINS......325
67 — FAMILY LOYALTIES ARE CHALLENGED......335
68 — THIRD TIME FATHER OF THE BRIDE......341
69 — CRIBARI FAMILY 2021: "UNCLE" WOLFE......345
70 — ONCE UPON A TIME THERE WAS...THE SIXTIES!...... 351
71 — NOW NONO......363
72 — FATHER OF A MOTHER......365
73 — WOLFE AND CAROLA's SECOND ACT...... 371
74 — SHIELDING HIS LOVED ONES......373
75 — A DREAM DEFERRED: DAD AS COLLEGE PROFESSOR......379
76 — THE MOST PAINFUL DAY......385
77 — TRIBUTES......391
78 — CLOSURE A HALF CENTURY LATER......395

IN MY FATHER'S HANDS...PERSONALITY TRAITS...... 405
ACKNOWLEDGEMENTS...... 407
ABOUT THE AUTHOR...... 409

— INTRODUCTION —

THE STORYTELLERS

***WE ARE THE CHOSEN.** In each family, there is at least one who seems called to find the ancestors, to put flesh on their bones and make them live again and to tell the family story and feel that somehow they know and approve.*

To me, genealogy is not a cold gathering of facts, but rather the breathing of life into all who have gone before. It involves pride in what our ancestors were able to accomplish and how they contributed to what we are today. It goes to respecting their hardships and losses, their never giving in or giving up, and their resoluteness to build a life for their family.

It is a deep pride and understanding that it was they who paved the way for us in so many ways so that we might be born who we are, so we remember them. With love and caring and scribbling each fact of their existence, because we are them and they are us.

So, I tell the story of my family hoping that one from the next generation will feel the same desire and take their place in the line of family storytellers.

Camille Cribari

Let this beautiful poem written by my sister Donna Cribari serve as a signpost for you, dear reader, to guide you through our dad's unique life journey.

My father walked thro' barren lands and smiling
blessed them
He laid his hands on hearts and they stirred
Touched minds with his wit and words
Brought aliveness everywhere with his eyes
And left the world crying for his lifeness

— PREFACE —

SENTIMENTAL JOURNEY

RECENTLY MY HUSBAND LOU drove my daughter Dana and me down to Mount Vernon for a Sunday visit to the place where my life began. It was a truly exhilarating and inspirational afternoon; my mind was already focused on writing dad's story. Although I had been back to my birthplace many times over the years, this visit had a much more powerful impact.

We drove past the places that dominated the first two decades of my life. As we went up Broad Street hill, the first place dad's family, the Benjamino Cribaris, made a home in this country, I was amazed at the drastic change in just the five years since I was there last. On the very spot where my grandparents lived and worked, the place where my grandfather established a successful ice cream factory, two ten story buildings were rising over the once residential haven. I felt personally invaded. Dad would have felt even worse.

We turned right on Gramatan Avenue, the main street that runs from residential Fleetwood to downtown Mount Vernon, still the busy business thoroughfare I remembered. "That's where the Fleetwood Bakery was," "that's where we went for ice cream": sense memories galore.

Down the hill to the Circle, the heart of the city, to the places I had recently been researching, places where my father lived, worked and played a century ago: The Community Church where my parents met in a Community Theater group, Hartley Park where there is a plaque in honor of dad's brother, Mario; the old Mount Vernon High School building where dad's teachers recognized his intellectual and verbal gifts, encouraged him to pursue higher education and recommended him for a scholarship to Columbia College which he received for all four years.

Now we were in the heart of the big city, overwhelming in its crowded streets and urban sprawl. Of course, I expected to see Proctor's Theater where dad used to drop me, my sisters and friends, every week for the children's Saturday matinee. Sadly, there are no more downtown movie theaters.

This is my grandfather Ankerson's drugstore on Fourth Avenue, Mount Vernon as it was in the 1940's. We found the exact spot across the railroad bridge, on Fourth Avenue, on the left side.

Gustav Ankerson was a respected leader in the community. How I loved to go to Nono Ankie's drugstore, jump up on a tall stool at the soda fountain and sip a chocolate ice cream soda.

One time, Nono let me go to the back of the store behind the curtain where the salespeople took breaks. We drove past the biggest theater ever, or so I thought at the time, Wood Auditorium, where as an elementary student I performed in the annual city-wide school celebration of the arts which presented the different cultures of Mount Vernon's student population in song and dance. I remember seeing fellow students dressed in Irish costumes, German leiderhosen. It deeply influenced my lifelong belief that the arts are what connect us best.

When I got home and googled Wood Auditorium I happily discovered that Mount Vernon school administrators are trying to re-establish that city wide arts event. I hope they do.

We found the building on First Street where dad had his law office; it ran parallel to the New York /New Haven, now Metro North train tracks. Dad's office was on the same block as the Eastchester Savings Bank where his father-in-law, nono Ankie, was a longtime trustee. I remember when I was old enough, I would walk to dad's office from the Public Library and wait for dad to finish seeing his clients so we could drive home for dinner together.

Across the train tracks from dad's office I saw the street where a home-style German restaurant used to be; it was where nono Ankie took us out to eat once a week for many years. It must have been after nana Ankie died because he was always alone. I remember the German egg noodles and apple strudel for dessert.

Next we backtracked to Fleetwood to search for the different family homes

My sense memory kicked in; I became a human GPS.

First, nono and nana Ankie's house, 138 Overlook Street. The house looked so small, overwhelmed by the lines of cars parked on both sides of the narrow two way street. Where were the wide-open sidewalks my sisters and

I paraded down to celebrate VJ Day, costumes and musical instruments provided by nana?

Still there, but they're un-parade-able.

Except for the 1920's-1930's style automobile, this is 138 Overlook Street the way I remember it. I found this picture in mom's keepsakes.

Onto the Cribari house, 468 North Fulton Avenue, blocked from full view by a huge yellow truck in its too narrow driveway. Memories from my life as a single parent emerged as we sat in front of the house where my young daughters and I lived for four years. Saints Peter and Paul, the church I was married in is across the street; so is Pennington School where my daughter Denise and I both went.

A pleasant surprise, Pennington is a bigger, better looking version of what I remember. I loved that school in the 1940's when I went there and then in the 1960's when Denise did. It looks like the Mount Vernon community still does.

On the other side of Pennington is the house where my first boyfriend Greg lived. "Turn left," I said, "I've got to find my cousin Roberta's house." One of many interesting coincidences in my family history, Greg and Roberta got married and their son Paul is a friend of my daughter Dana's.

She called Paul on her cell as we passed his father's, then his mother's house: another full circle.

It was easy to find the last house on our tour. The route to 317 Claremont Avenue was indelibly etched in my memory because I walked home from school that way every day for years. We weren't supposed to go to Pennington, we lived in a different district, but somehow dad pulled strings so we did.

Oh no, it's changed; our beautiful white house, it's yellow, garish. From its original Tudor, white stucco with dark brown wood-trim, to a mustardy yellow with light brown wood trim, ugh! A once wide open, tree-lined neighborhood was crowded with parked cars.

Let me remember it as I did when I wrote about that beautiful house at the turn of the century. *"A line of graceful white birches used to be on the front edge of the stone wall. They disappeared decades ago. I still see their silvery ghosts."* Here is dad and his girls amidst the beautiful birches we all loved.

I still miss those birches. Oh, how we loved to go up in the swing!

So many images arise… The long, narrow black asphalt driveway on the right side of the house curves right up into the one and a half car garage. There was a basketball hoop over the garage door, my younger sisters' delight. Not there? Or is it? I can't see from the street. I stare at that narrow driveway down which I coasted on my two-wheeler. Down which at sixteen I learned to back the family car, very carefully, just clearing our wall on one side and our neighbor's on the other. Narrow driveways still give me a nervous chill.

I long to ring the doorbell and ask the present owner permission to go into the backyard. So many memories, a huge, powerful rough-barked tree; I think it's an ash. One low-lying branch of its mighty, unreachable branches bears three little girls who reveled in "*Oh, how I love to go up in the swing, up in the air so blue. Oh, I do think it the pleasantest thing ever a child can do.*" Dad loved to recite from Robert Louis Stevenson's Child's Garden of Verses."

I know there's a huge, grey-pitted **meteor** right next to that tree even though it's hidden from my view by its massive trunk.

Yes, there's a meteor in our backyard! A meteor! It's definitely a piece of a meteor and it landed in our backyard thousands, maybe millions of years ago."

I'm sure of it. My father said so.

Camille's House
Mount Vernon, New York, U.S.A

HAIKU BY CAMILLE

There's the house, slow down!
That's the one I grew up in.
White stucco, brown trim.

Graceful white birches
Red, pink azaleas in spring
My phantom vision.

The picture window.
Dad's den, the "new" addition
Still there, yes, still there

I wrote this Haiku with my ESL students several years ago. They were asked to write haikus then draw their childhood homes. It's a wonderful pathway into childhood memories. Try it.

— 1 —

WOLFE WITH AN "E"

VOLFANGO FULVIO CRIBARI BECAME Wolfango, then Wolfgang before I was born. Volfango is the Italian form of Wolfgang. Dad was always troubled by his given name and often talked about changing it, but of course he never did. Cribari legend has it that my grandparents chose a godfather for each one of their eleven children. The godparent was given the unique privilege of naming his godchild. If you didn't like your name you couldn't blame your parents; convenient, yes?

Here are the Cribari family names in age order; Vittorio Emmanuel (Victor) Rosina (Rose), Volfango Fulvio (Wolfe), Hugo, Arnold, Romeo (Ray), Ermito Mario (Mario), Guido, Olga and Cornelia (Dolly). My grandparents' names are Eugenia and Benjamino Salvatore.

I've always thought that part of dad's success as an Italian American professional in mid 20th century America was because of his unique, unforgettable first name. Wolfe Cribari is an iconic name in Westchester County courtrooms to this day. When dad tried to legally change it to W.Edward the judge refused. He told dad it was because *everyone* already knew him as Wolfe.

"Wolf with an 'e'" led me to google *"The Social Wolf: Living with Wolves August 10, 2021.* What I found stunned me; so many of dad's outstanding social characteristics are shared by his wolf brothers. *"The alpha male wolf has quiet confidence, self-assurance: he knows what he needs to do and what's best for his pack (family)"* An incredible description of dad's alpha male lifestyle.

"He leads by example and has a ***calming effect*** *on his clan."* His nieces and nephews still speak of dad with warmth and love. *"The alpha male wolf devotes quality time to pack pups, whether wrestling or nurturing the little ones. We assume this is the female wolf's job, not so. Females run the show: where to travel, when to hunt, when to rest. Alpha male wolves show respect for females and share responsibilities."* Sounds like my parents Wolfe and Carola. *"No two species are more alike behaviorally than wolves and humans."* Dad would love these wolf-words that also describe my well-named father: *"territorial, playful, loyal, caring, and above all devoted to family."*

To complete the analysis of dad's name I am following his example and *reading the dictionary*. Mom said dad often just sat and read it. He had a library size one in his den; it was always open. I basically ignored it even though one of my favorite hobbies when I was ten or so was to play librarian in dad's library. I even created our own card catalogue from his massive book collection. Dad was thrilled I wanted to be around books even though I didn't like reading them yet.

Today I googled *adjectives, that begin with the letter "e"* to describe aspects of dad's character with the final letter of Wolfe. *Here are my favorites*...

> **e** is for *ebullient – bubbling with excitement.* When dad was into something, he was really into it. You heard it in the tone of his voice, saw it in his dramatic gestures, and the sparkle in his eyes.

e is for *eloquent – well spoken.* Dad kept copies of many speeches he gave to different organizations on a variety of topics. His language, depth of information and historic perspective create the epitome of this word's meaning.

e is for *empathetic – able to share in and understand someone else's feelings.* As evidenced in dad's reactions to family issues in correspondence and his summations to the jury, this quality shines through as it did in life.

e is for *exceptional – better than anything similar.* Dad's mentors, peers, clients and family agree he was one of a kind. In his obituary he was called a Renaissance man for his wide range of interests and expertise.

e is for *entrancing – very charming and interesting.* I believe dad developed this trait in his acting days; he was definitely both. Some people have one without the other: charming, not interesting; interesting, not charming.

Dad also had two other **e** traits that are rarely combined in one person: ***elegant*** (*graceful and poised*) and ***endearing*** (*cute and lovable)*

This biography is chronologically constructed through ***episodes.***

— 2 —

DAD'S IMMIGRANT ROOTS

AS A LIFELONG LANGUAGE arts teacher who continues to teach foreign born adults ESL (*English as a Second Language*) in a Zoom classroom, I've always searched for new ways for them to learn together and to feel empowered in expressing their thoughts and dreams in a second language. I often urge students to time-travel with a beloved ancestor and tell his/her story. That journey back through time always takes them into new and uniquely creative places and perspectives. I finally found the time to "practice what I preach."

A former ESL student and friend, Vania Amadeu, sent me these words of Elias Canetti, a Nobel prize winner for literature, 20 years ago. I was intrigued and kept them with dad's papers. They have served me well in this venture. Obrigada, Vania!

> *It is necessary to visit our people who have passed away, find them, without it, they lose themselves with amazing speed.*
>
> *When we re-meet them in their own place, they recover their lives. Suddenly, we remember everything that we assume has been forgotten regarding them, we listen to their words, we touch their hair, we see ourselves reflected in the brightness of their eyes.*

Before we had never been sure of their eyes' color, now we can recognize them without hesitation.

Maybe everything in them is more intense now than when they were alive.

These words triggered memories of nana Cribari's house on a quiet, tree-lined suburban street. Nana and her husband, Beniamino, immigrated to the U.S. at the turn of the 20th century, They lived in New York City for a year and moved to Mount Vernon in 1903, the year my father was born. They subsequently had **seven** more children. I'm sure the unsanitary conditions and potential danger of raising children in an overcrowded lower Manhattan tenement caused their move out of the city into the then bucolic suburbs.

Baby Wolfe

— 3 —

NANA'S ADVICE TO CAMILA

HERE'S A MONOLOGUE I wrote several years ago to try and recreate an actual conversation I had with Nana when I was a very young wife and the mother of three daughters, ages 1,3,5. Nana was in her early 80's as I am now. She is speaking to me at her son Wolfe's request. In typical dad fashion, he asked someone else, in this case his mother, to try and convince me to limit the size of my growing family. Nana never lost her very thick Italian accent.

> *Iffa knew then whata know now, a never woulda had all those kids, You hear me, Camila? A wassa justa you age when we got marry. A leava ma familia in Calabria anna we come to New York City. Ma, it wasn't the same for me. You know whatta mean? My father was a bigga man in Falconara, the mayor. Alora, the tears when me and Beniamino leeva for America..*
>
> *Ma America wassa da land a make a success. So many Italians come-a here. We no afraid a hard work, everybody helpa each other. Cuggini, gomare, so many paisani.*
>
> *Ma-shu de first years wassa bad. We didna speak English so good. There wassa plenty jobs, but no good pay. We hadda two keeds; Victor, Rosa, My beautiful baby Arthur, he die een Calabria afora we come America. A hadda leava ma home anna de bad feelings. Ma Calabria, dat's where you father was conceived, in Italy. Maybe dat's why he's so special. Un vero Italiano!*

Den we decid-a get outa big city. We tooka chance and move-a Mount Vernon.

Some friends live in Fleetwood. We come-a 'ere anna see how clean eet was, farms anna trees all-over dissa place. So peaceful.

A said before a never woulda had so many kids, but I guess God wanna dat-away, a new baby every two years 'til Guido. Before a knew we had Rosa and seven boys. Tanka God we hadda big house on Broad Street, but very crowded widda eight kids.

So wha 'appen? Two more afta Guido, girls, managia!

In Italy, no problem, everybody know. Ma in Fleetwood, wha happen ? Ma boys are men, dey wanna de own beesi-ness, no de fadda's. Ma our boys never lose-ah la famiglia, America change-ah everybody so fast, make-ah me e-scared.

Beniamino, he love-ah thees country, always. America, thees, America that! I love-America too, but no like-a ma husband. Italians come-ah here to find gold inna streets, no Beniamino. He hadda dream, always he keepa hees dream. But woman she have-ah keep close-ah home, cooking, cleaning anna take-ah care bambini. No time for dreaming.

Beniamino and me, we fight alla time. No fistah fights, justah scream. Too much noise, too much-a noise; sometime ah think ah won, but nobody win. Ah wassa Democrat, he wassa Repub-lee-cin, Eh, you know what make-e heem so mad? Ah senda ma wedding ring to Italy for Mussolini. Your grandfather he went-ah crazy dat time.

But my husband he wassa good man, people take advantage your grandfather. Eet drive-a me crazy. Your father he love-ah him so much. He's just like him with heesa dreams. Everybody want you father helpa dem an he always try, justa like Beniamino. I feel sorry, but I canna change.

When-a Victor take over Beniamino's ice cream business, what a mess. Beniamino knew he couldna run the business, but he let him try. We couldna afford to pay anyone to work in factory, justa family work, boys and girls.

De olda ways didna work in America. Ah teenk-a old ways wuzza right, but no Beniamino. Always, America right, Imma wrong. Ma now heesa gone, he die when you justah leetle baby.

Camila, listen to me. Three babies is enough. Donna be estupida like you Nana.

— 4 —

THE FAMILY LEGEND—NANA WAS RIGHT

Eugenia Manes Cribari, Nana Cribari to me, was always reminding her children that they were related to the notorious Albanian hero Prince Scanderbeg. I heard the name over and over again in my childhood during uncle Ray's incessant teasing of his mother. As I dug into my ancestors' roots I discovered that nana was indeed descended from that powerful medieval Albanian leader.

Here's the "Family Legend" as it might have been told if nana had better command of the English language. She was right, Uncle Ray!

> *Many generations ago, seven families fled Albania to escape a Turkish invasion. These were royal families, people of wealth and importance and they feared their conquerors would follow. Two of the seven families, Musacchio and **Manes**, had blood ties to the Albanian nobleman, Scanderbeg*
>
> *The seven families sailed around the boot of Italy and up that country's western coast to a point near the village of San Lucido. Beaching their boat, the families began life in a new land. The date of that migration was 1476.*
>
> *Then one day they were dancing in the meadow. They looked to sea and spotted Turkish sails. Fearful of discovery, the seven families moved*

> *further into the hills until they came to a large rock. Circling over the rock was a falcon, so they named their town Falconara and built their church upon that rock.*

A second authority on the subject, Signora Menina Manes who at the time, 1983, was an elementary school teacher in Falconara, said the Scanderbeg story was part of the curriculum she taught the village children. Menina's father Settimio, who was mayor of Falconara at one time, became interested in preserving the story of the village founding. He wrote a manuscript about it, *Cenno Storica*. Roughly speaking the title means "Historical Illusion." This is the author's way of saying that the legend of the seven families – as fascinating as it was – was nevertheless a legend. Cenno Historica has been translated into English and is the best, most precise summary of the founding of Falconara.

— 5 —

THE CRIBARI-MANES IMMIGRATION

HERE'S SOME HISTORIC DATA to set the scene for the Cribari-Manes family's first American home on New York City's "streets of gold."

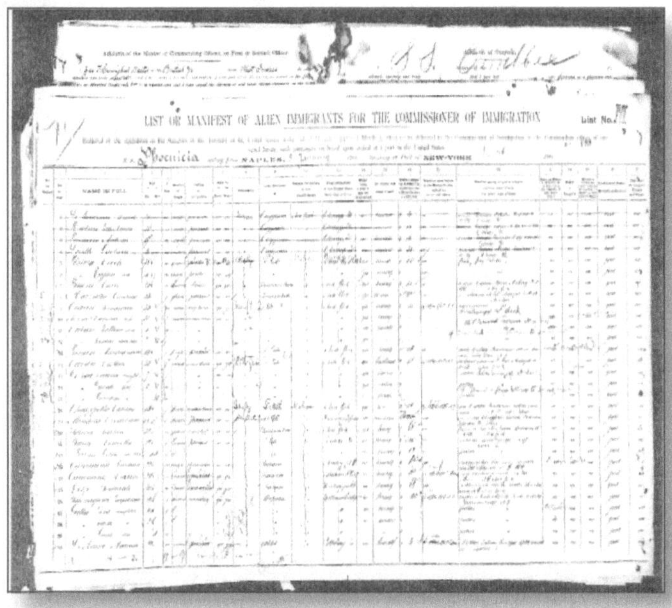

LIST OR MANIFEST OF ALIEN IMMIGRANTS FOR THE COMMISSIONER OF IMMIGRATION

S.S. Phoenicia ... NAPLES ... NEW-YORK

LIST OR MANIFEST OF ALIEN IMMIGRANTS FOR THE COMMISSIONER OF IMMIGRATION…MANIFEST OF S.S. PHOENICIA JANUARY 1903

Eugenia Manes, wife, and Beniamino Cribari came to America on the S.S. Phoenicia which sailed from Naples, Italy on January 9, 1903 and arrived at the Port of New York on January 26, 1903. They endured a seventeen day voyage in mid-winter Atlantic weather conditions. With them were their two children, Vittorio (Victor) Cribari, son, almost 5 and Rosina (Rose) Cribari, daughter, almost 3. Eugenia was two months pregnant with dad who was born August 6, 1903. Dad was what we would call an "anchor baby" today.

> *"The wave of immigrants who arrived between 1880-1924 found overcrowded tenements that had only been made taller to accommodate the newcomers, creating safety concerns. In fact conditions worsen during this period. Lack of running water, garbage piled up on streets, inability to launder clothes triggered spread of disease such as cholera, smallpox, typhoid and tuberculosis."*

No one in dad's family ever talked about their parents' reasons for leaving their homeland. Maybe it was because their second son, Arthur, had died there, nana and nono probably never knew what caused Arthur's death. Nana never wanted to go back to Falconara until dad convinced her to go thirty years later.

The choice to travel across the ocean in mid-winter must have been because the fare was cheaper. I'm sure they didn't go first class. What I do know is that they had two young children with them, Victor and Rose. Nana was pregnant with dad, which probably helped cause her to be more seasick than her family.

All their possessions were in a huge black trunk which was undoubtedly kept in the baggage hold. I have that 100+ year old trunk in my living room. Where did they keep their daily necessities? What were their meager cabins like? I can't imagine such conditions.

Then how did nana feel leaving the ship and walking through tumultuous New York crowds with two young children grasping her hands? Frightened and confused; not what she expected in the land of freedom and opportunity.

At best, life in New York City at the beginning of the 20th century was a culture shock for the record number of immigrants, 8,795,386, who arrived at Ellis Island. The city already had a population of 3, 400,00, a far cry from the Calabrese countryside nana and nono left behind.

Dad was born in New York City on August 6, 1903; the same year the family moved to the "suburbs," out of harm's way.

— 6 —

DAD'S FAMIGLIA

THE FIRST HOME FOR Wolfango Fulvio, third son of the Beniamino Cribari family was a house on Broad Street in the Fleetwood section of Mount Vernon. The house is no longer there.

That house provides the setting for a musical I started writing several years ago about dad's family. The characters and scenes I've included in this biography provide playful glimpses of an Italian immigrant family before World War II. First the large cast of characters:

CAST OF CHARACTERS
THE BENIAMINO CRIBARI FAMILY 1900-1930

EUGENIA: Late forties, small delicate boned woman. Independent in spirit dependent on her husband and children. Life in a new country with different social mores challenges her old-world values. She has little time for herself. Loves to cook, listen to opera.

BENIAMINO: Early fifties, powerfully built. Strong character, passionate and often in conflict with his wife's ideas politically. Devoted to his son, Wolfe, the embodiment of his American dream, who in turn adores him. Very expressive in Italian, not so in English.

WOLFE: Early twenties. In his last year of college, ready for law school. Ahead of his time, an idealist. Slender and physically energetic. Expressive eyes and hands. Totally dedicated to the welfare of his family and his goal to become a professional.

VICTOR: Late 20's, oldest son. Self-sacrificing, but often at odds with his domineering father. Smoldering religiosity which appears in contrast to the worldly priests he encounters. Dedicated to his mother and his younger brother Wolfe.

HUGO: Early twenties, rakish, witty. Dark-skinned like his father, sensual. Always involved with a woman or two. A wheeler-dealer. A great sense of humor with a charm that attracts the ladies.

ROSE: Mid-twenties, going steady with a non-Italian, hard working Irishman. Works at a routine office job, much of her free time is spent helping her family which she occasionally resents. Oldest daughter, surrogate mother care-giver.

ARNOLD: Late teens, slender and physically energetic. Just finishing high, going to college following in brother Wolfe's footsteps. Likes being involved in Hugo's schemes. Ladies man, appealing personality.

ROMEO: Mid-teens, a little chubby and attached to his mother. Neither an athlete nor a scholar. Great sense of humor, loves to pull pranks and tease. Likes to dance. A typical teen, "escapes" by sleeping a lot.

MARIO: Early teens, handsome, generous, often insecure. Sports are all for him and his younger brother Guido. Constantly seeking approval of his father. One of his mother's "babies." Protective of siblings.

GUIDO: Early teens, youngest of seven brothers. A combination of Rose's shyness, Mario's athletic prowess, Arnold and

Hugo's charm, Victor's seriousness and Wolfe's sensitivity. A tag-along to Mario and a charming nuisance for his older siblings.

OLGA: Ninth child, the child Nana is pregnant with in first scene

DOLLY: Tenth child, born after the time in which this play is set.

Patriarch Beniamino Cribari working near his Fleetwood home.

Here's the trunk nana Cribari brought to America. It's in my living room.

Nana with her two youngest daughters, Olga & Dolly.

Nana and Nono Cribari at their home on Broad Street, Mount Vernon. N.Y, aka Fleetwood. An Easter Sunday morning sometime in the mid-1930's.

If your nearest Drug or Confectionery Store

cannot supply you with

Savoy Ice Cream

COME TO OUR ICE CREAM PARLOR AND PARTAKE
OF A DELICIOUS DISH OF

Savoy Ice Cream

For the home as dessert, for bridge parties, school or social functions of any sort, just phone and we will deliver to your home this real treat.

Savoy Ice Cream Company

14-16 WEST BROAD STREET,

MOUNT VERNON, N. Y.

PHONES—OAKWOOD 9378, HILLCREST 4157

Right: Advertisement for Savoy Ice Cream Company 14-16 West Broad Street, Mount Vernon, N.Y. Nono's successful ice cream manufacturing company which was located next door to his home during the 1920's and 1930's

The Savoy Ice Cream flyer reads: *If your nearest Drug or Confectionery Store cannot supply you with Savoy Ice Cream come to our ice cream parlor and partake of a delicious dish of* **Savoy Ice Cream.**

For the house as dessert, for bridge parties, school or social functions of any sort, just phone and we will deliver to your home this real treat.

Savoy Ice Cream Company 14-16 WEST BROAD STREET, MOUNT VERNON, N.Y. PHONES OAKWOOD 9378 HILLCREST 4157

What an accomplishment for nono, a recent immigrant. I wonder who wrote the advertising copy for him; it was probably dad, he was the family wordsmith.

SHOP IN FLEETWOOD

Prompt, Courteous Service — Shop With the Finest Stores In Mount Vernon

Official Merchants Association Directory—Clip this directory and hang in a convenient place and save for future reference.

Automobile Dealers

AUBURN SALES AND SERVICE
FLEETWOOD GARAGE
Volpi Brothers, Inc.
AUTO REPAIR and STORAGE
10 West Broad Street
Hillcrest 3957 - Oakwood 1150
Mount Vernon, N. Y.

BANKS

FLEETWOOD BANK
Broad and Locust Streets
Mount Vernon
Opposite the Fleetwood Station

BAKERIES

Phone Hillcrest 4241
W. BRUST, Prop.
Fleetwood Bakery and Restaurant
Pastries of All Kinds
Birthday, Wedding and Special Made Cakes
564 Gramatan Ave.
Near Broad Street
Mount Vernon, N. Y.

BARBERS

Phone Oakwood 2679
James D'Auria
Fleetwood Barber Shop & Beauty Parlor
"Where the Promise is Performed"
Ladies and Children's Hair Bobbing a Specialty
574 Gramatan Avenue
Mount Vernon, N. Y.

BUTCHERS

"Conscientious Service"
The Fleetwood Market
James H. Braun, Prop.
We are the oldest established market in Fleetwood and invite your patronage.
Choice meats, fish and poultry.
Oakwood 5946. Prompt deliveries.
556 GRAMATAN AVENUE

COAL

Let Us Assume Your Heating Problems.
Telephone Oakwood 2871
Frank Cerchia
REAL ESTATE
General Insurance
703 Locust Street
Opp. Fleetwood Station
Mount Vernon, N. Y.

COATS—DRESSES

Fleetwood Dress Shop
Misses' and Women's Coats, Dresses and Hosiery
L. B. CAHILL
45 Grand Street
Mount Vernon, N. Y.
Oakwood - 2011

DRUGGISTS

...eetwood's First and Leading Drug Store
FLEETWOOD PHARMACY
L. Adler, Chemist
Phone Hillcrest 2422
562 Gramatan Ave., Cor. Broad St.
Mt. Vernon, N. Y.

DRUGGISTS

Free Delivery Everywhere
Try Our Drug Store First
Phone Your Wants
John B. Maffay's Pharmacy
20 Years a Registered Pharmacist
Opposite Fleetwood Station
Mt. Vernon, N. Y.
Phones Hillcrest 4272-4273
Quality - Service - Satisfaction

FRUIT MARKET

Gramatan Fruit Market
Choice Fruit and Vegetables
376 Gramatan Avenue
Mount Vernon, N. Y.
Oakwood 7847
D'Matteo & Triano, Props.

GARAGES

Our new telephone is

GROCERS

Gristede Bros.
Superior Grocery Stores
Gramatan Ave., and Broad St.
Near Fleetwood Station
Mt. Vernon, N. Y.
Tel. Oakwood 4614-4615
H. VOIGHTS, Mgr.

Telephones Oakwood 7222-7259
The Park View
GROCERY and DELICATESSEN
Fresh Fruit and Vegetables
A. KNOPP, Proprietor
47 West Grand St.
Mount Vernon, N. Y.

Phone Oakwood 7044
Orders Promptly Delivered
Fleetwood Dairy and Delicatessen
Choice Dairy and Grocery Products
228 Gramatan Avenue
Mount Vernon, New York

HARDWARE

The Fleetwood Hardware Co.
Theodore P. Schoen, Prop.
Dure Paints—Housefurnishings
Electrical Supplies—Tools
Glazing—General Repairs
Telephone Oakwood 4229
378 Gramatan Avenue

ICE CREAM

Visit our new Ice Cream Parlor at 16 WEST BROAD STREET
If your nearest store cannot supply you with
Savoy Ice Cream
come to our parlor.
High class chocolates
A complete line of smokers supplies
Phones Hillcrest 4157 - 1685-W
Oakwood 9378

SHOE REPAIRING

Telephone Oakwood 4380
Grand Garden Apartments
Sassonia Shoe Repairing Co.
Shoe Shine Parlor
Shoes Repaired—Hats Cleaned
Genuine Materials and Workmanship Guaranteed
Satin Shoes Dyed
Personal Service Our Specialty
All We Ask Is A Trial
691 Locust Street
Near Fleetwood Station
Mount Vernon, N. Y.

TAXIS

Stand—Fleetwood Pharmacy
Hillcrest 2422-3932
Office—Hillcrest 3062
C. A. MARSH
Fleetwood TAXI Service
Service Day and Night
44 Crary Avenue
Mount Vernon, N. Y.

Oakwood 0777
Holbrook Hall Taxi Service
BONDED
Cor. Gramatan and Fleetwood Aves.

Tailors-Furriers

If you desire high class workmanship plus prompt service at reasonable prices, just phone
Hillcrest 1687
Holbrook and Westchester Garden Tailors, Cleaners, Dyers and Furriers
445 and 472 Gramatan Ave.
"for men and women who know."
PHIL WEISS, Prop.

Morton Cleaners

SCENE ONE: MUSICAL ABOUT THE CRIBARI FAMILY

The Cribari's Broad Street home and the wooded field known as Schusser's Farm across the street. Suburban New York 1920's

A split set: stage R is a front porch, a flight above street level of the three story house. Stage L is a field, empty space. Impressions of the rest of the house are extended walls, props upstage of the main set that fade off into blackness.

WOLFE has just learned that his mother is pregnant again, it is her ninth child. He is shocked and angry. He *dashes out of house, jumps off porch, and frantically runs off L.* EUGENIA *enters from the same direction, calling after him.*

EUGENIA:

Wolfango, Wolf, you no letta me feenish. Vieni qui . comma back ere. NOW!

(*to others off R)* Victor, Hugo, Mario, getta you brother. He's gonna inna da woods. (*HUGO enters*) Tell imma coma backa talka me. *(pushes HUGO off as MARIO enters.)*

VICTOR:

(From offstage R.) Why don't you leave him alone, ma? Let him go. Maybe he wants to be alone.

HUGO:

(Starting off L) Alone? Why's he so special? Alone? In this house? Hey, Wolfe, come back, who the hell do you think you are? I'll find him, ma. *(yelling)* Wolfe, *fer* Chrissakes, come back here... *(Exits running)*

MARIO:

(Running after HUGO) Hey, Hughie, I'll find him for you. Can I drive the truck tomorrah if I find him? Wait up. *(Bumps into his father Beniamino who enters R)*

Oops, oh hi, pop! (*Exits running)*

EUGENIA:

(*walks out on porch, sees Beniamino*) Ai, Beniamino, when dey's a problem you no here. Imma bad guy again. I tolla Wolfango about the baby. He yella me anna run away. I send Hugo, Mario go find him!

BENIAMINO:

(Interrupts her with a loud, piercing whistle. Both he and Eugenia wait almost nonchalantly for the return of HUGO and MARIO which is immediate.

HUGO:

(Out of breath, pushing MARIO ahead of him as a shield) We saw him, pop, he was headed for Schusser's field. I coulda caught him, but you whistled.

MARIO:

Some of the guys were starting up a game already, pop. Can I go? They're choosing up sides. Is it all right, pop? Ma? Huh?

BENIAMINO:

Go inside, tutte due! Washa you hands for dinner. *(Both boys look at their mother, hesitate slightly)* Vai!!! *(They run into the house)* Eugenia, Why you always take-ah tings in you own hands? I tella you I talka to him. Issa betta I tella him. (*He puts his arm around her, they go up to the porch as the lights fade and half the set disappears in darkness)*

WOLFE:

(Runs on from UL and falls on his knees LC) Why? Oh God, why now? They're too many of us already! *(Strikes ground with his fist in anger)* Too many! Too many wops! (*Sneering sarcasm*) Guinea bastards, they throw their pants across the bed and nine months later! (*Laughs cynically*) God! They're right, they're right. Breeders, that's all we're good for, guinea breeders. For what? To be ground up and served as... meatballs!! (*a manic laugh*)

How could they do this? Now, of all times. Just when I got the scholarship to Columbia and ...She said God wanted it this way. What way? What does God have to do with it? Sweet Jesus, (*looks up to heaven*) if you want another wop, send it to Lily and Pierre. *(Looking up to heaven*) What could Jesus possibly want with another wop? Jesus, hah! An only son! He sure had it good. Father Mike told her God wants a new soul, another *(sneers)* Catholic. It's easy for him to say how great it feels to be part of a big, happy family. He comes here once a week to eat ma's spaghetti marinara, smoke pop's cigars, drink his brandy and leave. **God** wants mom to have another baby? Really! What hypocrites! How can mom fall for it? She's no fool. Pop hasn't seen the inside of a church since I don't know when. It's not true about God! It's true about us wops, even the best of us, no better than studs, brood mares. I can't stand it. I can't think of them that way!

(*During the last part of the monologue, BENIAMINO enters, goes to WOLFE and puts his arm around his shoulder*)

BENIAMINO:

Imma sorry, Wolfango. Imma sorry you mother no letta me tell you.

WOLFE:
It doesn't change anything, does it? *(stares at him)* Does it?

BENIAMINO:
No, ma, I coulda tolla you better. I coulda tolla you nunga you worry.

WOLFE;
Oh no, I won't worry, pop. *(yells)* How the hell can you say a thing like that?

BENIAMINO:
Wolfango, caro figlio, you are too old, too soon. Somaday you understand. *(sings in Italian accent)*

Leave age to age's cares, seek your own truth.
Before you know, cares of manhood steal the joy of youth.
So full of love, it seems, but a man must have a dream
Be kind to dreams, my son, we must have dreams.

— 8 —

EARLY EDUCATION

BENIAMINO RECOGNIZED HIS SON Wolfango's unique gifts and love of learning. During my research into dad's early years I found eight of his carefully preserved high school report cards. They are a real treasure because they reveal the subjects in which he excelled which in turn led him into a profession where he could use them best, the law. Here's one of dad's report cards from junior year. The name Wolfango was on his 9th and 10th grade report cards. It became W. Edward in his junior and senior years. I wonder how he was able to do that without legally changing his name.

For the first half of his 3rd year, he got straight A's in all his Academic subjects, but a C in Physical Training. The grades stayed the same for the second half in all but English II and American History which both went from A to B+, but Physical Training went up to a B. Dad took 5 Regents finals, the test scores don't reflect his straight A classwork, however he did get an 87 on Biology Regents. Biology grades became a future subject for a masterful letter Dad wrote to Doni.

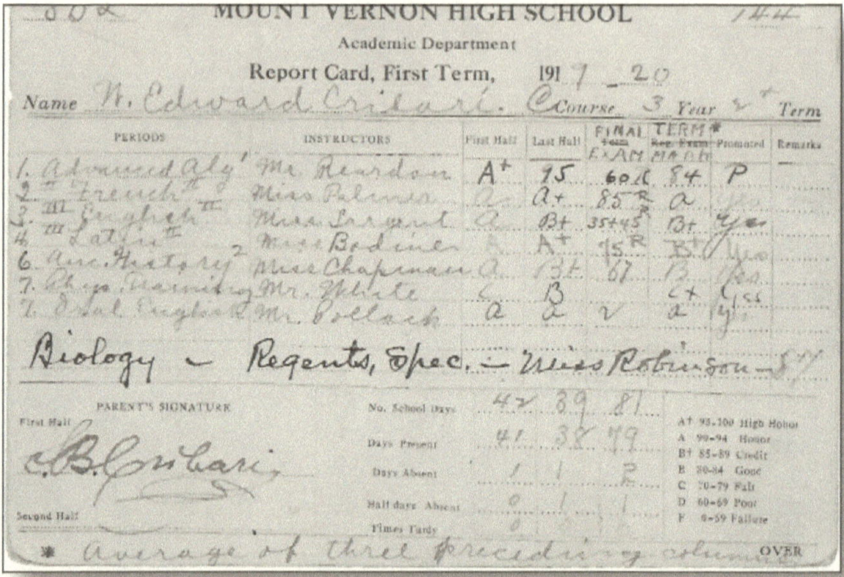
MOUNT VERNON HIGH SCHOOL

Academic Department

Report Card, First Term, 1917 – 20

Name W. Edward Crilari [illegible] Course 3 Year 2nd Term

PERIODS	INSTRUCTORS	First Half	Last Half	FINAL EXAM	TERM MARK*	Promoted	Remarks
1. Advanced Alg	Mr. Reardon	A+	95	60 R	84	P	—
2. French	Miss Palmer	A	A+	85 R	A	Yes	
3. English	Miss Sargent	A	B+	35+45	B+	Yes	
4. Latin	Miss Bodine	A	A+	95 R	B+	Yes	
6. Anc. History	Miss Chapman	A	B+	67	B	Yes	
7. Phys. Training	Mr. White	C	B		C+	Yes	
7. Oral English	Mr. Pollack	A	A		A	Yes	

Biology – Regents, Spec. – Miss Robinson – 87

PARENT'S SIGNATURE

First Half C. B. Crilari

Second Half

No. School Days	42	39	81
Days Present	41	38	79
Days Absent	1	1	2
Half days Absent	0	1	1
Times Tardy	0		

A+ 95-100 High Honor
A 90-94 Honor
B+ 85-89 Credit
B 80-84 Good
C 70-79 Fair
D 60-69 Poor
F 0-59 Failure

* Average of three preceding columns

OVER

He also told my sister Bill about rushing up a flight of stairs to see his grades at Columbia College and how his heart was pounding in fear of losing his scholarship. His advice " just get through."

I'm sure of it. My father said so.

— 9 —

"America, I Love You; You're Like a Papa to Me"

WOLFANGO CRIBARI WAS THE shining light of Lady Liberty's torch in the eyes of his patriotic, passionate father Beniamino, My father adored both his parents, but had a special connection to his father that his nine siblings didn't. This is an assumption based on unfavorable comments made by one of my aunts in her later years. It is also supported by my mother who always said how much she loved her father-in-law. Eugenia described her husband as a dreamer, but so was her beloved son Wolfe.

Beniamino's achievements as an "American" entrepreneur were remarkable considering his limitations in language. He started an ice cream manufacturing company – Savoy Ice Cream – in a building that was adjacent to his residence in Fleetwood, Mount Vernon. And according to the family, it became the ice cream of choice in upscale restaurants and country clubs in Westchester County during the 1920's and 1930's

Wolfe's achievements in the most language-based professions he could have chosen, acting and trial law, required the very gifts his beloved father never had time to refine. Dad never heard English spoken without a strong accent by either parent (nono and nana were busy just surviving), yet dad's diction is incredible.

I knew my grandmother Eugenia for 25 years as a physically weak but powerful woman who made fantastic meatballs and spaghetti every Thursday and Sunday for her sons, daughters and grandchildren. Though a loving grandmother to her 15 grandchildren, she always scared me a little. I still don't know why. One thing I am sure of, my father was her favorite. How that affected her relationship with her other nine I'll never know.

In going through my Dad's memorabilia, I came across this article about Nana Cribari in a 1929 edition of *The Fleetwood News*. It truly surprised me.

> *This very purposeful organization was founded by Mrs. Eugenia Cribari of Fleetwood as an auxiliary to the Italian Civic Association and had its beginning with a small group of women who held their first meeting on June 5, 1919 at the home of Mrs. Elena Blasi 133 Broad Street… The major part of the association's activities has been along charitable lines. …established the first school of Italian in the city…one of its first achievements was the commemoration of the sexcentenary anniversary of Dante's death. The association presented the Mount Vernon High School a bronze relief of the Italian poet.*

Nana Cribari was what we now call a "community activist." Where did she find the time?

I have always been sensitive to the plight of the immigrant and have spent the best teaching years of my life helping them acquire and refine their adopted language, English. I wish nono Cribari had the time and opportunity to take a class like the one I teach. He would have been an enthusiastic participant. I don't know if nono had as strong an accent as nana did; she never lost it. It didn't matter, accent or not, she ruled!

What do dad's parents and today's immigrants have in common? They were trying to fit into a culture their parents never experienced.

Beniamino and Eugenia Cribari's ten children, were raised in strange new surroundings in which "the child is father to the man." Dad and his siblings were their parents' American dreams in the flesh. Born American, the Cribari children were their parents' pathfinders. The life story of Wolfango

Cribari reveals how well he lived out that role for his immigrant parents and his own family.

Both my Italian grandparents were leaders in their suburban Italian-American community. Beniamino was involved in political groups, Eugenia in cultural ones. Dad passionately supported their efforts to become Americanized and often helped them find programs that inspired immigrant Italian audiences.

In this speech dad gave to the ICA – Italian Civic Association – during World War II, I discovered how dad used his storytelling skills and patriotic fervor to inspire and encourage his Italian neighbors who were faced daily with the fact that their country of origin was at war with their country of choice. I've included excerpts only.

> **I want to open my remarks tonight by recalling a story for you that I heard from my mother.**
>
> **A father had three sons who were approaching manhood. The father had a flourishing shipping business, and it had been his ambition to have his sons carry on and enjoy the fruits of his labor. However, each son wanted to take up a different vocation.**
>
> **One day, the father and his three sons were walking in the woods. The father told each boy to bring him four sticks. The boys did what their father told them and each one gave his four sticks to his father. The father handed each son one stick and asked him to break it in two. This was easily accomplished. The father then handed each of the three boys three sticks and asked them to put the sticks together and break them. Not one of the brothers could break them.**
>
> **The father gathered his sons to him and said, "My sons, alone the sticks were easily broken, united they were strong." The lesson we can learn from this story "in unity there is strength." The very name of our country exemplifies the power of union, The United States of America, not the States of America, the United States of America.**

One of our greatest statesmen once cried out in one of the darkest moments of American history, "United we stand, divided we fall."

So, my friends, I say to you tonight and let it be the ever brilliant shining constellation to which we turn our eyes, let us have unity in our organization here – unity of spirit, unity of purpose and unity of power.

We have within the confines of this organization the potentialities of great things. We stand for the highest ideals of our country and it is our unceasing effort to bring the people of Italian origin in this city into contact with these ideals. But, my friends, we cannot accomplish our ends single-handed and alone. We must cooperate one with another.

We are bound together by our common ideals and aspirations. We stand as a unit, for if we are to consider ourselves as individuals we are no longer an association. As an association we are a mighty force that will carry forward the high purposes for which we strive and upon which we have founded and built our present success.

Let us now adopt as our slogan the battle cry of The Three Musketeers: one for all and all for one. I thank you for your kind attention and the opportunity to have addressed you.

Reading Dad's speeches from the 1930's and 1940's reinforced what I always knew about my father's social, political thoughts and feelings. I never had the time or inclination to read them until Covid forced me into an insulated environment with free time to go through dad's significant memorabilia.

The instant accessibility of historic data via computer and cell phone also enriched my research and the ability to share dad's pertinent writings on Facebook. I recently presented parts of this speech that dad wrote and delivered to **new citizens** in Judge Davis's courtroom, White Plains, New York during WWII, 1943 to be exact.

The significance of the timing is obvious, we were fighting the Italian army in World War II. There were probably very few new citizens from Italy in the 1943 group he was addressing. Nevertheless, dad introduces himself as "the son of immigrants" relating to his immigrant audience but also unafraid to be Italian. No question about his "Latin" looks. (*read "guinea" in those days*) But I'm sure his passionate love of country overshadowed any initial prejudice towards him that an audience might have felt.

Dad's lifelong notion that "we are all immigrants" is clearly expressed. He never lost sight of who the authentic, under-credited builders of America were. This speech sums up how a first generation American felt about his countrymen who during this speech were fighting against Italy, his parents' homeland.

> **Today a priceless privilege and trust has been bestowed upon you. I can sense with deep feeling the pride that you must feel.**
>
> **I am the son of an immigrant who many years ago threw off the shackles of the old world to seek opportunity and freedom in this country. My beloved father's life in this country was one of hardship, sweat and toil. A working man, all his life, ten children to support and with practically no time to enjoy the fruits of his labor, he told me of his great happiness in the opportunity America afforded him and his children to be free and to do as they pleased.**
>
> **I need not tell you of his endless gratitude that, despite his lack of means, this great country gave his children: the opportunity of education and a profession. Do you wonder then about the great love for America that immigrants develop despite the hardships that many have had to undergo?**
>
> **It seems just yesterday, does it not, that your ship came to rest opposite the lower tip of Manhattan Island. You were filled with happiness and yet with fear. There rising before you, silhouetted against the simmering red hot glow of lights, were ramparts of steel and concrete. You could see no passage that led beyond. You expected no friends to greet you.**

There you were, an immigrant, face to face with the great, prosperous, powerful America - a little problem come to its shores.

What a problem America seemed to you. A problem as great as life itself. Pacing up and down late into the night on the crowded boat, you tried to visualize what might confront you on the next day. Further than that you dared not think. Doubts arose to torment you. What would this new country be like? Would you pass inspection? How would you make yourself understood? Could you make a new start in life?

Nowhere in man's history has there been such a country as America. Never before did the lovers of freedom, high and low, ignorant and educated, dark and light, come together not knowing each other, but drawn by the same dream, however expressed, to make a new nation. Had this idea been planned it would have been called fantastic. Men would have thought of a thousand reasons against it. But it is an instinct of man's being. It stirs in him as the blood stirs and he does not know why. It is the instinct of life.

America appreciates the many gifts you bring to its altars. You have brought your music, your poetry, your art, your culture, some touch of your home, field or forest. All of these will become part of America. You have also brought hands with which to work, minds with which to conceive, hearts filled with hope – stout hearts to drive live minds, live minds to direct willing hands.

At the gate of America you left behind other things that America doesn't want. Hatred of old time neighbors, national prejudices, traditional fears. They are inconsistent with the American idea of freedom.

At the altar of America you have sworn yourself to a single loyalty. You have bound yourselves to sacrifice and struggle, to plan and work for this land.

Today we are a multitude of people on a pilgrimage, ordinary people filled with such hope as has never caught the hearts and imaginations of any nation on earth before.

Our land, our people, our flag. Our land, a continent. Our people of all races. Our flag, a symbol of what humanity may aspire to when wars are over and barriers down. We must be dedicated and consecrated anew, to die for if need be.

— 10 —

AN ARTISTIC LEGACY: LOVE OF ACTING, MUSIC, AND THEATER

ONE OF DAD'S DREAMS came true in his early twenties right in his own backyard. He joined a community theater group and spent the little free time he had while going to college, law school, working part time jobs, onstage at the Community Church with the Community Players of Mount Vernon. His natural gifts as an actor led him to be frequently cast as leading man or villain; his ethnic looks made him a hometown Valentino. It also led him into a transformative relationship with an older woman who was his leading lady in all of the Players offerings. She was known as Lady.

Ironically dad never talked with us about his acting days, but he did tell us about the first time his father went to see him onstage. Dad was playing a villain who is killed at the end of the play. It was a typical melodrama of that era like *East Lynne*, but it was in English and although Beniamino loved theater, his only experience was with plays in Italian.

When Wolfe was "killed" at the end of the play, Beniamino was overcome. The reactions of the audience, especially his wife Eugenia and daughter Rose, so unnerved him that Rose ran backstage to get dad to come out front to show his father he was still alive. Dad's "death scene" must have been pretty powerful because although the acting style of the time was melodramatic, dad was probably a "method' actor before its time. The acting reviews he got are proof of his skills.

One of the reviews of his acting in a popular community theater play, "Little Italy," pays him the highest compliment an actor can hope for. This from the New York Herald Tribune, May 5th 1928

> *"Florence Aitken Tompkins as the young wife and* ***Wolfango Cribari as the street singer, gave fine restrained performances, never once allowing themselves to approach the danger of burlesquing their characters."***

I recently read "Little Italy" It's such a parody of Italian immigrant life that I wonder why dad didn't refuse the part. If there is such a thing as Italian "racism," the Italian characters in that play are the epitome of it.

Here's a dramatic scene I wrote that imagines dad's artistic and personal relationship with Lady, Mrs. Tompkins, his co-star in the theater group.

— 11 —

SCENE TWO: MUSICAL ABOUT THE CRIBARI FAMILY

A rehearsal hall at the Community Church, Mount Vernon 1927

A rehearsal is in progress. In the middle of a scene, a cast member "breaks up" and the scene falls apart. The play, is ***"Little Italy"*** *which won an award for best community theater production in the annual Westchester County tournament that year.*

The scene's leading lady, LADY, is an educated, cultured woman in her late 30's, WOLFE, her leading man, in his early 20's, is angry and over-reacts unexpectedly.

WOLFE:

(screams) For chrissake, can't any of you take this seriously. *(Silence)* When you're ready maybe we can get through this scene without some damn fool messing up. (*stalks offstage)*

LADY:

All right, everybody, let's take a five minute break, then we'll pick up where we left off. (*The rest of the cast exits, looking back to see how* LADY is *handling her temperamental co-star.)* Wolfe, can I talk to you a minute? (*She goes to edge of stage, he joins her and they sit on the apron*) O.K., let's have it. There are only a few rehearsals left. We can't afford this outburst. This isn't like you.

WOLFE:

It, it isn't just the play. It's everything, You're the only one I can talk to.

LADY:

Why? What is it, Wolfe?

WOLFE:

I don't know. I can't stand the attitudes. Who do they think they are?

LADY:

Whose attitudes? What, what is it you want from them? *(pause)* What do you want from me?

WOLFE:

A chance, the chance to get started.

LADY:

Started on what?

WOLFE:

I need time, time to myself. I have enough pressure, exams, law school, home, enough without this.

LADY:

Without what? What happened? It can't be that missed cue…

WOLFE:

Jesus Christ, no (*deep breath*) Mom's pregnant again. She's having it in November.

LADY:

Oh, I see.

WOLFE:

You see? You do? How could you? You don't even have a clue what it's like living the way we do. I feel so rotten, I made a real scene at home, right before I came here, I, I… (*starts to choke up as other actors return to stage*)

LADY:

Wait, Wolfe, wait, they're starting the scene again. Maybe rehearsing is good right now. Something you're totally involved in.

WOLFE:

Yeah, I know, it's what I love more than anything, more than…

LADY:

Please don't look at me like that, it makes me want to hug you, Not a good idea and we both know it, don't we? (*They sing about forgetting, escaping reality)*

April 29, 1927

THE DAILY ARGUS, MOUNT VERNON,

Scene in the Community Players' Fine Production, "Little Italy"

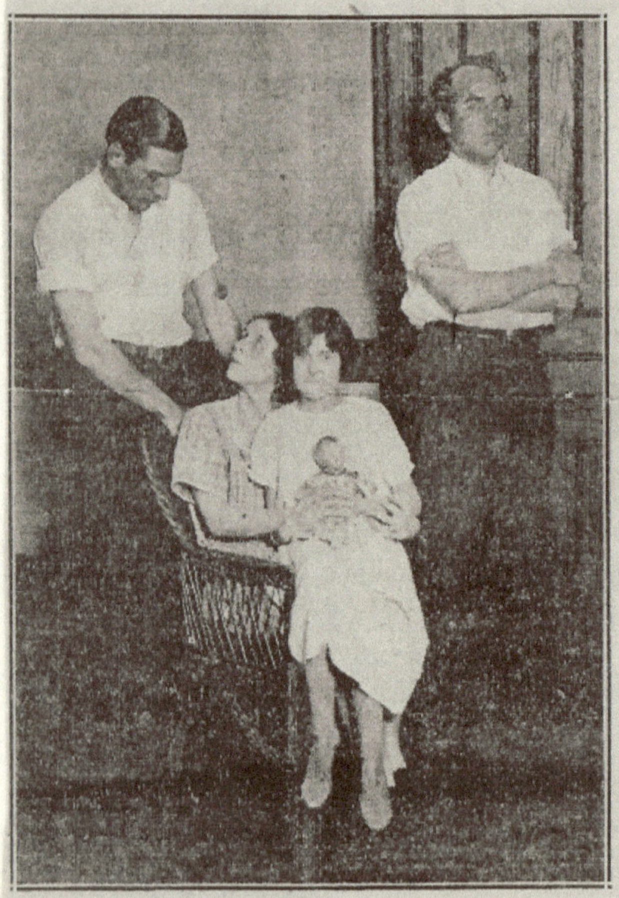

Photo by Iris Studio.

A scene in "Little Italy," the play presented last evening at the Westchester Woman's club by the Community Players, in the tournament being held under the auspices of the Westchester County Recreation commission, and which was selected by the judges as one of the plays to be repeated in final competition for the cup.

— 12 —

COMMUNITY PLAYERS STAR

THIS NEWSPAPER PICTURE OF dad with Mrs. Tomkins as they appeared in the play "Little Italy" is undoubtedly in character considering the seriousness of both actors' attitudes toward the art of acting.

If you analyze it on a more personal level, you can see a young man seeking the advice or approval of a woman who is the mother of a child, Mrs. Tompkins had two daughters. The child has little connection to the two-some. The woman's husband, off to the side and uninvolved, is clueless as to his wife's relationship with the other man. This is a real merging of onstage-offstage life for both.

Here's another review of "Little Italy," which I discovered in a "Looking Backward" column of The Daily Argus, Mount Vernon, 1927.

> *The auditorium of the Westchester Women's Club resounded with applause when the Community Players were awarded the silver cup offered by the Westchester County Recreation Commission for the best play presented in connection with the Westchester County Little Theater tournament. Mount Vernonites were especially jubilant as they realized that the Community Players of their city had been successful in the competition, the more so as a particularly high grade of amateur productions had prevailed during the tournament and because among the entries were some of the most representative drama clubs of the county.*

> *"Little Italy," the prize play, was done in a remarkably artistic manner. The delineation of types so true to life was an outstanding feature.* ***Wolfango Cribari put great stress upon the emotional scenes.*** *George Pendleton played his part with accuracy and earnestness and with a sensitiveness that were highly commendable. Mrs. Florence Atkins Tompkins essaying of the young wife's role was exceedingly meritorious.*

When the Players' production of "Little Italy" made the county-wide finals this review of the lead actors' performances also appeared in a New York newspaper. *"The performance of "Little Italy" left one literally entranced. Florence Aitkin Tompkins played her role with skill and* assurance, *put into her part a shimmering beauty…*

Wolfango Cribari in the part of Michele did a dramatic piece of work. His portraiture was vigorous.

SUBURBAN LITTLE THEATRE PLAYERS MAKE CUP BIDS

By FORREST DAVIS.
(Chairman of the judges.)

It was suburban night in the Little theatre tournament at the Frolic. Commuters who catch the 5:15, hurry through dinner and dash to rehearsal in the village hall gathered from four nearby points for the third event in the week long Belasco cup race.

Mount Kisco and Mount Vernon were invading Broadway with amateur wares. So, likewise, were Elizabeth and Jackson Heights. They brought their own public, for the most.

Wolfgang Cribari

The Jackson Heights Players dared that tricky hazard for nonprofessionals, a medieval costume affairs. It was "Prison Bars," by Carl Bixby.

The trifle was given enthusiastic treatment by O. J. Gude jr., Octavia Hicks, the author, and Horace Canning.

In contrast, Eugene O'Neill's tale of avaricious madness, "Where the Cross Is Made," closed he bill. Dealing with he phrenetic influence of overdue treasure on a seafaring father and son, it was made vital by the Y. M. H. A. Maskers of Elizabeth.

A triangle drama expressed in the flambuoyancy known as Latin, "Little Italy," by Horace B. Fry, furnished the Mount Vernon Community players their vehicle.

George Pendleton, Wolfgang Cribari and Florence Aitken Tompkins acted the roles energetically. A child, Adele Ritchie, played a bit.

Miss Martia Leonard, inspiration of the Brookside Open Air theatre of Mount Kisco, wrote the play for her group. "A Tale Retold," it was another restatement of the Adam, Eve and Lilith triangle, epigrammatic and well handled by Robert Hugh Hamilton, Jane King and Gertrude Connell.

Troupes from Columbus, O., Poughkeepsie, Ardrossan, Scotland, and Decatur, Ga., appear tonight.

This article appeared in the DAILY NEWS on May 10, 1928 it refers to the play that dad's Community players presented that year for the Little Theatre tournament in New York City,

> *"It was suburban night in the little theater tournament at the Frolic...A triangle drama expressed the flamboyance known as Latin "Little Italy " by Horace R. Fry furnished the Mount Vernon Community players with their vehicle. George Pendleton, Wolfgang Cribari and Florence Aitken Tompkins acted their roles energetically. A child, Adele Ritchie, played a bit."*

If you Google Wolfango Cribari you'll find him listed on IBDB (*Internet Broadway Data Base*) Credits: Broadway: Little Italy May 09, 1928. Performer Wolfango Cribari (Michele) Play One Act Revival. Dad was on Broadway for one night.

Here's a dramatic portrait of Wolfango Cribari in his 20's in a different role. The painting is entitled "Crib as Lonnie." Dad was obviously **not** typecast in this role It doesn't mention the play in which the character of Lonnie appears. The painting was obviously a prop for the play. It also reveals dad's ability to overcome stereotype casting.

This portrait, an oil pastel, was created by a relative of Mrs. Tompkins named Atkins. It hangs over the piano in my home. I see him everyday as he looked in his twenties: black slicked back hair, long face, prominent nose, large ears and dark soulful eyes. His eyes: I've never met anyone else who had such eyes. They expressed what he was feeling even when he didn't want them to: often dancing with joy or sparkling with humor, then sad and pensive; simply mesmerizing.

Dad believed his most distinctive feature was his prominent Roman nose. He was obsessed with a fear that one of his children would inherit his schnozz, as he called it. I especially remember dad literally pushing up the end of my baby sister Bill's nose every night before she went to bed determined to prevent her nose from having a hook. Maybe it worked, she doesn't!

Here's a vaudeville style skit I created from a story dad used to tell us.

Dad: Do you want to know how I got this hook on the end of my nose?

Camille: Yes, daddy, I do.

Dad: You know nana and nono had too many children – ten of us. We had to sleep in two big bedrooms, upstairs in the house on Broad Street. There wasn't any heat upstairs so we brought a few heated bricks and put them in blankets at the bottom of our beds.

Camille: Bricks in your beds?

Dad: Hot bricks.

Camille: Didn't you get burned?

Dad: They were wrapped in a blanket. In wintertime it was so cold we had to sleep with our clothes on under the blanket. That was my problem: my nose was so big it used to stick out from under the blanket. If I had a little cold that night and my nose was running, a big icycle grew on the end of my nose.

Camille: Ewww!

Dad: That's how I got the hook.

Camille: No, it isn't.

Dad: Only the nose knows!

I'm sure of it, my father said so

By the way, he adored Jimmy Durante.

— 13 —

MRS TOMPKINS – MENTOR, MUSE…MORE?

AMONG DAD'S PAPERS WAS this poem. Although it is typed and not in her recognizable handwriting, the poet's identity is clear to me, it was Mrs. Tompkins, dad's co-star in community theater who was also a gifted writer.

To Wolfango.

A little bit of sternness in your eye,
A little worried pucker on your brow,
A transient smile, coming when cares go by,
A hard face softened, I don't just know how.

A temperamental face, each varied mood
Too violent and quick, now gay and kind,
And then again discourteous and rude,
All indications of a restless mind.

Too moodily depressed now and again,
Pondering o'er questions which no doubt you'll find,
Far greater men have pondered all in vain,
Because they're far beyond the human mind.

Swiftly the melancholy hour passes, while
Your keen eyes soften to a mild caress,
The hard mouth changes to a reckless smile,
A pessimist turned jester, one would guess.

Too reckless in your search for happiness,
Too eager to find depths where shallows are,
Too moody to find peace in loneliness,
Too quick to think each fire-fly a star.

Sensitive and keen, and much too prone to reach,
The heights of joy, the lowest depths of grief,
But slowly Life's experience will teach,
That all sensations, gay or sad, are brief.

It certainly wasn't written by one of dad's male friends and it was definitely not written by my mother. The images in this verbal "portrait" of my father are identical to how Mrs. Tompkins viewed the young, gifted and passionate young man who she loved and lost. I'm sure she wrote it. Since it's not easy to read here's a transcript below:

To Wolfango

A little bit of sternness in your eye.
A little worried pucker in your brow,
A transient smile, coming when cares go by,
A hard face softened, I don't just know how.

A temperamental face, each varied mood
Too violent and quick, now gay and kind.
And then discourteous and rude,
All indications of a restless mind.

Too moodily depressed now and again.
Pondering o'er questions which no doubt you'll find
Far greater men have pondered all in vain
Because they're beyond the human mind.

Swiftly the melancholy hour passes, while
Your keen eyes soften to a mild caress,
The hard mouth changes to a reckless smile,
A pessimist turned jester, one would guess.

Too reckless in your search for happiness,
Too eager to find depths where shallows are,
Too moody to find peace in loneliness,
Too quick to think each firefly a star.

Sensitive and keen, and much too prone to reach
The heights of joy, the lowest depths of grief,
But slowly life's experience will teach,
That all sensations, gay or sad, are brief.

This describes dad's twenty year old self so honestly; she knew him well. It also reveals a quasi parental concern for dad's welfare. He kept it with her letters his whole life.

Mrs. Tompkins (Lady) was not just dad's leading lady, she was mentor/teacher for the young, naïve Wolfango. In one of her letters to dad she recommends that he read this obscure poem written by poet Thomas Moore.

I googled it and here is an excerpt. It clearly describes how she felt about ending their mutually inspirational relationship.

from *Lalla Rookh*
by Thomas Moore

"How sweetly," said the trembling maid,
Of her own gentle voice afraid,
So long had they in silence stood,
Looking upon that tranquil flood—
"How sweetly does the moon-beam smile
To-night upon yon leafy isle!
Oft in my fancy's wanderings,
I've wish'd that little isle had wings,
And we, within its fairy bow'rs,
Were wafted off to seas unknown,
Where not a pulse should beat but ours,
   And we might live, love, die alone!
Far from the cruel and the cold,
   Where the bright eyes of angels only
Should come around us, to behold
A paradise so pure and lonely.
Would this be world enough for thee?"
Playful she turn'd, that he might see
   The passing smile her cheek put on;
But when she mark'd how mournfully
His eyes met hers, that smile was gone;
And, bursting into heart-felt tears,
"Yes, yes," she cried, "my hourly fears
My dreams have boded all too right—

We part—for ever part—to-night!
I knew, I knew it could not last—
'Twas bright, 'twas heav'nly, but 'tis past!

I love this wonderfully illustrated logo of the Community Players where dad discovered his lifelong passion for acting, it could have been created today. Its energy and whimsical style also provides insight into the talented people, like dad, who were involved in the Community Players.

My sisters and I knew from dad's family and mom that he had been a ***really good*** amateur actor in his twenties. We knew him as a comic actor in church shows and as an enthusiastic audience for the many plays and musicals he watched us perform in. He always gave us positive, useful reviews with constructive criticism for our performances and the overall productions. I never felt they were father-daughter based, but from one performing artist to another.

Which brings me to the startling discovery I made more than a decade after dad died, a box of letters from his co-star, Mrs. Tompkins, stashed away in a box at mom's Port Chester home. I asked mom if she knew about the letters.

"Yes, I did."

We all heard about Mrs. Tompkins growing up because once in a while mom brought up her name and Dad reacted in typically dramatic style. Now, I had access to 40+ letters she wrote to Dad. I read them in one sitting.

From the first, I felt an underlying tension that must have always been between them. I tried to imagine dad's letters to her. I was intrigued. I called mom and asked her if she read any of them.

"No, I didn't"

I was stunned. No woman I know would have kept love letters from her husband's former paramour, moved them to her new home after he passed away and not read them. But I believed mom. She told me dad told her all about his relationship with Mrs. Tompkins years ago and that there was never an "affair." She believed him. But, she never read those letters dad kept for more than 30 years.

I certainly did. The 40+letters Lady wrote dad between 1925-1927 were dramatic enough to turn into a two-person play. At least I think so. See what you think. Here are four from different stages of their relationship:

> ***Letter #1: 3/17/25 Mount Vernon, New York.***
> *I have a "day" at the Drama Department of the Women's Club on Thursday, April 9th, in the afternoon. I should like very much to put on Theresa Helburne's "Enter the Hero" – principally because I know the part and I just haven't time to learn anything new right now. Would you like to play the man in it? The part is not long and it's a good part. I think you would enjoy playing it. But I'm wondering about college – could you get away that afternoon? I do hope it will be possible and that the idea will appeal to you. We would only need a few rehearsals. The others in the cast – two women – have played in it before. – so we'd just need a bit of polishing off as 'twere! Will you telephone me.*
>
> *Cordially yours,*
>
> *Florence Aitkin Tompkins*

> ***Letter #5: 6/29/25 Mount Vernon, New York***
> *My beloved one – what can I say to comfort you. When I am in such sore need of comfort myself – somehow I must get hold of myself if only because I know you will be happier if I am. Our peace and consolation*

will come from realizing that the days pass surely – and I am yours and you are mine. Our sorrow comes because we love each other – but I would not forego the love because of the tears it brings.

Pietro, beloved, I thank God for you,

Lady

Letter #11: 7/17/25 Westport, Ct.
My dear – I am so sorry – there aren't any words to tell you how much. My heart is more than ever with you in these sad hours, and I am just fairly aching with the desire to ease things for you. But I know, only too well, how impossible that is. For some reason hard to understand, we all must needs fight our own battle with suffering alone.

There's this, however – because you have a mind and heart sensitive to things of the spirit; because your eyes are strong enough to see visions, this passing of your friend from one place to another will not long hurt you as it does now.

When you go into the woods and feel God there, he will be there, too, part of the universal glory. This will not seem any comfort to you now, I know, the physical parting is so cruel, but, dear heart of mine, in God we all live and move and have our being – whether we be living or dead, as we call it, only some are not hampered any more by this cumbersome body. They walk with such freedom, and in such light and beauty, that it is breath-taking to think of it.

Or, so it seems to me.

Good night

Letter #42: Monday night eleven o'clock, August 22, 1927
As perhaps you have surmised – and perhaps as you wish – we have come to the parting of the ways.

> *I can't bear to let it go by default as it were. We have been too close: I love too much the spirit which I am still convinced is really you, to let this moment slip by in cowardly silence. I want to clear away any shadow of doubt – if I can – of my sincerity, my agonizingly deep feeling.*
>
> *It seems as though I cannot help you anymore. That whatever influence for good I may have been to you is gone. That means something else is gone too – there is no more spiritual contact between us apparently. And I can stand no other kind if that first is gone...*
>
> *As for your treatment of me – I am quite willing to admit that many of the small cruelties* ***are*** *small and that in* ***themselves*** *they are not important, but as an indicator of the fact that your love for me is not what it was two years ago, they cannot be mistaken. To me there is only one justification for a secret love affair – and that is a great and all-inclusive love....*
>
> *I pray you may live up to the best that is in you – that best which I loved and adored – which I still love and adore and will forever.*

Here's another way to look at that unique triangle of Wolfango, Florence and Carola; from 1925-1927 *(the same years as the letters)* Carola was also a member of the Community Players. It's where she and dad met. It was the beginning of the Wolfe Cribari theater family that continues almost a century later.

Mom had her version of the theater triangle: Mrs. Tompkins never cast her in a leading role, she always got the part of the maid; **anti**-type casting, believe me. Mom led us to believe that Mrs. Tompkins, who was also Carola's singing teacher at that time, was responsible for Carola's casting problem.

While Mrs. Tompkins was a member of the board for the Community Players, she didn't cast the plays in which she starred and Carola was cast as a maid. But you can't blame Carola for being annoyed at being cast as a maid because the three "players" in this romantic melodrama were always: *Florence: leading lady; Wolfango: leading man and Carola: supporting role.* They were constantly interacting, literally and figuratively.

Here's evidence: Carola at far right as the maid and Mrs. Tompkins seated center stage. No sign of dad. It speaks a thousand words.

— 14 —

COLUMBIA COLLEGE SPORTS FAN

SPORTS WERE ON A par with acting for dad in his twenties. At Columbia College he belonged to the Philo Dramatic Club, another detail I never knew. There's also evidence in his keepsakes that dad had an unfulfilled wish to be a champion in some line of sports. I never knew this. Only this picture from his college days is evidence that he engaged in a sport. I believe he was on the Columbia Regatta team during his sophomore year because he earmarked a description of the team's activities in his college yearbook. He actually kept this oarsman picture on his dresser for as long as I can remember. I know it wasn't swimming; he was a terrible swimmer.

I recently went through dad's 1925 Columbia University yearbook and discovered new details and writings about dad's college years.

On a page of average senior statistics, I compared dad's to his classmates:

Height – 5 ft. 10 inches	*Dad – 5 ft. 11 inches*
Weight – 151 pounds	*Dad – 145-150 – guessing on this one.*
Age - 21	*Dad – 21 in June 1925, 22 in August 1925*

Underneath Wolfgang E. Cribari, Mount Vernon, N.Y., his formal yearbook picture, a yearbook staffer wrote:

> *We didn't know there was such a place as Bronxville until Crib fell into our midst. Strangely enough his hobbies range from dramatics to criminal law. If you ever want to witness an enjoyable piece of acting, ask Crib to repeat, "Is that a crime?" Crib is the best little monologue artist in the class and he has entertained a great many of us with this gift.*

Three famous names emerge as dad's classmates at Columbia: Richard Rodgers. Lou Gehrig, and Red Grange. Richard Rogers, class of 1923, is acknowledged as the composer of a comic operetta, "Half Moon Inn" which his alma mater produced at a New York City hotel. In the yearbook, his last name is spelled Rogers, not Rodgers.

The Columbia yearbook staff wrote the following about Lou Gehrig who dad always talked about. *"No one was more famous for his performances on the gridiron and the diamond than Lou Gehrig."* Gehrig was acclaimed the leading college baseball player that year (sophomore year, 1922) and shortly after the end of the season was signed by the New York Americans.

Red Grange was credited with giving Columbia football the best season in its history. *"This year (1925) Columbia football reached a new peak."* Dad was a diehard fan of Columbia's football team, he idolized Red Grange who started at Columbia. Dad kept expecting his alma mater to live up to its 1925 heights. It never did. We always rooted for Columbia during football season and sang the Columbia Lions' song,

Roar, lion, roar
And hear the echo in the Hudson Valley.
Fight on for victory evermore
While the sons of Knickerbocker rally round
Colombia, Colombia
Shouting her name forever,
Roar, lion, roar
For alma mater on the Hudson shore.

I have a funny memory to illustrate dad's zealous loyalty to Lions football.

Dad, mom dressed in her new luxurious mink coat, my sisters and I are all sitting high up in Columbia's home stadium at Bakersfield near the Harlem River Bridge. It's starting to get cold out, it's football season in New York. I didn't want to be there, I was a teenager. Dad is really excited about this year's team and their great coach, Lou Little.

It 's the second half and the Lions are winning, but the other team, I think it was Cornell, scores a touchdown and ties the score. It getting colder and I don't like football anyway. It's no fun, but my sisters don't seem to mind,

Mom and dad both have little silver flasks with them and keep taking sips of whatever was in them to "keep themselves warm." Dad keeps yelling advice to Coach Little from high up in the stands. Mom gets tired of his yelling and tells him to keep quiet, he's giving her a headache.

Next thing I know mom is unsteadily, but carefully, walking down the stadium's steep tiered steps toward the fenced off player's bench where Coach Little is sitting, head in hands. She tries to open the gate to get to his bench.

Apparently, she thought she should personally remind him to "do something" so her husband's beloved alma mater would win the game. Before dad could go after her, two men escorted my elegant, mink-wrapped, slightly tipsy mom back to her seat. Dad was laughing his head off. I was mortified.

I had no idea who won that game until my good friend Janet Davis found a copy of the program cover for October 30, 1948 in her research on Colombia College's football season.

Cornell beat Colombia that day 20-13. Here's the program cover. Thank you, Janet.

— 15 —

WHAT WOULD YOU LIKE TO BE? SURPRISE!

DAD WAS THE PROVERBIAL "self-made man," the list of jobs he worked at while studying to become a professional proved the extent of his drive and passion. Dad worked his way through four years of under-graduate study at Columbia College and three years at Columbia Law School. He had to earn the money to pay for his education in any and all ways possible. As a young man, he attracted the attention of the local media. This is what dad told whoever interviewed him for the *"What Would You like to Be?"* column.

During his years in college and the law school he spent his summers at a variety of jobs to earn money for the next semester's expenses. Dad ran a trolley car from Subway (the last stop on the NYC subway in the Bronx) to New Rochelle one summer and got home from the run at three o'clock in the morning. I distinctly remember riding on the trolley that ran alongside dad's law office in Mount Vernon. Dad loved trolleys and was nostalgic about them when trolleys became obsolete.

He also drove a truck three summers, worked in a drug store, painted scenery in Lee Lash Studio, spent one summer with General Optical and one with the Westchester Lighting Company. One vacation he fulfilled a childhood ambition and worked as a train announcer. For some reason dad didn't include the work he and his brothers did at the family's Savoy Ice Cream store and factory. He never stopped! It's remarkable that he had time to study.

But study he did every spare moment he had. Dad was on a yearly scholarship and always anxious that his grades would drop and he would lose his only chance for a college education. He never forgot the anxiety those days caused him which is apparent in the memories Bill aka Carola Cribari, pianist, music teacher, composer in Heidelberg, Germany shared…

"One story I always tell my pupils is his (dad's) way of putting NO PRESSURE on us academically or with my piano lessons. As I brought home good grades he would look at my report card and make a face and throw it on the ground and say "this is a terrible report card." Thereafter there might be a note he left overnight for me (he often did that) telling me how proud he was.

Regarding my piano lessons, I tell my pupils that I never really practiced but just played piano (I wanted to be outdoors and playing ball instead). He said he didn't care if I practiced. I would always have to have one lesson a week with my teacher coming to us. It was brilliant psychology in both cases.

With the grades it was because he was terrified to get bad grades and lose his scholarship. He described climbing up three flights of stairs to see the grades posted on the bulletin board at Columbia. He said his heart was racing wildly until he saw his grades were good enough to keep the scholarship. I think he resolved never to put us under that pressure.

I was always scared of math tests. The eighth grade Regents tests came. Dad knew I was scared. He wrote me a long letter showing me how to take a test. It was brilliant. I remember to this day a few points (I wish I could find the letter) …

Do not go ahead of the first question. If you do you may panic and not be clear-headed, Stay with each question until you feel you did the answer then go on to the next one. *Wow! As I write this it's a lesson for life!!! I actually followed his advice step for step.*

I remember still being scared I would fail the test. He must have called up Mother Mary Daniel and told her how scared I was because shortly after the test she called me over to tell me I got a 92 on the test. She told me not to tell the others because she wasn't ready to give out the grades

— 16 —

ENTER STAGE RIGHT: CAROLA ANKERSON

BEFORE CAROLA ANKERSON KNEW Wolfango Cribari was on the same planet, she was in school every day with his brother Hugo. Here is an adorable school picture with Carola, first row staring at the camera, fifth on the right, a big bow in her hair.

The dark-skinned little boy second from left in the back row is dad's younger brother Hugo. Carola and Hugo were in fourth grade at Lincoln School in Mount Vernon, it's still there. No words were needed in 1915 to describe the difference between the two classmates who would later become family.

The children who separate Carola from Hugo look predominantly Anglo. Not only is Hugo's place in the back row symbolic, he looks so out of place you want to hug him.

Good news, neither Hugo nor Carola ever let anyone "get the better of them." Each in his/her own way did just fine.

"Carola... Ca-roo-la!"

That's the way my father would call up the stairs while the rest of us waited for her to change her mind about which dress to wear or re-do her hair.

Physically mom was almost my exact opposite: petite, dark brown eyes, light blonde hair. She loved to reminisce about her natural chestnut color hair, "before I started to color it." I remembered it too.

Both unique and typical of her time, she was a complex, gifted beauty. A family friend, Bob Carney, Art's brother, once called her "an iron butterfly." Another friend of our family, Ricardo, described my 75 year old mother as a "coquette." Strikingly beautiful as a young woman, she was the product of doting parents and from her early teens lots and lots of boyfriends. My sisters and I know this, not because my father said so, but because Doni still has the pictures of those boyfriends. Mom kept them in a silver topped box underneath her bed forever.

Carola left high school at fifteen, traveled to France to study the violin, worked in her teens as an artist's model in New Rochelle, taught ballroom dancing at Arthur Murray's in New York City; basically, followed her dreams!

LY ARGUS, MOUNT VERNON, N. Y., MOND

May 5 1930

TERNAL—PER

Engaged To Wed Local Man

MISS CAROLA ANKERSON

Mr. and Mrs. G. H. Ankerson, of 128 Overlook Street, announced on Saturday, the engagement of their daughter, Carola, to Wolfango E. Cribani, of Mount Vernon.

In my mind's eye, mom will always be the carefree "flapper," dancing the Charleston, listening to Gershwin play the piano, staying out late and sleeping until noon. She sat next to George Gershwin while he played his latest songs. One of her favorite memories.

This is mom's engagement photo May 5, 1930. She turned 25 on May first. Mom's independent spirit "allowed" her to marry my father who was from a vastly different world, a struggling immigrant family.

Both of them obviously believed "love conquers all."

Mom already had her own identity as an artist, concert violinist, before she became a mother. She was always off somewhere learning something new: how to play the organ, how to design and sew fashionable clothes. She went to The City once a week for as far back as I can remember leaving domestic responsibilities to a string of different ***maids***.

Mom was never the idealized Donna Reed mother of the 1950's even though she dressed the part. In fact, one of her outstanding traits was her taste in clothes: she was always dressed to perfection in the latest style with the right shoes and matching accessories. Neither my sisters nor I inherited her gift of garb.

Of course, she went to the hairdresser weekly until just a few weeks before she passed. Well into her 80's she wore stockings and heels every time she left the house. She made sure her daughters were well dressed and always bought our clothes for us, much to our chagrin. No jeans and sneakers in our closets. But there were lots of unworn fancy dresses just hanging there.

Always in the moment, mom didn't like talking about the past, ever. I'm sure she wouldn't mind my including this picture of her and her parents if I don't mention a date. She was twenty years old at the time.

Here as you can see from these childhood pictures, my mother Carola: like her name, was not plain Carol, but Carol with an "a." Carola…active, adorable, attractive, and appealing! Yes, she was!!!"

One time I tried to interview mom about the day she arrived in Paris to study abroad. She just happened to arrive the same day Lindbergh did after the world's first transatlantic flight, May 21,1927. I asked her: What was it like to be an eyewitness to such an historic event? Her initial response: "*It was too crowded. We couldn't get a taxicab.*"

I persisted so mom found herself in the moment.

"I arrived in Paris in 1927. I don't remember the date (it was obviously Lindbergh's) But I went on the ship and he flew. It was the first one across the ocean. They made a fuss over that flight. I never liked history.

I stayed at this nice hotel. The girl I went with went out on a date, so I had room service. So I wasn't out in public that night. The same night I was left alone in the hotel, was the night Lindbergh arrived.

Gradually, mom started to re-live her time abroad…

I went on a train down to Switzerland and Italy. I liked Italy, the people were singing in the streets. I met some people. I always met people. I met a guy on the ship, family of Lionel trains. Also someone named Gump, San Francisco Gump. I played at the ship's concert with G. Bombashek, he played the piano for me. I went first class. Students got a discount. I played St. Saens "Le Cygne" (The Swan) and the Song of India.

I went to Europe to study the violin at Fontainbleau. Went to live in the Palace and I practiced in the Palace four hours a day. That's where I met a very well known composer, Roy Harris. He used to take me to tea. We rode bicycles, picnicked in the woods .I only stayed for half the course because I got sick. I got very weak. I guess I was doing too much.

Before I went to Fontainbleau I was doing the Charleston in Paris. I guess I burned the candle at both ends. My white blood cells were down. I was too sick to enjoy first class. I had to go home so I went second class. The purser was very nice to me. I was only in Fontainbleau six weeks, part of the summer. Teacher in Fontainbleau, Maurice Evite.

Waynie (Wayne Tinker) came over to see me when I was in Fontainbleau. Your father met me when I came back. I think he came down with my mother and father to the ship.

Bomboshek took me to a party where I met George Gershwin and he sent me to my singing teacher, Louis Ashenfelder. Gershwin was at a party on West 57th Street on the south side apartment. Lots of opera stars were there too. I was interested in hearing him play the piano. He was very nice. When I used to pose when I was very young, I drove to New

Rochelle to pose for artist Donald Tieg. He always played "Rhapsody in Blue" for me so I was really happy to meet Gershwin.

I was taking singing lessons and I was doing pretty well. I got a job in the chorus in Greenwich Village and I'd go down in the hottest weather. I was in the chorus singing, but I was also going to do a violin solo. But I lost my voice, strained it.

I took singing lessons from Mrs. Tompkins at one point, before I went to Louis Ashenfelder. He had lots of connections. But I lost my voice, so I gave that one up. I remember buying my mother that orange tea set with the money I made posing for artists. I think I had a few others in New Rochelle, but not Rockwell. My mother let me get out of high school..

Mom used her considerable artistic gifts in a variety of venues. As a child she danced with her younger brother Paul at a Bozeman, Montana vaudeville theater, she studied in France to be a concert violinist, and was cast in an off-Broadway musical by producer Ned Weyburn in New York City. When she first met dad she was already a well-known violin soloist for local groups like the Rotary Club, Women's Club and Community Players. She eventually left acting to her Barrymore-esque Italian friend Wolfango.

When she was 23 years old, mom's parents took her on a cruise to Hawaii probably because of her 'buddy' Wolfe (dad cautiously signed his letters that way). Ironically, mom said it was dad's letters that attracted her. Carola Ankerson and parents Bertha and Gustav are listed on the manifest of the S.S. Malolo which sailed from San Francisco July 28, 1928 and arrived in Honolulu August first. Mom said her parents took her on that cruise to get her away from dad. My sister Bill remembers mom telling her that Elfrieda, mom's older sister, advised her to *"take him (dad) as a lover, don't marry him."* Neither ploy worked.

Fast forward six decades: Here's Carola with her great grandson Stephen Lucas when he was a kindergartener.

"How come I don't sound like Carola when I play?" was five year old Stephen's wise observation. Stephen was learning from the best! Another family legacy.

Back to the courtship: Dad wrote this letter to mom weeks *before* Mrs. Tompkins wrote him the letter ending their relationship. It was at the very beginning of mom and dad's romance (as dad might have called it). It was also just a year before mom's parents decided to take her on that Hawaiian cruise.

Dad was an up and coming lawyer and mom was teaching dancing, taking violin lessons in NYC and modeling for New Rochelle artists. They were testing the waters; dad alludes to "Torches," a play the Community Players were presenting, which means he was still performing with Mrs. Tompkins.

The letter has an apologetic, humble feeling especially if one considers dad's usual assertive, dynamic style.

August 10, 1927
Carola dear,

Please forgive me for not calling you or writing you sooner. We went out to the Archer's summer home in Pa. and gave "Torches" (a play done by the Community Players) out there and didn't return until this morning.

I want awfully to see you, Carola, and I was just wondering if you could find an evening free this week. In any case tomorrow night I am going to drop off a choice bottle of wine which will make you strong enough to stay up until ten in the evening.

I hope you are going to permit me to see you at your home.

I have a club meeting at 8:15 so I'll have to run along right after,

but I want you to please permit me an evening later in the week.

Faithfully,

Wolfe.

As further evidence of Dad's pursuit of my mother, here are three notes he sent her that mom kept with the love letters.

This is to certify that the undersigned belongs body and soul to Carola Ankerson and undersigned certifies that he values her love more than his life and would gladly give it up for her.

Wolfango E. Cribari

Once and for all, I prefer no one to you! With all my love, Wolfe

Just a line to let you know that I love you more than anything in the world. I'll be with you wherever you are.

This is a real historic find. It's a 1920's version of a greeting card which dad obviously included with a string of pearls he had delivered to mom's home.

Carola

Dearest, may these little pearls be a constant reminder that of all the many million girls I'll never love but one – just you. Wolfe 1929

To the sweetest girl in all the world with all my love from her buddy Wolfe.

"Buddy" again. In March of the same year, 1929, dad wrote this pleading letter asking Carola's forgiveness for breaking a date at the last minute. The reason was he forgot he had a rehearsal for a play he was in. Maybe he did forget, but once again the Community Players and Mrs. Tompkins 'interfere.'

I'm sure Carola was fully aware of dad's predicament.

Dearest

I learned for the first time last night that there is to be a dress rehearsal of the "Yellow Triangle" at the McDonald Club tomorrow, Saturday night, in preparation for a performance at that place Sunday night.

I didn't know this at the time I arranged to see you the other night, dear, and again I must ask your forgiveness. I am writing you instead of phoning you for fear that over the telephone you might not understand.

Would you like to come down to the McDonald Club tomorrow night? I realize perfectly that it won't be very much in the way of entertainment for you and I'm terribly sorry . If you would like to come won't you please call me tomorrow. If not, my not hearing from you will indicate that you would rather not.

Again I ask your forgiveness and pray you understand my position

after having promised to perform down there a month or so ago.

With all my love,

Forever your own

Wolfe

I'm sure she didn't go to the rehearsal, but how could she resist his passionate appeal for forgiveness? She didn't, they were married the following year, 1930.

Unlike dad, mom never kept her old boyfriend's letters except dad's. But she did keep their *pictures*. We all knew about mom's pictures. I can only imagine my parents arguing about those pictures over the years. Mom was really good at reciting their names, always with an innocent, yet provocative giggle.

We all loved the name of boyfriend Wayne Tinker. Dad called him Waynie Stinker. So did we. Dad used to say it was a good thing that mom didn't marry Waynie; their children's names would have been "Harris Tinker and Gladys Tinker." Mom dropped him for dad.

Interestingly enough there is one letter from mom which dad kept. She found it after he passed. She says she hated writing letters and admits it in this one.

Wolfe dear,

Though I'm not in a suitable mood to write a letter, I shall make an attempt. First, of course I understand your attitude Saturday evening and I'm not angry with you, so please don't worry about that any longer, if you really have been worried. I'm very sorry you couldn't talk to me, but evidently fate didn't think it best. However when your exams are over I hope to see you. Your letter was very sweet, thank you.

If I had thought you indifferent surely your letter would have changed such a thought – so everything's perfectly satisfactory, isn't it?

Have been so busy since Monday morning I'm positively exhausted. Mrs. M.'s suicide Monday a.m. naturally upset this household as she was a very good friend of mother's. Poor mother. The funeral was this noon and mother went way down to the cemetery-down past Brooklyn someplace-and she's been helping.

Monday afternoon we went to N.Y. to break the news to Mrs. M.'s aunt, as she has a weak heart and the shock might have been too great had they told her over the phone – there are so many things to do when someone dies, too. I should have gone to the funeral, but I just couldn't – have only been to two and they are so terrible.

Well, I must change the subject. Posed yesterday afternoon for another New Rochelle artist – it's not so easy, but I enjoy it. Leave for Dartmouth tomorrow night and will have to be back Monday, beginning about nine.

Life is one thing after another. Please write again. I wish I could write as good a letter as you do. I'm sure you'll pass everything, so I won't wish you luck, otherwise I would.

My best,

Carola

Mom and dad's courtship was not exactly typical in that there wasn't much time to "see each other." The following letters reveal the frustration they undoubtedly shared. The first one dad wrote from the Mir-A-Lak Inn in Lake Placid, N.Y. and the second from his Mount Vernon office after he returned home.

> ***Wednesday***
> *Dearest,*
>
> *Your voice over the phone a few moments ago was like an angel's from heaven. Oh, honey, you don't realize what I have gone through this last week without word from you. It has been a torture of mind for me imagining every conceivable thing. Then your sweet assurance this morning made a complete change in me.*
>
> *Just a little more proof added to the already great amount indicating how utterly devoid of happiness and inspiration my life is without you, honey.*
>
> *Gosh, I'm happy for the first time in weeks. Gee, it was sweet of you to call me, honey, and if you could only have seen what the few words with you over the phone did to me, honey. I almost tore the roof off the place and darn near drowned Dave who was taking a bath at the time.*
>
> *Gee, I wish I went with you, dear one, it has seemed like years since I've held your dear self in my arms and felt your dear heart beat against mine. I'd give everything I've got if I could suddenly be transported to you up there in Maine, beloved. I can't wait until I see you, darling.*
>
> *Can't you make an appointment at a certain place where I can call you over the phone when I get home to the office? Please do this, dearest, and let me know in your letter when and where I can call you. Don't forget.*
>
> *I'm glad you called me a "big bum" over the phone, dear. That's nothing to what I really am, Honey. I should have stayed with you, darling.*
>
> *Leaving today for home, stopping at Saratoga and will be in tomorrow night. I received another telegram from the office this morning and there*

is no question about it, dear, I must get back by Friday. But, I'm coming up over Labor Day, dear, to bring the sweetest girl in the world back home to her buddy.

All my love to you, darling girl, and until eternity and then some.

Always your own,

Wolfe

Write me, dearest, if you want me to do any work when I'm back. Also don't forget to let me know where I can call you and when.

Good-by, sweetheart, for a while.

Saturday afternoon

Dearest,

Gosh, honey, you ought to see where I am writing this letter. My desk is piled about a foot high with mail and documents I was unable to get through this morning due to the pressure of many interviews that took up all my time from nine to one.

I returned home last night at about six and didn't come down to the office, dear. I was pretty much tired, disconsolate and unhappy. I haven't been able to enjoy a peaceful night's slumber since I left you. I found your dear letter awaiting me at the office. Honey, I deserve every word of censure that it contained.

Believe me, darling, you certainly let me off easy. But, honey, I've had punishment enough for not having stayed with you. If you could only feel a trifle of the sadness that has been mine at the recollection of the wonderful hours we could have had together if I had not acted impulsively, you would realize, I am sure, how remorseful I have been.

(For two pages dad explains why he didn't go to Maine to visit her)

Honey, perhaps I do wrong in writing you so much. You state in your letter my absence gives you an opportunity to think away from any influence I might have. But, dearest, I miss you so and I know you will forgive me.

The only way I have to at least spiritually feel you near me is by writing to you. I shall try not to write too often.

I love you honey and I'm desolate without you. Smile for me, just once now, dear. That's the girl, you're so sweet, dear. Yes, I wish I were with you.

All my love to you, honey,

Wolfe

— 17 —

CAREER CHOICES: THE LAW AND POLITICS

WOLFANGO CRIBARI WAS ALREADY recognized in his mid-twenties by older professionals for his considerable language and intellectual skills. Dad's theatrical co-star Mrs. Tompkins was undoubtedly sparked by his witty, passionate and dramatic style of communicating. His verbal prowess proved to be equally effective in his chosen profession, the law. But law was not Dad's first choice. He wanted to be a doctor, the dream of many young men of his time. Dad's two best friends followed that professional pathway. The story Dad often told about the event that changed his life's goal from medicine to law is typical of the wonderful stories I grew up with.

In his first year of medical school at Columbia University; Dad was required to take a course in which students observed an operation in progress. In Dad's case it was an operation called a mastoidectomy. (I googled it, it's complicated and it still takes 2-3 hours.) Apparently, while in the midst of the required observation, Dad fainted dead away and had to be revived. So much for med school and "Doctor Wolfango."

I'm sure of it, my father said so.

Ironically, when I was a child I was prone to severe ear infections and on many occasions Dr. Cerchy (Dr. *Camillo* Cerchiara, my father's best friend for whom I was named) was frequently called to our house to "lance" my ear to drain the infection. Dad was never in my bedroom when the "lancing" occurred. I never knew why until I was an adult and he told me about the frightening operation that detoured his career path.

My father's local celebrity as amateur actor and community activist soon caught the attention of the local Democratic party. Dad was asked to run for Mount Vernon Supervisor in 1927, just two years after he had opened a law practice; another feather in the ambitious young man's cap. He ran as a Democrat, but lost the election and chose not to go the political route ever again. Years later, he became a Republican.

Here is his campaign bio as published in the local paper.

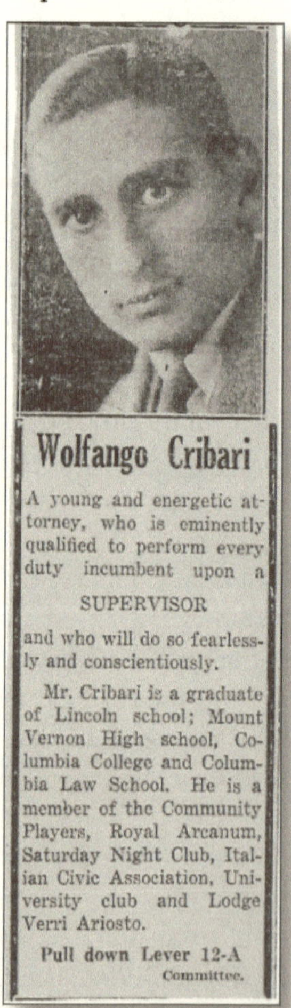

Wolfango Cribari

A young and energetic attorney, who is eminently qualified to perform every duty incumbent upon a

SUPERVISOR

and who will do so fearlessly and conscientiously.

Mr. Cribari is a graduate of Lincoln school; Mount Vernon High school, Columbia College and Columbia Law School. He is a member of the Community Players, Royal Arcanum, Saturday Night Club, Italian Civic Association, University club and Lodge Verri Ariosto.

Pull down Lever 12-A

Committee.

N.Y. State Supreme Court judge, Judge Humphrey J. Lynch, sent him a letter of encouragement after his political setback. Some of his words of advice are as relevant today as they were a century ago.

> *My dear Mr. Cribari December 5, 1927*
>
> *I want to congratulate you particularly upon the splendid run that you made going as you did so far ahead of the ticket, which speaks well of the esteem in which you are held in your native city. I am sure I do not need to tell you that you have remarkable talent that I am sure will be of great service to you in the profession that you have chosen and I am looking forward with great anticipation to see you struggle your way up the ladder until you arrive at the position of being one of the leading trial lawyers in this County*
>
> *There are things more important in life than being elected to public office. It was a wise statesman who said, "I would rather be right than President," and I think you and I can both take inspiration from that quotation.*
>
> *I want to impress upon you the importance of not losing faith in the principles of our party. We can put Westchester County in the Democratic column within the next three years.*

Dad's life in his twenties was as hectic at home as it was in college, politics and the theater group. This scene is a snapshot of those days. My uncle Guido told us another version of this incident that remains a family mystery.

SCENE THREE: MUSICAL ABOUT THE CRIBARI FAMILY

The Savoy Ice Cream parlor. Next to Cribari home, Broad Street.

An afternoon in Spring, 1928

MARIO is at the front window of the ice cream parlor signaling like mad to GUIDO who comes running in, rips off his baseball jacket, runs behind the counter, splashes some water on his hands and puts on his white uniform jacket.

MARIO:
Guido, where the hell have-ya been? Mom was just here and I told her you were out on a delivery.

GUIDO;
We went into extra innings. Thanks for covering for me. Any customers?

MARIO:
Nah, it's been quiet. But that's the last time I'm covering for you.

GUIDO:

I already thanked you. What the hell else d'ya want? You're gonna have to thank **me** pretty soon.

MARIO:

What're ya talkin' about?

GUIDO:

You'll see. I'm gonna bring in a big counter business.

MARIO:

Sure!

GUIDO:

The guys said they were gonna stop by on the way home, for eskimo pies.

MARIO:

Jeez. I hope you didn't offer to treat the whole team.

GUIDO:

Who said anything about treating? I'm bringin' in customers.

MARIO:

The guys on your team are the customers? Forget it!

GUIDO:

Not my team. Augie heard me talkin to Joey and he's bringin' the whole varsity, first string! Wait'll you meet 'em. (*He is interrupted by HUGO's entrance. HUGO is already dressed to go out for the evening.*)

HUGO:

Hey, Guido, mom wants ya. (*GUIDO runs off towards the house)* What's up, kid? Where are all the customers? Did you try the new slot machine?

MARIO:

No, pop says we're not allowed. Hey, Huey, isn't that Arnold's tie?

HUGO:

(Adjusting the tie smartly) Looks pretty good, huh? With Wolfe's shirt.

Say, kid, Gen loved those fancy forms we had Saturday night, you know the rose shaped ones with the strawberry ice cream…

MARIO:

Yeah, so!

HUGO:

How 'bout wrapping me up a few of those fancy forms to take to her?

MARIO:

Ya got $3.50?

HUGO:

Ah, come on, this is family.

MARIO:

Gen? Family? That's not what mom says. (*HUGO gives him a meaningful look*) Ah gee, Huey, you know everybody's always chiselin' pop outa ice cream. That's why we can't make a dime even though everyone says Savoy's the best stuff around. What other ice cream business has the owner's sons pickin' the tops off the strawberries, hand dippin eskimo pies… (*GUIDO enters on MARIO's diatribe)*

HUGO:

All I asked ya for was some lousy fancy forms.

MARIO:

(continues where he left off) ..waitin on customers every day after school, makin' home deliveries to regulars who complain if one drop melts.

HUGO:

By the way, when do you start makin' deliveries tonight?

MARIO:

Why? Ya gonna help out?

GUIDO:

Hey, Mario, ma says we can close the store early and eat dinner at five cause there's lots of special deliveries tonight on the truck.

MARIO:

That's great. Maybe Wolfe'll let me drive the truck. *(Hands a package to HUGO he had been putting together)* Here's your fancy forms, Huey.

HUGO:

Gee, thanks! Gen'll love them. (*Starts to exit, runs into two suspicious looking men at the door.)*

MOBSTER #1:

Hey kid, we got a work order here for Savoy Ice Cream. We got to pick up a defective slot machine.

MARIO:

(*Looks at the "work order"*) Savoy Ice Cream, that's us. Yeah, here's the slot machine. Pop just bought it from a friend he used to know in Italy. It cost a fortune. *(Realizes his mistake in next minute)*

MOBSTER #2:

You guys must be in the chips.

MARIO:

(*Pokes GUIDO to say something, GUIDO remains dumbstruck*) Well, we just made the last payments on it. Last time pop tried it, it worked fine.

MOBSTER #1:

C'mon, Augie, Let's get it in the truck. We still got a few more jobs.

(*They pick up the slot machine, put it on a hand truck and leave the shop in a hurry.*)

MARIO:

(*Shouts at men as they leave*) Hey, wait! We've gotta call pop, he's out on a delivery. (*To Guido*) Pop didn't tell me they were coming to pick up the slot machine, did he tell mom?

GUIDO:

How am I supposed to know.

MARIO:

(*Realizes what just happened*) Omigod, we're in for it. Maaaaa!!!

I wonder if dad ever got involved in finding the ones who stole the machine.

N. Y. GIRL, 20, LOSES DEATH CELL CALM

Doris Becomes Hysterical On Eve of Last Appeal.

By JOHN O'DONNELL.

Montreal, Que., March 13.—The 20-year-old American girl, who is known to her jailer nuns by the single name of Doris, lost her death cell calm today and gave way to hysteries on the eve of the clemency appeal to save her from the noose of Canada's hangman next week.

She impatiently summoned her lawyers to the Fullum st. jail.

She ordered and received the fancy dishes on which she and her fellow-condemned, young George McDonald, had once dined in

R. L. Calder Doris "McDonald"
Former crown prosecutor and condemned girl.

Broadway cabarets and Montreal hotels. She even demanded a name under which to mount the scaffold. But the last request went unfulfilled.

For Doris has proved to the nuns and her confessor that she was never married to McDonald, the young confidence man with whom she has been found guilty of murdering a Lachine taxi driver last

the mother who lost her in infancy.

Her Westchester marriage to Buster Allen was annulled.

J. A. Le Gault, counsel for the condemned pair, arrived in Ottawa tonight to make his clemency appeal for the American girl to Minister of Justice La Pointe tomorrow. R. L. Calder, former crown prosecutor, was summoned by Doris to her cell today, but business had taken him outside the province and he will not meet her until the end of the week.

The girl, who has felt that she had been abandoned by every one except the mother whom she does not care to see, Mrs. Hazel Snyder of Chicago, was cheered by word that her Mount Vernon counsel, Wolfgang Cribari, would arrive in Montreal Monday and be with her until her sentence had been commuted or she had mounted the steps of the scaffold in Valleyfield prison.

— 19 —

FIRST CRIMINAL CASE MAKES INTERNATIONAL HEADLINES

DAD BEGAN HIS LAW practice at age 25. At the end of his first year of practice, 1928, he took on a case The New York Journal described as one of "nation-wide interest." It involved the defense of Doris Palmer MacDonald, a society girl from dad's hometown of Mount Vernon, who was already in a Montreal jail for her part in the murder of a Canadian cab driver when dad became involved.

DAILY NEWS

Montreal, Quebec March 13, 1928.

The 20 year old American girl, who is known to her jailer as Doris, lost her death cell calm today and gave way to hysterics on the eve of the clemency appeal to save her from the noose of Canada's hangman next week.

The girl who felt that she had been abandoned by everyone but her mother whom she does not care to see...was cheered by word that her Mount Vernon counsel, Wolfgang Cribari, would arrive in Montreal Monday and be with her until her sentence had been commuted or she had mounted the scaffold in Valleyfield prison.

Doris was under sentence to hang. Dad joined a local committee to help save her in February 1928. The Julia Palmer McDonald Case became a national news sensation. Julia was referred to as "sex-mad, gin-mad, jazz-mad" These images were at the center of her case and dad set out to connect them to a plea of insanity.

Press reports began to hint at Julia's conversion, *"She was consoled by the gentle nuns at L'Agile Sainte Marie Convent in Montreal."* This in contrast to the press's original depiction of Julia as mad-cap flapper and in stark contrast to the murdered man's widow who was pictured in the newspapers with her seven fatherless children. Like today, sensationalism sells!

Julia Palmer's husband, George McDonald, a former U.S. Navy sailor, was under sentence to hang for the murder of the cab driver on March 23, 1928.

Dad traveled to Montreal two weeks before Julia's husband was scheduled to be executed. *"Wolfango Cribari, Mount Vernon attorney, volunteered his services without compensation and at great personal sacrifice made several trips to Montreal and Ottawa."*

DAILY NEWS
Montreal, March 17

Doris Bares Her Soul As Death Nears

By JOHN O'DONNELL

Montreal, March 17.—While her two attorneys, one American and one Canadian, were battling separately in Ottawa and Montreal today to win life-giving clemency from the British Crown, young Doris Palmer, American flapper-bandit condemned to hang, made two confessions in her death cell in the Fullum st. jail.

One was made to the French-speaking chaplain of the prison. It was a necessary religious prelude to the holy communion which

(NEWS photo)
Wolfgang Cribari

the American girl will receive at the prison mass tomorrow on what may be the last Sunday the girl will spend on earth.

Her other confession, a detailed account of what took place six months ago when Adelard Bouchard, Lachine taxi driver, was shot down by the revolvers of Doris and George McDonald, was made to Wolfgang Cribari the Mount Vernon attorney, who is now the spearhead of the American campaign for clemency.

Cribari was obviously depressed as he realized the weight of the public sentiment behind the silent pressure which is steadily pushing the girl and George McDonald toward the scaffold of Valleyfield prison, where both are scheduled to die next Friday morning.

"I can't realize that this young girl is going to die," Cribari said as he left the jail. "I don't think she herself completely understands.

While her two attorneys, one American and one Canadian, were battling separately in Ottawa and Montreal today to win life-giving clemency from the British Crown, young Doris Palmer, American flapper-bandit, condemned to hang, made two confessions in her death cell in Fullum St. jail. One was made to the French speaking chaplain of the prison. It was a necessary religious prelude to the holy communion which the American girl will receive at the prison mass tomorrow on what may be the last Sunday the girl will spend on earth.

Her other confession, a detailed account of what took place six months ago when Adelard Bouchard, Lachine taxi driver, was shot down by the revolvers of Doris and George McDonald, was made to Wolfgang Cribari, the Mount Vernon attorney, who is now the spearhead of the American campaign for clemency.

Cribari was obviously depressed as he realized the weight of the public sentiment behind the silent pressure which is steadily pushing the girl and George McDonald toward the scaffold of Valleyfield prison where both are scheduled to die next Friday morning.

"I can't realize that this young girl is going to die, Cribari said as he left the jail. "I don't think she completely understands."

Dad's goal was to get George McDonald to corroborate his wife Julia's claim that *"I didn't do a thing."* After visiting Julia's husband in jail Dad was able to obtain McDonald's statement and it literally saved Julia's life. Here it is:

> *"To whom it may concern, This is to certify that my wife Doris Palmer McDonald now in jail in Montreal is innocent of the murder of A.Bouchard. I swear to this, my God in heaven. She had not one thing to do with this murder. The Denver confession is untrue." Dad brought a copy of the condemned man's last message to Doris in her cell. George's affidavit absolved her of any guilt in the murder.*

CANADA SPARES LIFE OF DORIS

Mercy for Girl Spells New Hope for McDonald.

By JOHN O'DONNELL.

Montreal, Quebec, March 19. —Doris Palmer McDonald has been saved from the scaffold of Canada.

Formal announcement of the government's decision to grant the young American girl the boon of the king's mercy will not be made until Wednesday or Thursday, but the powers have decided she shall not die.

The news today came down from the house of parliament building in Ottawa and even penetrated into the nun-guarded death cell of Doris in the Fullum st. jail.

Her Fate Links His.

The fate of George McDonald, the lover, who until yesterday shielded himself behind his common law wife and then absolved her of blame, is still in doubt. Probably next Friday dawn he will mount the eighteen steps leading to the death platfrom of the century-old gibbet and give his life for the crime of which he and Doris were found guilty—the murder of a Lachine taxi driver, Adelard Bouchard, last July.

Third Slayer Hunted.

McDonald has two chances for life, and both are imbedded in the final disposition of the fate of the titian-haired girl. After the commutation of Doris' sentence to life imprisonment is announced a plea will be made for a new trial for the girl—a trial at which McDonald's appearance as a witness will be necessary.

His second chance comes from the desire of his enemies, the police. They wish to keep him alive while there is a chance of capturing the third member of the murder band, Ralph McMullen. There is fear that the poor health of Doris may lead to her early natural death, and with her and McDonald eliminated there would be no one who could identify McMullen. Canadian detectives are still confident of his early capture, probably in New York City.

Will George McDonald be spared? Read tomorrow's Pink and other editions of THE NEWS.

(NEWS photo)

Wolfgang E. Cribari of Mount Vernon, N. Y., attorney for Doris McDonald, and J. A. Le Gault, her trial attorney, in conference over her case in Montreal.

DAILY NEWS

Montreal, Quebec, March 19

Doris Palmer McDonald has been saved from the scaffold of Canada.

Formal announcement of the government's decision to grant the young American girl the boon of the king's mercy will not be made until Wednesday or Thursday, but the powers have decided she shall not die.

The news today came down from the house of parliament building in Ottawa and even penetrated into the nun-guarded death cell of Doris in the Fullum jail.

"Think of Me Often," MacDonald's Last Message to His Young Wife

Sent Letter to Former Mount Vernonite Few Hours Before Execution—Attorney Describes Scene When Reprieve Came This Week.

"I'm going to say good-bye, Doris, as I think I am going. Think of me often if you go free."

GEORGE."

These were the last words to his wife, Doris Palmer MacDonald, written by George MacDonald, only a few hours before he went to the gallows in Canada this morning, for the murder of Adelard Bouchard, taxicab driver.

Excerpts from MacDonald's last letter, full of pathos, were given exclusively to the Daily Argus this morning by Attorney Wolfango Cribari on his return from Canada, where he had spent the past week in connection with the appeal which finally won a reprieve for the former Mount Vernon girl.

The story of how Mrs. MacDonald, formerly Julia Doris Palmer, of this city, broke down when told of her reprieve, and of her reaction last night to the approaching death of her husband, was also told today by Mr. Cribari in an interview with the Daily Argus.

Prior to leaving Canada last night, Mr. Cribari secured a copy of MacDonald's last letter to his wife. The letter, written from Bordeaux jail just before the doomed man was taken to Valleyfield to be hanged this morning, began as follows:

"Dear Doris—

"I am sorry to say that from now on, I hold no chance for life, so all I am going to do from this hour, is to get ready for a good and holy death."

Continuing, MacDonald told of how his father had come to visit him, and of how he had broken down and wept.

"I hope I can have mother ready for the news," the letter continues. "I will have to pray hard for strength for her. I hope if you go free, you will always follow the rules of the Holy Catholic church. . . . . . I will try and guide you from heaven—I will go to heaven, as I will die in a state of grace. From this hour on, my thoughts are going to be of God alone. . . . . . You will say a prayer for me, for I will need it."

Calmly resigning himself to his fate, MacDonald continued:

"I guess I will not get an answer to this, as I think I will be in another world by then. Don't think Doris for a minute that I am afraid to die—far from it. If God wants me, and I think He does, I will be glad to go Him. I prayed to God for help and strength on the last days, and I got it."

The doomed man then concluded his last earthly epistle with the plea that Doris think of him often.

When MacDonald arrived at Val-

(Continued on Page Six)

Atty. Wolfango Cribari

Thus Dad's career path became clear. His face recognition skyrocketed and his reputation as a talented, even unconventional, criminal defense lawyer was launched.

> *Wolfango E. Cribari, brilliant young attorney of Mount Vernon, who has been staging an untiring fight to save the girl said yesterday,* ***"all hope lies in the hands of Minister LaPointe. He alone can save the girl."***

Minister La Pointe did "save the girl," Julia Palmer, from the gallows.

Here is how Dad summed it all up after the fact:

> *I am convinced the Canadian authorities would* ***not*** *have commuted her sentence. Before I left, there was handed to me an official announcement from Ottawa indicating that the reprieve had come through merely in the natural course of Canadian justice and not because Julia Palmer was a woman and least of all because she was an American.*

Julia's final words to my father:

> *"Mr. Cribari, how may I show you my gratitude for your unexpected help? I do thank you again and again."*

Dad's comments to the press about Julia's Mount Vernon neighbors' adverse reactions to her commuted sentence:

> ***"The law in this case was more merciful than those who call themselves Christians."***

This is an unconventional comment even for my father; it means Doris's critical Mount Vernon neighbors.

What a dramatic start to dad's career of defending others.

Husband Holds Doris' Fate

MONTREAL.—Urgent requests for the presence of Wolfango E. Crebari, Mount Vernon, N. Y., attorney acting for the McDonald defense committee, marked the dawning of the last eight days of life for Doris Julius McDonald, sentenced to hang at Valleyfield on March 23 with George McDonald, her husband, for the murder of Adelard Bouchard.

W. E. Crebari.

A wire to the Mount Vernon attorney from the assistant Mother Superior of the Women's Prison, brought the reply that he would be in Montreal by Friday morning at latest, to remain here until the question of life or death is settled.

Doris pins her sole hope of reprieve on the possibility of McDonald issuing an affidavit clearing her of participation in the crime. Immediately upon Crebari's arrival a conference of lawyers will be called to devise a means of obtaining McDonald's story of the Bouchard killing.

J. A. Legault, K. C., Doris' trial attorney, said he had interviewed the Minister of Justice at Ottawa, but his conference had shed no hope on the case.

Both Doris and McDonald will be moved to Valleyfield on Wednesday to await execution on Friday.

ATTORNEY IS URGED TO COME

Former Julia Palmer Wants to See Him In Reference to Case

HURRIED CALL SENT

Wolfango Cribari to Leave for Montreal Tonight—Will Remain Sometime

Montreal, March 15.—(INS) — Urgent requests for the presence of Wolfango E. Cribari, Mount Vernon, attorney who is acting for the MacDonald defense committee, marked the dawning of the last eight days of life for Doris Julia MacDonald, sentenced to hang at Valleyfield on March 23 with George MacDonald, her husband, for the murder of Adelard Bouchard.

A wire to the Mount Vernon attorney from the assistant mother superior of the women's prison brought the reply that he had been delayed at home by his practice but that he would be in Montreal by Friday morning at latest and would remain here until the question of life or death is settled.

Doris pins her sole hope of reprieve on the possibility of MacDonald issuing an affidavit clearing her of participation in the crime. Immediately upon Cribari's arrival, she will summon a conference of all her array of legal talent to devise a means of obtaining MacDonald's story of the Bouchard killing.

J. A. Legault, K. C., her trial attorney, returned from Ottawa late Wednesday night with the news that he had interviewed the minister of justice but that his conference had shed no hope on the case.

Until Cribari arrives on Friday, the door of her death cell is barred to all counsel except R. L. Calder, K. C. She has refused to speak to anyone else until the Mount Vernonite arrives to advise her.

On Wednesday both girl and lover will be moved to Valleyfield to await execution on Friday.

Mr. Cribari will leave Mount Vernon tonight.

— 20 —

WOLFE & CAROLA— DIFFERENT WORLDS

AVVOCCATO WOLFANGO FULVIO CRIBARI married Carola Emilia Ankerson on June 10th 1930. As I wrote this fact I stopped short and realized that this was all I knew about the most important event in their lives to date. A phone call with my sister "Bill" (Carola Helen is on her birth certificate, my father gave her the nickname) helped me remember and filled in a few details.

First a little background from that most unreliable of all sources, family lore. My father's mother, Eugenia Manes Cribari, was a practicing Roman Catholic and a pillar of Sts. Peter and Paul Church in Fleetwood for her entire life. My mother's mother, Bertha Lehrkind Ankerson, was an Episcopalian. I believe mom was baptized Episcopal. I'm sure dad was baptized Catholic. Historic Episcopal St. Paul's Church in Mount Vernon was the bride's family's choice for her wedding.

Neither dad nor mom were church-going people, so where their marriage ceremony took place was not a problem they anticipated. They should have because Eugenia refused to attend her son Wolfe's wedding because the ceremony was to be held in a NON-Catholic church.

Anyone raised Catholic in the mid-20th century will understand why I put NON in caps. I was raised Catholic, terrified of committing the grave offense of attending any other church but Catholic, "the true faith." I guess nana Cribari felt the same way, but the bride's family traditionally makes the decisions. It must have been awful for everyone.

I'll never know just how difficult a time it was for my parents. I do know that to pacify nana Cribari, dad and mom were married a second time in the rectory of St. Peter and Paul Church by its pastor Father John Delaney. One other thing I do remember mom saying about their wedding, which my sister confirmed, is that mom wore a peach colored wedding dress because she "didn't look good in white." I don't have any pictures, but no matter what color, Carola Ankerson must have looked exquisite!

"I would like to be a millionaire" ... Avvocato Cribari,

When I was growing up in the 1940's and 1950's the name of **Wolfe Cribari** was well-known and respected in his hometown of Mount Vernon; he was a local celebrity! When his Italian clients occasionally arrived on our doorstep I heard them ask for Avvocato Cribari a name I never understood. Mount Vernon's Italian community sought him out and jumpstarted his career in a way high profile cases couldn't. His Italian immigrant roots gave him a unique standing in his chosen profession. Proof is in the fact that dad was only 28 years old when he was featured in the weekly Daily Argus column, "What They Would Like To Be," August 15, 1931

Recently married and a proud graduate of Columbia University Law School, dad had the "world on a string." His first response to the column's title question," I would like to be a millionaire" not only sounds superficial, but selfish, two words that don't belong in the same sentence with my father's name. Read on, you'll learn more, as I did, about his early career.

> *"Especially I would like to be a millionaire in order that I might shower on my mother and father all the luxuries and happy times that wealth can reasonably bring, to recompense them in a slight degree for their sacrifices and unselfishness in my behalf when they were in need as much as I...If it had not been for the wonderful sacrifice of my parents I would not have attained anything I have acquired...I enjoy fulfilling other people's wishes and get a vicarious happiness from other people's good fortune."*

He said he would also like to be a millionaire because an independent income would ***allow him to practice the law "in which he is most interested, for which he is best fitted and which appeals to him most."*** A final reason dad gave is that he would like to have his own private golf course, tennis courts and not have to stand in line.

I'm sure of it. My father said so.

He was the most difficult person I ever stood in line with, *ever!*

— 21 —
DISCOVERING ROOTS

IN OCTOBER 1933, WOLFANGO and Carola Cribari set sail on the Italian cruise line Rex for a late honeymoon trip to Italy. It was basically a visit to dad's relatives in Calabria, Falconara Albanese. No stops in Rome, Florence or Venice on their travel itinerary. This trip on a luxury ship came at a time when Italy was thriving under the leadership of Benito Mussolini, Nana Cribari's hero.

I love looking at their eyes in this passport picture, I see fear, vulnerability, exasperation, but also a real determination; their body language is one of togetherness. It had to be because it wasn't just Mom and Dad setting sail that October day, Nana Cribari went along with her son and his new bride. Why their European honeymoon became a threesome is at the top of my list of things I wish I'd asked my parents to explain.

Here are a few scenarios: Dad was doing well enough financially to pay for all three tickets. Carola loved to travel and was willing to share her good fortune with her new mother-in-law. Nana Cribari accepted the invitation never considering herself a fifth wheel. Dad was way too enmeshed in his role of "favored son." Dad persuaded Carola that his mother's presence in Italy would benefit them, she spoke the language, knew the customs. Or **all** of the above!

Learning about the early days of mom and dad's marriage really made me appreciate mom's strength more than ever. Carola Ankerson lived up to the literal meaning of her maiden name, she was dad's ***anchor.*** I believe he knew it. Mom was always there when he felt insecure, when he questioned himself. A new metaphor to define their undefinable bond.

Here is a photo of mom and dad on board the Rex in October 1933. Mom is third from left; dad is on the end at right. The others are obviously shipmates.

Nana is not in the picture, she obviously gave them their "space."

They both look very happy.

Thank you, dad and then mom, for taking such good care of these now ninety year old photographs. They're family treasures.

The next one is of the steamship Rex. The second one is of a touring car mom and dad were photographed in during their trip. They are in the second row on the left. I don't see nana Cribari in that picture either.

This is nana Cribari's family in Falconara Albanese, 1933. Taken at the same time as those that follow.

My very favorite picture of dad. In his mother's homeland, probably Falconara Albanese, October 1933.

All dressed up in a business suit and necktie riding on a donkey. He looks so "at home" and comfortable.

I post this on Face Book every year on his birthday and get the best comments. It makes people happy!

Nana Cribari with her father Joseph Manes, dad's grandfather, and a woman who has been identified by family members as Joseph's mistress.

Nana's whole family with Joseph its central character. That's nana over her father's right shoulder.

These remarkable photos have stood the test of time because they were valued by both my parents.

Here's mom in the beautiful native costume of her Italian American husband's mother's hometown of Falconara. She looks right at home and loving every minute.

Mom was already enamored by the Neapolitan songs which she learned to play on the piano to accompany my father's singing.

Another picture of Joseph Manes, on the balcony of his home.

His folded hands remind me of my dad's long, tapered fingers.

An inherited feature of dad's which I share.

A legend about Joseph is that he died in his nineties when he fell out of a tree. I wonder if the Manes family in Italy has any other stories about our colorful ancestor.

— 22 —

FAMILY TREES—ROOTS

WHEN MY PARENTS CELEBRATED their 25th wedding anniversary, I gave them a memory book which included a page for their respective family trees. I assumed neither one was into "roots" because neither one wrote anything on that page.

I did some research and created these family trees:

Groom's Family Tree
Wolfgang Edward Cribari

Father's side
Father:
Beniamino Salvatore Cribari
Grandmother:
Carolina Chiapetta Cribari
Grandfather:
Bernadetto Cribari

Mother's side:
Mother:
Eugenia Manes Cribari
Grandmother:
Rose Riggio Manes
Grandfather:
Joseph Manes*

Bride's Family Tree
Carola Emilie Ankerson

Father's side
Father:
Gustav Herman Ankerson
Grandmother:
Helen Paulsen Ankerson
Grandfather:
G.P. Ankerson

Mother's side:
Mother:
Bertha Lehrkind
Grandmother:
Emilie Lambach Lehrkind
Grandfather:
Julius Lehrkind born 1842

**The only ancestor dad and mom met during their 1933 trip to Calabria.*

In contrast to dad's immigrant parents, mom's German/Danish parents were born here. Mom told me a few stories she heard from her mother's Lehrkind relatives. I wrote down these highlights. This is mom's voice…

My grandfather Julius came here when he was 17 years old. He was very poor when he came here. His daughter Bertha (Carola's mother) was born in Davenport, Iowa. She met Gustav Ankerson there when he was working at a soda fountain. Then her family went out to Bozeman, Montana to live. She took a trip to Germany to find her father's family which is written about in her diary.

Julius ran away from home three times, one time he got a job as an apprentice in a brewery in Schleswig Holstein. The final time he stowed away on a ship that was bound for America. He arrived during the Civil War and was given an opportunity to enlist for money, but he refused.

I remember my grandfather, Julius, eating at the table, he ate big quantities of food. He didn't talk much. He wanted my father, Gustav Ankerson, to work for him, but my father turned down the job because he thought the brothers (Bertha's) would have been jealous. Mother couldn't stand the heat in the northeast so until I was 16 we went to Montana every summer.

Family traditions in Bozeman:

They always entertained us. They killed chickens. I remember when I was eight years old, I wanted to be in the circus and ride a horse. I didn't ride in Montana. Picked berries – sarvis berries, little bigger than blueberries. They had asparagus plants, orchards, We rode in a carriage pulled by horses. At ten I went to Yellowstone in my grandfather's Cadillac. Harm drove."

Harm was mom's young uncle. The only child of her grandfather Julius's second marriage, he was just five years older than she was. Mom traveled with Lou and me to Montana to see him in 1988. We loved meeting him and his wife Jean and seeing the Lehrkind Mansion and Museum dedicated to Harm's father and mom's grandfather Julius.

Here's another Lehrkind story from mom's memory.

> *"On August 26, 1927, Aunt Til (Lehrkind) was at cousin Anna's and saw Lindbergh flying toward Milwaukee while she was sitting on Uncle Hugo's porch in Le Claire, Iowa"*

I have to question mom's, or Aunt Til's, memory about the August date even though the year is accurate. Mom was in Paris on May 21, 1927 and witnessed the landing of Lindbergh's first transatlantic flight. Maybe Lindbergh was back in the U.S. later that year because the flight Aunt Til witnessed couldn't have been the historic first.

Mom's memory always served her well, but she said she *didn't like history!*

Programma

PARTE I.

1. INNI NAZIONALI

SINFONIA - Poeta e Contadino .... *Suppè*

SELEZIONE - "Traviata" .... *G. Verdi*

Orchestra Prof. S. Buoniconti

---

2. BACI E CAREZZE - Marcia .... *A. Salmaggi*

ALL'OMBRA - Mazurka .... *O. Di Bello*

Orchestra di Mandolini - Prof. L. Consoli

---

3. "TORNA A SORRENTO" *De Curtis*

AIDA MARTIGNETTI

"YOU'VE GOT WHAT GETS ME", *Geo. Gershwin*

BABY GLORIA MARTIGNETTI

Signorina Fanny Zimbardi al piano

PARTE II.

Il Romanzo di Un Farmacista Povero

Commedia in Quattro Atti di Edoardo Scarpetta

PERSONAGGI
(In Ordine di Comparsa)

CARMENIELLO - *servo di Elisa* .... Prof. A. Borloso
ELISA BONE' .... Ines Lampignani
FELICE .... Avv. Wolfango E. Cribari
NANNINA - *Fioraia* .... Marie Aprea
D. ANTONIO - *Capo giovine di Farmacia*, A. Pizzutello
CONTE SAVERIO CHICHIONE .... Vincent Petrillo
TOTONNO - *servo di Saverio* .... Avv. F. R. Sirignano
VENDITORE DI GIORNALI .... Frank Pirone
ALESSIO - *Dentista* .... Avv. Joseph Reitano
CONCETTA - *sua moglie* .... Josephine Gargani
GIUSTINA - *loro figlia* .... Rose Pirone
SERVO DEL DENTISTA .... Frank Pirone

Al quarto atto suonerà selezioni di violino la signora CAROLA A. CRIBARI accompagnata al piano dalla sig.na Theresa Pizzutello

---

BALLO — Orchestra Prof. S. Boniconti

— 23 —

CAROLA AND WOLFE'S FIRST ARTISTIC COLLABORATION

HERE IS A PROGRAMME for Grande Recito e Balle (*Recital and Dance*) to benefit La Cronaca Illustrata, an Italian newspaper published in Mount Vernon.

It is testimony to dad's undiminished desire to continue acting. It also spotlights his wife Carola's excellent reputation as a concert violinist; they were both featured in this all-star presentation. Mom and Dad had only been married for two years at the time, practically honeymooners.

I recognized names of a few other participants in this event, several were my parents' lifelong colleagues and friends: P.R. (Patsy) Sirignano, a N.Y. Supreme Court judge; Joseph Reitano, a respected Westchester politician, and Vincent Petrillo of the Petrillo Contruction family, one of dad's major clients for many years to come. Theresa Pizzutello, the sister of Carola's best friend, Mary, accompanied Carola on the piano.

— 24 —

A MAN OF MANY WORDS

BY HIS LATE TWENTIES, dad was married, had college and law school degrees and a promising law practice. He was the first and only professional in his immigrant family that both adored and were awestruck by him. Dad's early achievements dominated their lives, parents and siblings alike. Their adoration helped create the man he became.

Dad met his match in Carola Ankerson. She also knew what she wanted early in life and allowed nothing to get in her way. Her parents never denied her anything. They allowed her to quit school in tenth grade, sent her to Paris for a musical education and ultimately supported her choice of the son of Italian immigrants as her husband. Such a choice was a first in the Ankerson-Lehrkind families who were of northern European, mid-western backgrounds.

Mom said she was first attracted to dad by his letters. I'm sure that wasn't the whole story. As a fellow member of the Community Players she watched dad in a variety of onstage performances over several years. He had matinee idol status in the group, I can't help comparing dad to one of his favorite fictional heroes, Cyrano De Bergerac, not just the prominent nose, but for his exceptional way with words. Those words worked for dad, but not for Cyrano. Cyrano did something dad never would have done. Cyrano wrote letters to his love Roxanne for *another man*. When Roxanne discovered it was Cyrano's letters she fell in love with, not the other man's, it was too late. Cyrano died of a broken heart.

I always smile when I recall dad's impromptu recitations of Cyrano's dynamic monologue, "Enorme mon nez" (*Enormous, my nose)* both in French, a language he studied and loved, and in English. You can see the verbal humor dad was so fond of in these excerpts from that monologue. I've only included five of Cyrano's 17 witty nose metaphors; dad used to recite them all. Like Cyrano, he adored role playing and flowery, eloquent language.

Viscount: Sir, your nose is very big...

Cyrano: Is that all? You might have said at least a hundred things.

Aggressive: Sir, if I had such a nose, I'd amputate it.

Considerate: Take care, your head bowed by such a weight lest head o'er heels you go.

Practical: Put it in a lottery. Assuredly, 't would be the biggest prize.

Descriptive: Tis a rock, a peak, a cape. A cape, forsooth, 'tis a peninsula.

Dramatic: When it bleeds, what a Red Sea!

My mother and father's relationship can also be compared to another classic love match, Katherina and Petruchio in *Taming of the Shrew*. Let me make it clear, mom was **not** a shrew. To the contrary, I never heard her yell at my father unless he started it, but he did lots of yelling.

When I was in my early teens, I distinctly remember the main cause for his frequent outbursts was the butcher mom bought the meat from. Dad's dramatic complaints made me afraid the butcher would become grounds for divorce; that's how serious their arguments always sounded to me. Nobody ever won those dinner time fights.

Here's the scenario: One night dad would praise the tenderness of the veal mom served him and the next night he'd rant and rave that she must be having an affair with the butcher to allow him to sell her such stringy veal. It didn't matter whether mom defended herself or remained silent, it always escalated into all out war.

Then one day it was over! It just stopped. Maybe mom got a different butcher. Or maybe she finally found the words to calmly tell dad to go buy his own meat, find his own butcher.

— 25 —

DAD'S HOROSCOPE 1/26/39

"Horoscopes merely indicate tendencies, remember you are still 'master of your Fate and Captain of your soul."

I'M SURE DAD'S FAMILY and friends would have been surprised to know that he believed in horoscopes. Not necessarily the ones you read in the daily newspaper, but those that connect date, time and place of birth to personality traits, natural talents, weaknesses and positive and negative signs to look for in the future. The 3 page horoscope I found in dad's papers is extremely comprehensive and in many aspects amazingly accurate. His earthly path, already written in the stars, began to reveal itself in the third decade of his life.

> *"Your great energies are harnessed to a definite and well-controlled purpose. You know what you want early in life and you see to it that nothing, and nobody gets in your way. You can appear passionate and ardent in love, but this is merely an expression of your generalized intensity and your desire to dominate."*

Dad's horoscope also describes his Venus (*love*) connection. It helps explain his "butcher fixation," just one of many of jealousy-based issues that exploded into fights. Why was it always during dinner? My answer, he had a captive audience!

"An emotional nature alternately repressed and explosive, apparently somewhat conventional and cold, but actually very independent and erratic. An idealist in the realm of love, full of theories about sex and human relations in general which complicate relationships that to other people are much more simple. Can be swept off (his) feet by an idea, an ideal, a theory more quickly than by the physical beauty of an individual."

Dad seems to have always had one eye on the future, his interest in horoscopes and one eye on his past, his connection to his heritage. I found several articles from Cronaca Illustrata, an Italian weekly newspaper among his memorabilia. I was surprised because I don't remember him speaking Italian, even with nana.

Dad's early success in a profession that required an exceptional command of language was another aspect of his horoscope that was a part of who he was.

"You make demands of the world, and in seeing to it that your demands are acceded to, you achieve success. Your great strength is unswerving purpose with the energy necessary for its accomplishment, and these qualities will take you as far as your imagination can reach."

A reporter from the Cronaca Illustrata, September 5, 1935 issue, saw this in dad when he interviewed him at age 32. Dad was already considered "a prominent Italian-American." He described dad perfectly in unique, flowery prose: *carattere dinamico* … dynamic character; *un tipo che si stacca immediatamente dalla massa*… a type who immediately stands apart from the crowd ; *"piu italiano di questo?*…more Italian than that?

Admittedly a stereotype, but in dad's case it was his reality. These words from his horoscope underline the same traits.

"Energy is the keynote of your nature. You have a sort of quivering intensity toward some goal not too well defined, and tend to spend your energies in nerves and in emotional and sensational matters. Your passionate nature in any case is strong – love, anger, hate, fear, all the personal passions can take strong hold of you."

Having researched and carefully preserved his 1939 horoscope, source unknown, means dad really felt it was as he would say ***"on the money."***

His self-awareness didn't help him control his jealous streak, but it worked for him as avvocato (*advocate, lawyer*), and through my eyes, as a singular, distinctive father.

CRONACA ILLUSTRATA

ITALIAN WEEKLY NEWSPAPER

The Italians of the County Are over 65,000

GIOVEDI' 5 SETTEMBRE 1935

NEW YORK 64 Spring Street Tel.: CAnal 6 — 2826

Personalita' Italiane nel Westchester

L'Avv. Wolfango Cribari

E' uno spirito irrequieto, come tutti gli spiriti che considerano il limite dello spazio un insulto alla intelligenza. E' un carattere dinamico, che alla cultura ed alla preparazione, accoppia in felicissima armonia le caratteristiche tipiche della razza latina. Intemperante nelle discussioni, caldo d'eloquenza nelle perorazioni, drammaticamente sentimentale nell'oratoria. E' un tipo che si stacca immediatamente dalla massa, e fra virgulti e ginepraı, a forza violenta della fede che sente nelle proprie convinzioni, tuona nella voce, si impone coll'energia, e crocifigge colla logica.

Più italiano di questo?

Ha nel passato e nel presente della sua famiglia calabrese, uno scenario dal quale attinge colore ed ispirazione. La gentile mammina sua, la signora Eugenia Menes, gli ha insegnato quello che modello significa per la donna: come madre, come sposa, come atomo in quella immensa e necessaria azione femminile che viene svolta dalle nostre dame nella contea di Westchester: figliuola del Cav. Giuseppe Menes, il quale ancora serve da cinquant'anni il comune di Falconara Albanese, nella verde, rude Calabria, in qualità di segretario Municipale, la mamma di Wolfango fonde in un unico carattere gentilezza, dolcezza femminile, ed energia, impetuosità calabrese.

Dal padre, l'amico nostro Salvatore Beniamino Cribari, Wolfango ha ereditato l'immenso amore per la terra d'orgine, lo sforzo strenuo che l'immigrato nostro ha dovuto materiare per

mocratico, nelle cui file ha portato sempre la voce potente dei bisogni degli Italiani: senza ambagie e senza troppo riguardo per chi mal vedeva le continue affermazioni italiane nel campo politico, ha sostenuto, anno per anno, la necessità che il partito riconoscesse la potenza, l'efficienza e la lealtà del voto italiano. E fu alfiere di queste delicate idealità, quando anni fa, in una battaglia tempestosissima, portò il colorito della sua candidatura a Supervisor, sulla scheda del suo partito. Ha coperto la carica di Commissario della Ricreazione Pubblica della città di Mount Vernon, per nomina del Sindaco Bateman.

E' oratore convincente, caldissimo

— 26 —

DECADES OF HOPE, LOSS AND CHANGE

THE ITALIAN NEWS REPORTER also describes dad as *"in felicissima armonia la caretteristiche tipiche della raza latina"* = in most felicitous harmony with the typical characteristics of the Latin race. This article also gave me new insights into nono Cribari's roots. He came from an educated family in Calabria; Francesco Cribari (*dad's uncle*) was a *"benemerito"*-well-respected professor.

"Con el brillante scenario L'avv Cribari non poteva non dare al magnifico contributo alla scena." With such a brilliant background, lawyer Cribari can't possibly not give a magnificent contribution to the scene.

— 27 —

BROTHER LOVE

WHILE THE 1930'S WERE years of growth and looking ahead for dad, he never lost his love for theater and acting. He didn't have time to perform himself, but he loved to go to the talkies. It was during the 1930's that the silent films he had always enjoyed acquired voices. I believe that his innate love of language and acting inspired him to write a manuscript synopsis for a screenplay called "Brother Love" which is included as he wrote it. I'm not sure if he ever sent a copy of this to a studio called Cosmopolitan Photoplay Studio in NYC, but here it is. Script No. I007

TITLE: "BROTHER LOVE"
AUTHOR: E.W. CRIBARI

Cast of Characters:

Mrs. Roger...	a widow
Sam and John Roger...	her sons
Nettie Wells...	the pretty sweetheart of Sam
Pearl Moss...	the girl over whom John loses his head
Richard Ross...	Pearl's sweetheart
Nettie's uncle	
Court attendants	

TIME: PRESENT
PLACE: A SMALL WESTERN TOWN

Mrs. Roger and her sons, John and Sam, live happily in a pretty little home in a small town. Mrs. Roger is an ideal mother and is worshipped by her sons, especially Sam, who is a college student. While attending college, Sam meets a pretty and vivacious girl named Nettie Wells. She is wealthy and although she loves Sam, her main thoughts are for enjoyment,

Nettie's father does not confide his financial downfall to her, and he soon dies leaving her supposedly penniless. John, the older of the sons, has been the main support of this little trio. He has recently fallen in love with Pearl Moss, a girl of disputable character. In order to give her all the things that her heart desires, John finds it necessary to give his mother less money every week. Mrs. Roger finds it hard to get along and Sam is obliged to leave college and seek work.

Nettie forgets all about John after he is gone. Sam finds work in a nearby grocery store, but Mrs. Roger has to work too, so as to make ends meet. Pearl feigns love for John so as to get all she can out of him. In reality she loves Richard Ross. Sam is informed of Pearl's double love affair, and tries to persuade John to give Pearl up. But to no avail. John's love is staunch and true.

On his way home after a meeting with Pearl, John passes the back of the grocery store and sees Sam putting away the day's receipts. John goes home, seeks seclusion in his room and plans to rob the grocery store. Mrs. Roger and Sam both notice that John is acting queerly and think it is over Pearl. Mrs. Roger tries to console John.

The following night Sam calls on Pearl for an explanation of John's attitude. He finds her in the company of Ross. The latter resents an offense Sam gives Pearl and they come to blows. Ross pulls a gun on Sam, but Sam deftly kicks it out of his hand, gets it and uses it to hold him at bay. Sam leaves the house, pockets the gun. On his way home, he notices a light in the store and the back window open. On looking closer he sees his brother. He goes to the drawer to see how much money his brother has taken.

A policeman happens to pass, notices the open window and light and investigates. Policeman flashes light on Sam and puts him under arrest. He searches him and finds the gun which makes matters worse. Sam is about to explain, but stops so as to shield John. His mother is informed and rushes into the jail and thrusting herself into Sam's arms begs him to tell the truth. He refuses saying, "Someday, Mother dear, you will understand."

Sam is tried and sentenced to three years imprisonment. On kissing his mother she faints in his arms. Turning he embraces John and asks him to leave Pearl and look after mother. John confesses that he is a coward, but Sam silences him. Things go from bad to worse.

The little home is sold and Mrs. Roger and John go to live in smaller quarters. John is still madly in love with Pearl and in consequence gives his mother no money. For lack of proper nourishment, Mrs. Roger weakens and dies. In his letters, John does not let Sam know of his mother's death because he realizes that he was the cause.

Pearl makes known her intention to marry Ross. John is furious with jealousy. She will not as much as let him into her home. On the date set for the wedding, owing to good behavior, Sam is freed. He immediately seeks his mother at home, but fails. Neighbors inform him where they moved to. Sam enters John's room and finds him cleaning a revolver. Sam asks for mother and on hearing the sad news, he grabs John by the throat. John flees, and Sam falls into a nearby chair and sobs convulsively

John runs all the way to Pearl's home, enters unawares, and just as the guests are drinking to the bride's health, John shoots her twice. She falls dead. John picks her up in his arms, kisses her frantically and swoons. He is arrested and tried and sentenced to die.

Sam tries to help John, but in vain. Sam is left alone. Nettie Wells has had a hard life since her father's death. She is forlorn and desperately seeks death in the cold waters. Sam is unhappy and seeks

> solitude. He sits on the pier thinking of all that has happened and hearing a splash turns and sees the form of a woman in the still water.
>
> He jumps into the water and swims to shore with his burden. He is amazed to recognize Nettie and takes her to his two room apartment in the basement, where he gradually nurses her back to health. When she recovers, they marry. Sam gets a steady job and they soon move to better quarters. Just about this time, an uncle of Nettie's locates her and tells her that a miscalculation has been made. Her father has left her a neat little sum. Sam and Nettie embrace and look forward to better times

Not my favorite, dad, sorry! This is a silent picture scenario in a talkies body.

Dad's screenplay must have been written after the death of his beloved father Benjamino in January 1937. The mother in the play is a widow.

— 28 —

THE PATRIARCH: BENIAMINO SALVATORE CRIBARI—A GREAT AND GALLANT MAN

MY MOTHER ALWAYS SPOKE of nono Cribari with affection. I'm sure nono was enchanted by his lovely, charming daughter-in-law. Depending on which of nono's ten children you spoke to, nono Cribari was feared, admired, resented and worshipped, quite a range.

I know dad adored his father and was undoubtedly devastated by his untimely death; the worst moment in his young life. Not only did dad lose a beloved parent, he took on the responsibility for his widowed mother in addition to that of his own growing family. I was seven months old when nono Cribari died so I have no memory of him nor the powerful changes his passing must have brought for everyone.

I researched nono Cribari's life by reading, translating and trying to interpret the Italian obituary. After comparing it to another in English, I discovered that many of nono's most notable traits were definitely passed down to his devoted son Wolfango.

Giovedì, 14 Gennaio, 1937.

E' morto a Mt. Vernon Salvatore Cribari

Uno dei più noti e fieri patrioti italiani di Mount Vernon è sparito dalla scena della vita, rapito all'affetto dei suoi da un male ribelle a ogni risorsa della scienza medica, alle 6.47 P. M. di venerdì scorso, 8 Gennaio, 1937. Salvatore Cribari, pioniere della comunità di Mount Vernon è morto come visse: serenamente; chiamando a nome la diletta consorte, i numerosi figli che volle vedere rispettati ed ammirati, col pensiero alla sua Sanfili (Cosenza) ove sempre desiderò tornare, perchè Salvatore Cribari nei suoi 45 anni di America amò soprattutto la sua terra natale e sempre ebbe l'orgoglio, la tenacia, l'onestà scrupolosa

SALVATORE CRIBARI

Here are excerpts from nono's obituary from the Italian newspaper Cronaca Illustrata the week following Beniamino's death, January 8, 1937.

They are testimony to the respect he received in his adopted homeland.

E morto un grande galanuomo = a great and gallant man has died.

Beniamino was also admired as a business pioneer who lived out his American dream for less than 30 years. *pionierer della communita de Mount Vernon*=a pioneer in the community of Mount Vernon.

Italianissimo con la parola nei consessi, nelle associazioni, sempre all' Italia, al suo popolo, alla sua storia ed ebbe per il Duce aconfinata ammirazione …

A true Italian with his words at meetings, in associations, always Italy, its people, its stories and he had admiration for Il Duce.

La suprema ambizione di dare al figli educatione professionale…

His main ambition was to give his children a professional education.

Fondo la Savoy Ice Cream Co., e per anni I suoi celebri spumoni e gelato ebbere la supremacia in tutte le magioni aristocratiche della contea…

He founded the Savoy Ice Cream Company and for years his celebrated spumoni and gelato were supreme in all the wealthy homes in the county.

Here's an envelope nono addressed to Wolfango, with the name of his business.

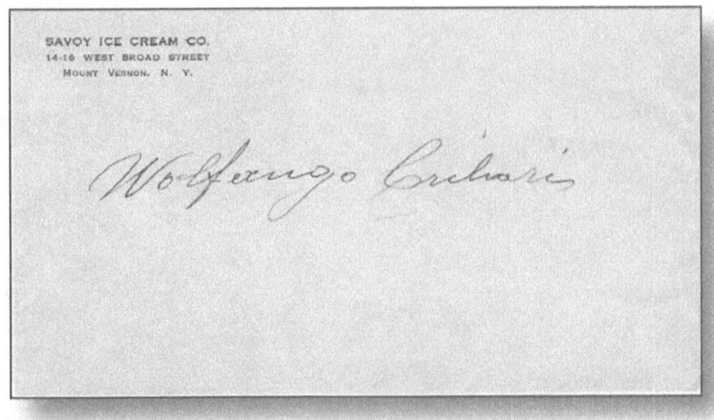

The reference to Il Duce in the obituary really surprised me. There's no way nono would have liked to be associated with the future Il Duce. A family story I often heard proves it. It goes like this:

Sometime in the 1930's nana sent her wedding ring to Italy's Mussolini (*Il Duce*) who she obviously admired and supported. Two details are sure: Nana's bold gesture happened before Mussolini was allied with Hitler in 1939 and was definitely before nono passed because his reaction is an integral part of the story.

When nono found out what nana did he was furious. It was her **wedding** ring. When I asked nana if it was true decades after the fact, she just laughed. Another Cribari legend I wish I knew more about.

This picture of Beniamino and his cousins, Benedetto and Vittorio, was taken in Italy. Benedetto sent it to nono in Mount Vernon as a memento of nono's "ultima volta" (*last return*) to Bucita, Calabria. I believe it was in 1929. Nono definitely made that ocean voyage back to Italy without nana; he may have made others. Dad kept several letters from members of his father's side of the family; here is a postcard from dad's grandfather "Tuo nonno Guiseppe" (*your grandfather Guiseppe*). A great grandmother (me) meets **her** great grandfather through a 100 year old postcard. Wow!

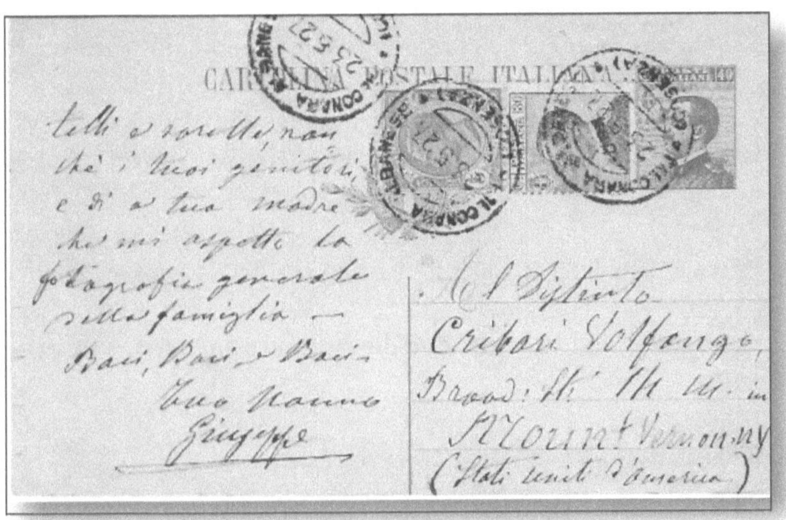

tutti e sorelle, non che i tuoi genitori, e di tua madre che mi aspetta la fotografia generale della famiglia — Baci, Baci e Baci — tuo Nonno Giuseppe

Al Distinto Cribari Volfango, Broad: St. 114 in Mount Vernon NY (Stati Uniti d'America)

Nono Cribari died in 1937, two years before Mussolini joined Hitler; when Mussolini was still an Italian hero as my grandparents' admiration reflects. Mussolini, the fascist's "new man" said he was prepared to fight should the need arise, but cleverly advocated a return to the ancient Pax Romana with its expansionist goal to create "*Italian living space in the Mediterranean area.*" I heard this as a child, "Mussolini made the schools better and the trains run on time." Italian-Americans pre-1939 bought it.

Dad's nephew and godchild, Stephen Cribari, wrote about our grandfather of whom *"he knew very little"* in his short story, "The Oregano Factor" *Nonno worked hard to establish a business that died with him. I would like to know why he found life so hard that he chose to die before I was born. He was physically explosive but otherwise silent, based on the few stories I've heard.*

I had to go to Italy, specifically Cosenza, to learn that my grandfather's people might be found in one hill town, my grandmother's in another, west, about three quarters of the way toward the Mediterranean. I spent a summer among these towns, Bucita, San Fili, Paolo, Falconara Albanese, San Lucido. Most of the area was settled by Greeks hundreds of years before Christ. In Falconara Albanese I learned that nonna was of Albanian origin and that nonno was Greek. Thank you, Stephen for finding our family's roots.

I only heard dad mention Il Duce once. I was about nine years old; dad was reading the morning newspaper. I used to look over his shoulder at the pictures on the front page. That morning I looked and saw a scary picture of dead bodies hanging upside down in the middle of a street. They were Mussolini and his mistress I discovered years later. Crowds of people were around them.

Dad stood up, folded the paper in half and slammed it on the table.

"Look what they did to **Mussolini**." he said and went upstairs to get ready for work.

I never told dad I saw that horrible picture. I can still see it.

— 29 —

SUGAR CUBES ON THE WINDOW SILL

WHEN MOM TOLD ME dad didn't want to have children I was shocked because of all the fathers I knew, dad was the best; so much fun to be with, so interesting to listen to. Even his many nieces and nephews couldn't wait to be around dad during holidays and on weekend visits. We all loved dad/Uncle Wolfe, he was silly, sang songs, played games, recited silly poems, told stories; ***engaged us.***

The feeling was mutual. Dad loved children. Nobody knows who the child in this picture is, but it shows his joy at being around children. Judging from the clothes, this is in the early 1930's before he had children of his own.

Mom was right, dad was wrong. He was destined and well equipped emotionally and intellectually to be a father. Whatever fears and doubts he had that stemmed from his own childhood never interfered with his innate ability to nurture. My mother must have sensed it, she left a lot of the nurturing, traditionally a maternal role, to dad. He was the one who got up and comforted us in the middle of the night when we were sick.

Dad used to say he was thankful he had three daughters and no sons. According to one of his creative "superstitions," the way to guarantee your children will be girls is to put a sugar cube on your kitchen windowsill. I never tried it for my own three daughters, but dad said he did and it worked.

I'm sure of it, my father said so.

I'll never know if " the sugar cube" idea was an old wives' tale dad heard. It might have been just another one of dad's "whoppers." I distinctly remember him saying that he wouldn't have been a good father for boys. Maybe that had something to do with the fact that he was raised with *six* brothers.

I can only imagine what dad's childhood must have been like. Over the years my aunts and uncles let it be known it was nothing short of chaotic. It had to have been. Their modest three story, three bedroom home housed ten children, seven boys, three girls and two parents. Loud? Boisterous? Overwhelming? Of course. A real problem for my scholarly, self-conscious, introspective father.

Whatever his doubts and fears, let it be known that Wolfango Cribari was an amazing father to his three daughters; we adored him and still do. I'll never believe that he wouldn't have been the same great father to sons.

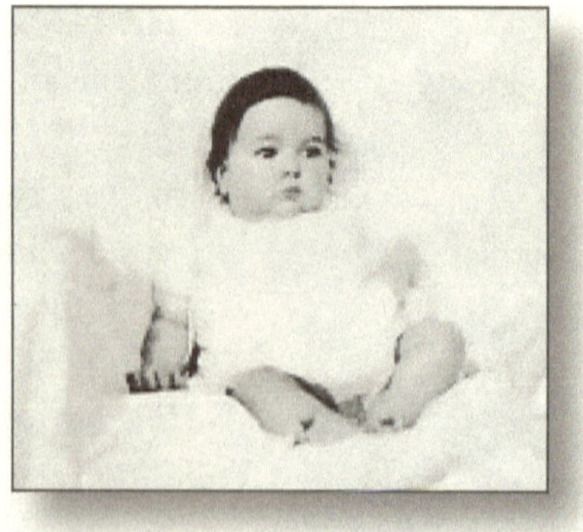

Baby Mia – Camille Carola

I was the first, "Baby Mia " Camille Carola– born June sixth, 1936: At 8 lbs, 14oz, 21 inches long, I was not an easy baby for my petite mother to deliver.

My mother was healthy and strong, but no one knew I was going to be a breech. Poor mom in hours long futile labor, I was going the wrong way.

Fortunately, Dr. Cerchy, dad's best friend and mom's doctor, had small hands and was able to turn me around so I could be born normally. As a thank you gift from my parents, I was named Camille after my savior, Dr. Camillo Cerchiara.

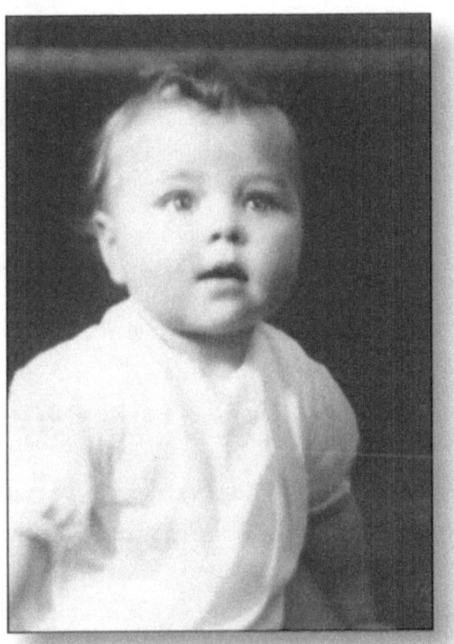

Baby Doni – Donna Marie

On the right, my sister Donna Marie, born April 30th, 1939 at 7 lbs. 11 oz, 19 inches long, second daughter for Wolfe and Carola. Thankfully no breech.

Mom tried several interesting ways to encourage Bill's arrival. She was late. One of mom's ideas was to try tap dancing. Mom, dad, Doni and I, were living at 395 Westchester Avenue so I envision my overdue, very pregnant mother tap dancing in the hallway. It eventually did the trick.

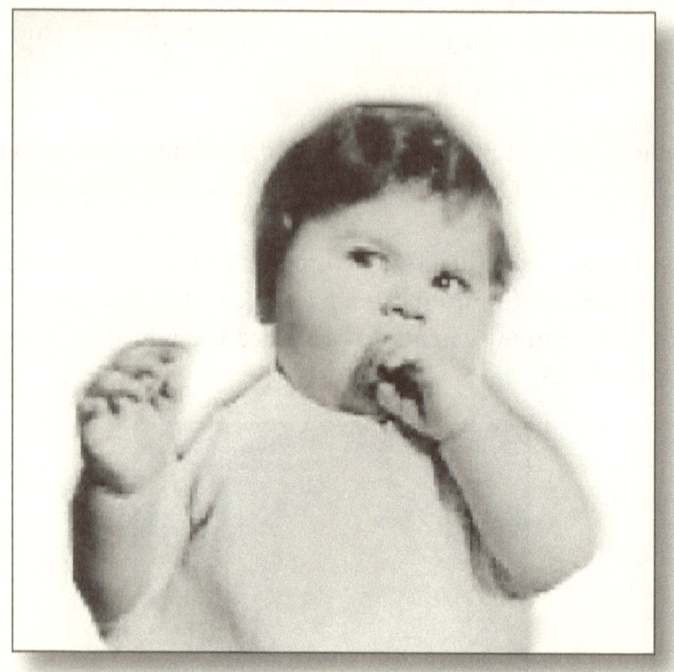

My youngest sister, Carola Helen, was born February 18th, 1942.

She was the biggest at 9 pounds 4 ounces, 21 inches long.

She also has the distinction of having been given the most nicknames. Dad called her Snookie, Goldberg and finally Bill.

Bill spent the first week or so of her life in the hospital waiting for her two sisters to get over the chicken pox.. Her quizzical expression in this picture seems to ask, "Is it safe for me to come home now?"

This picture of my christening in front of Saints Peter and Paul Church, Mount Vernon is a 1930's beauty. I am being held by my godmother, Rose, dad's oldest sister. Others from left to right: Nana Ankie, my mother's mother, Rose, Father Delaney who baptized me, my mother Carola peeking over Father Delaney's shoulder, my father Wolfe next to his best friend Dr. Cerchy, my godfather; Nono Ankie, my mother's father, Nana Cribari, dad's mother, partially hidden by Mary Cerchiara, Dr. Cerchy's wife.

It must have been a hot summer day judging from the brightness of the picture, my June birthdate and the clothes. The religious tension that effected my parents' wedding plans six years before is not apparent in this scene.

I love to imagine what was going on in the minds of my two grandmothers and my mother and father on this happy occasion. Nana Ankie is standing slightly removed, head high and proud, admiring her first granddaughter. Nana Cribari's face is literally hidden, perhaps she didn't want to reveal her victory smile: that day I was baptized a Catholic.

Mom's lovely relaxed smile is apparent, but she is behind the priest who six years before proved himself her friend and ally by marrying her and dad in the church rectory. It's ironic that my beautiful, first time mother allowed herself to be upstaged. Did she temporarily abdicate her new parental role to Rose? If you didn't know, you might think Rose was the mother. Dad, like nana Ankie, is standing tall and proud, also somewhat detached, closer to Dr. Cerchy than to his wife. Consider the trauma of his first child's breech birth and the role his best friend played in its happy ending.

Missing from the picture are my grandfather Beniamino, Rose's husband Jim Synnott, Miss De Rosso, my nurse, mom's sister Elfreida Barnett and dad's youngest sister Dolly. I learned from my baby book that they were *"later at the house"* Mom also made sure to mention that *"all had champagne."*

My baby book, still in good condition after eight decades, has been a limited source for telling dad's story from my early years. It obviously wasn't a priority for mom to write in it except for her detailed listing of who gave gifts, and the specific gifts they gave.

All parents know how the birth of a first child throws your marriage into chaos. For my parents the chaos started with my breech birth which was only weeks behind them on my christening day. My mother's optimism and my father's fearful nature are seen in the picture as are the feelings of all the participants in this happy, though slightly edgy celebration.

— 30 —

AND A LITTLE CHILD SHALL LEAD THEM

THIS ETCHING WAS ON my father's tall dresser for as long as I can remember. It is entitled "Peace." I don't know where he got it or who gave it to him but it must have had special meaning for him.

I believe it was one of dad's lifelong goals to find peace in domestic life. It says "*and a little child shall lead them.*" In our home, dad definitely let little children lead him. Not one of his three daughters was ever denied a thing. Even if mom was against one of our demands, she would defer to dad "*Go to the court of appeals:*" A clever and appropriate response.

It was rare that dad had a court case that involved a child, but in the last years of his life, he had one that affected him powerfully.

FAST FORWARD...twenty-seven years.

— 31 —

DEFENDING PLAYLAND, CRYING AT HIS SUCCESS

ONE OF DAD'S MOST unforgettable cases, one he often spoke about, proved to be a real test of dad's protective, quasi-maternal love for children. His reaction to winning the case reveals the depth of his connection.

I've used excerpts from a transcript of dad's Closing Statement at the trial which took place in May 1963 in a Westchester County courtroom. It shows dad at his best. In this thought provoking scenario dad was not the attorney for the injured child-plaintiff, but was defending the place where the injury occurred, Playland Amusement Park, Rye, New York.

Here are the vital facts: A young Catholic school girl, Carmela, from New Jersey, was on an end of the year class trip to Playland. While Carmela and her friends were on the park's Magic Carpet ride, Carmela got scared, jumped up out of her seat, grabbed a friend by the hand and started to run to find the attendant near the exit. The ride's pathway was dark, she had no idea where the exit was.

Question (Dad): Did you see the attendant?

Answer (Carmela): *Yes, I did.*

Question: But this time you didn't have any talk with him, and he didn't talk to you.

Answer (Carmela): *He refused to help me, He saw me hysterical.*

Question: But I mean there was no conversation?

Answer (Carmela): *He saw me hysterical.*

Question: There was no conversation?

Answer (Carmela): *No, but he saw me hysterical, most logical.*

Question: But there was no conversation?

Answer (Carmela): *No.*

Question: As you started to go over the rail, he was no longer there, was he?

Answer (Carmela): *There was no more aid or assistance, so that's my whole reason of jumping.*

Question: Well; he wasn't there any more?

Answer (Carmela): *I can't answer that. He could have been there. I can't answer that*

Dad to the jury: I don't know, honestly, ladies and gentlemen, where all this started from, but I have a strange conviction. This poor girl, unfortunate girl, came out on this balcony, scared to continue, and her girl friend didn't abandon her, after holding her by the hand from the time they started up to the Dizzy Room.

(Dad refers to friend, Miss Forte's testimony)

Question: Did you have her by the hand all the way through the Dizzy Room?

Answer (friend): *Yes.*

Question: And right out into the balcony?

Answer: (friend): *Yes.*

Question: And as you stood out in that balcony, did you have her hand, Miss Forte?

Answer (friend): *No, I let go of her hand when we got to the light.*

Dad to the jury: Now, Miss Forte was uncomfortable on the witness stand, you remember that. And there's a reason for it, because what really occurred was that Miss Forte told her, *"Stay here, and I'll go down and get some help."* Not that they screamed for anything. This is why the police records are honest and accurate. What happened? You know where the key is and I have a sneaking suspicion that many of you picked it up, The key, ladies and gentlemen, is in a little thing that Carmela said, which her honest face proved to me beyond a question of a doubt that this poor unfortunate girl was so coached way, way back, that she was giving a parrot-like story on the witness stand.

The sign, do you remember the sign? A sign which said, "If scared, call attendant." Can you imagine sticking those words in this poor kid's mouth. Everyone in there would be screaming for attendants because everyone was scared. Naturally, that's what it was there for.

Carmela became frightened; couldn't go back or couldn't go forward. So she jumped from the balcony. There it is, big as life, right in the cop's report, a policeman who I challenge Mr. G. (*the lawyer for the plaintiff*) to tell you is inspired by any ulterior motive.

Listen to this: They charged us, in this bill of particulars, with having caused this child a severe personality reaction, with tension, mental depression and paranoid fixations. You think

> I'm kidding you when I suggest to you that somewhere along the line, way back, somebody has got something awful on his conscience in this case.
>
> Paranoid fixations we caused in a child that has been in mortal illness from the day she was born, under constant medical treatment, from the time she was two months old, and for seven solid years, constantly in the offices of doctors.
>
> Why didn't they leave her alone?
>
> Why did they let her go there?
>
> I'm done. Let me repeat what I said at the outset; if ever a jury were put to an acid test, to resist sympathy and emotion, believe me, ladies and gentlemen, you are that jury. Because with all that has happened here this poor child isn't to blame. You heard her on the stand, doing the best she could to parrot some kind of story.
>
> So much for the actions on the part of those who would sacrifice the well-being of anybody, including a child that's involved with those terrible things. If you want to give her a verdict because she is sick, well, I can't stop it. But, if you do, remember, you will strike at the very heart of our system of justice in this country, where jurors are expected to be courageous, to do their job as they see it and leave the sympathy outside of that jury room. I'm just as sorry as anybody in the world for this poor kid. These are law courts, that's another matter.
>
> Thank you for your very rapt attention.
>
> I deeply appreciate it.

Mom told Doni that dad cried when he won this case against a crippled young woman's claim that Playland was liable for her injuries due to one of their rides.

The jury decided the young girl had been coached to present a scenario in which it appeared there was negligence. As the partial transcript above showed dad proved that was no negligence on Playland's part. Here are the key words in his statement: **"I'm just as sorry as anybody else in the world for this poor kid. These are law courts, that's another matter."**

I'm sure of it, my father said so.

The last decade or so of dad's trial career was spent as a lawyer for a respected insurance company. That career move guaranteed a predictable income for his golden years. I wish he had been around for them.

Camille, Carola, and Donna

— 32 —

DADDY'S LITTLE GIRLS

W**ITH THREE LITTLE GIRLS** who worshipped the ground he walked on, dad was given a second chance to experience the joys of childhood through his own adoring children. Throughout his life, dad overcame his parenting fears and truly delighted in his children and grandchildren, **all girls!**

As the eldest, I had the privilege of being his test case. Here are some unforgettable childhood scenes that flash through my mind to this day.

Scene One, I'm in my bedroom upstairs, tucked in for the night. Dad has just finished reading me a story from *Journeys Through Bookland*, an anthology of the world's best known children's legends, myths and fairy-tales. I have the book on a shelf right next to me as I type these words.

Dad read stories better than any other dad in the universe. That is not an exaggeration. He didn't just *read* the story, he acted it out, changing voices for each character, ad-libbing in funny voices, interpreting words I didn't understand with facial expressions and gestures. I never felt like I was just listening, I was part of a show.

Even at two or three I found a way to get him to read "*a few more minutes.*" He knew I was doing it, but he enjoyed reading so much, he happily read "*one more page.*" Then he'd crease the top corner of the page we stopped on, close the book, kiss me goodnight, turn out the light and go downstairs where mom was waiting at the piano to join him for the next scene.

Scene Two. I am snuggled under my covers, my bedroom light is out, but the hall light is on and my bedroom door is wide open. Dad and mom are downstairs. Mom is playing the beginning of "their song" on the piano. Dad's sweet, soothing tenor joins in.

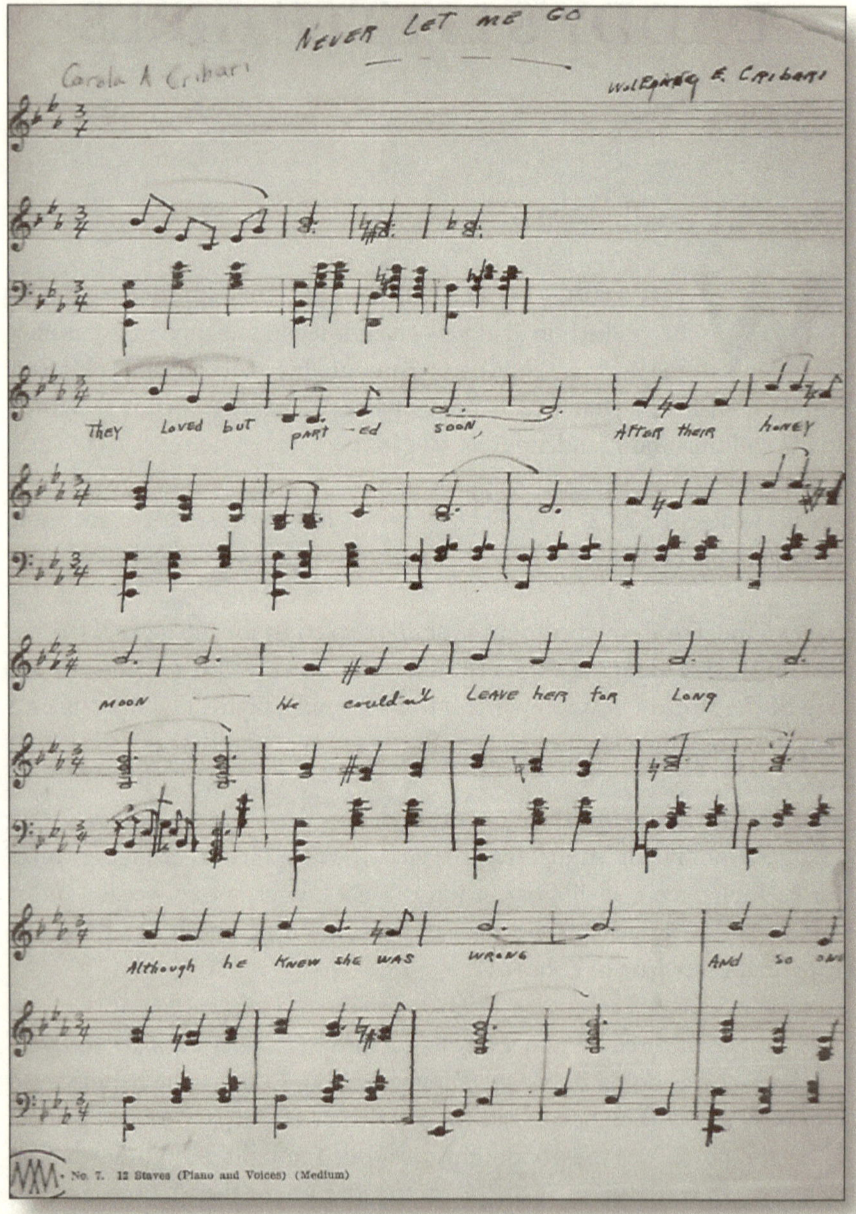

Never Let Me Go

by Carola A. Cribari & Wolfgang E. Cribari

Oh my darling can't you see that we should never part.
and that you will always be forever in my heart.
Don't ever leave me, I couldn't try to be without you,
I'd sooner die. I love you.

Dry the tears on your dear face and let's forget our woe.
Hold me tight in your embrace and never let me go.

Don't bother googling it, it never made the Lucky Strike Hit Parade. But it was number one on my parents' nightly hit parade because they wrote this song together. Obviously dad wrote the overly dramatic lyrics and mom the lilting melody. Their song also had this cryptic verse which I never heard them sing:

They loved, but parted soon after their honeymoon.
He couldn't leave her for long although he knew she was wrong.
And so one day he came to sing her this refrain.

What followed was any number of romantic favorites and show tunes. My sisters and I were silent listeners absorbing the words and music of familiar favorites we can still sing from memory.

Every so often, dad surprised us by singing an aria or a Neapolitan song. It was usually at mom's request. I still have their "Neapolitan Songs" songbook in my piano bench. In those wartime days, the only time I heard Italian was when dad sang those beautiful songs.

I wasn't always awake for the finale, but I can hear still dad singing

"See you in my dreams, hold you in my dreams.
Someone took you out of my arms
Still I feel the thrill of your charms.
Lips that once were mine, tender eyes that shine.
They will light my way tonight. I'll see you in my dreams."

Off to dreamland.

Down Rose's street and under the bridge to Nana's House we go.

— 33 —

PARENTS, SIBLINGS, WIFE & CHILDREN

THE STROLLER IN THIS picture is one of the leading players in this story. When I found this picture of my cousin Joan and me (*ten years and one and a half*) I was thrilled. Doni had it all these years with her family pictures. The stroller is clearly 1930's style, made of a wicker type material. This is the first childhood memory I ever wrote about.

Dad is pushing me in the stroller. We're taking our regular walk from our house on Ridgeway Street to nana's on North Fulton. It was cold out because my legs and feet are covered by a blanket; I'm cozy-warm.

Whenever dad walked me over to nana's, he always went the same way: he turned at the end of our block, walked down to the end of the street to the open field that edged the newly built Cross County Parkway. Dad liked to push me fast. It was fun, fun, fun! I could feel a cool rush of air on my face. I jumped up and down with delight as my stroller turned into an exciting new "ride." Maybe I was two and a half.

We were in the field at the top of a small hill of wild flowers and tall brown grass alongside the fenced off parkway. Dad stopped and put his foot on the pedal to keep the stroller from rolling down the hill. He started picking up dried leaves and grass, making them into a nice big pile. What was he doing? Was this a new game?

Dad took a small pack of little sticks out of his coat pocket. He rubbed the sticks together and beautiful golden lights started to shine in his hand. He dropped the pretty shining sticks one by one onto the pile and lights started to dance up, up, up. There was a lot of smoke and dad started to wave his hands around. It didn't go away. The yellow and gold dancing pile got bigger and bigger…more smoke.

Then dad was pushing me so fast I could hardly breathe. I tried to catch my breath, but the air smelled funny. I started coughing. Dad was running faster and faster. He didn't stop under the bridge like we always did. He just kept running all the way to nana's house. He stopped, lifted me out of the stroller, left the stroller on the sidewalk and carried me up the front steps into nana's house. Moments later, we heard sirens.

He never told anybody.

This story emerged from my subconscious when I was thirtyish and had three daughters of my own. It might have been right after dad died. The detail of the memory amazed me because I thought childhood memories weren't accessible from such an early age. No one but dad and me ever knew about this bizarre incident so I couldn't have "heard about it."

What was going on in dad's life at the time? I know we were still living on Ridgeway Street so my sister Donna (Doni) was either newborn or six months old. The fire-starting could have taken place in early spring of 1939. Doni remembers mom saying that she and dad used to fight a lot when she was pregnant with her. What they were fighting about we'll never know.

The year 1939 matters because I wonder about dad's state of mind and question his ability to act as a responsible parent. His erratic behavior truly puzzles me. Was he having a mini-breakdown?

During the same time my parents had to face a difficult decision about the deformity I was born with, a split palate. It wasn't the worst kind, but there was separation through the upper part of my palate causing the milk to come out through my nose while I was feeding

It's a wonder I was as chubby as this picture with mom shows. Dad couldn't face being at the operation I underwent when I was a toddler so Rose's husband, uncle Jim, drove mom and me and probably Rose to NYC for the operation. I believe dad's fear of loss influenced how he handled family crises.

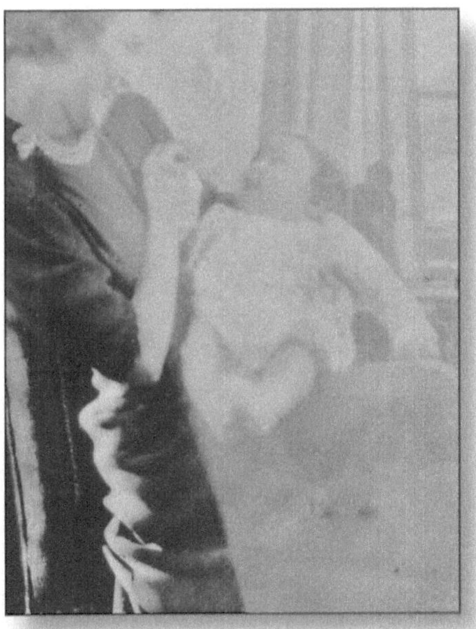

Mom with baby "Mia." Mom was the one who wanted to have children. It took being a great-grandmother for me to get complete perspective of what s loving and unique parent mom was.

Thank you, mom, for convincing dad to be a father. You obviously saw the side of him that became the nurturing, fun-loving parent he was.

As I look at this photo I see in you what you saw in him: fun-loving, nurturing. But you were the disciplinarian and often overshadowed by your dynamic spouse. On the other hand, you were delighted by your daughters' devotion to the man you loved.

— 34 —

WORLD WAR II ITALIAN-AMERICAN LAWYER

IN THE LATE 1930'S and early 1940's. Dad's life was overloaded with responsibilities not only to his wife, growing family, and recently widowed mother but also to his successful, time consuming law practice. Dad's burdens were confined to his hometown but another, more troubling problem was brewing on the world stage for Avvocato Cribari: his Italian background.

Dad was the quintessential first generation Italian; the chosen one in a large immigrant family. His struggle to improve his family's status dominated his short sixty-three years on this planet. He became the first professional in his family, a lawyer. He helped his paisani, he helped his family, anyone who asked. He loved to give. In 1939, a huge stumbling block emerged.

That year the United States was already aligning itself with Great Britain and France against two aggressive European fascist governments. Dad's parents' adopted country was bracing for war with Nazi Germany and their recent ally, Mussolini's Italy, their native land. In those days anyone with an Italian last name must have been justifiably unnerved. I have no evidence from anyone in the Cribari family as to the effect it had on their lives. It must have been devastating.

Recently I discovered that many Italian families in certain parts of the country were required to go to intern camps like the Japanese. That didn't happen to Italians in our area, but my husband's Italian-American family experienced the same feelings of isolation and alienation as dad's. Angelina Bruni DelBianco, my husband Lou's mother, used to tell him that during World War II a neighbor in suburban Port Chester constantly berated her family with ethnic slurs. The harassment only stopped when the neighbor saw Angie's brother Carmine walking home in an American army uniform.

It was the 1940's, a time of nightly blackouts, air raid sirens disturbing the peace. For me, above all, that decade meant family, lots of family, especially the Cribari family. I have come to realize that my sisters and I were in a unique position during our growing up years, we were the grandchildren of Italian **and** German grandparents while the U.S., our native country, was fighting a World War against both families' native lands.

By number and frequency of interactions alone, my father's family, always a force to behold, dominates my wartime memories. The Cribaris, originally 12 people living under the same roof, were now down to six, three men and three women, Nana, Olga and Dolly, Victor, Mario and Guido.

Nono had passed away and Rose, dad, Hugo, Ray and Arnold were raising families of their own; they all still lived in Mount Vernon. Nana Cribari, our Italian-American matriarch, by 1942 had two stars on the window flag of her suburban American home representing her two sons who were off fighting a world war against her native land.

I was in elementary school and clueless as to how nana felt. She was totally dependent on her American citizen sons who were required to sign up for the draft. Five of her sons, all above draft age, were exempt.

Nana must have been shocked when her oldest son Victor, in his early 40's, enlisted in the Seabees and was sent to the Pacific. She was undoubtedly relieved that her youngest son, Guido, was rejected for service because of a punctured ear drum.

Mario was either drafted or enlisted. He served as driver for General Mark Clark, saw action in the landing at Utah Beach and earned 3 battle stars.

Mario is pictured with nana and me when he came home after the war in 1945.

Here's another wartime picture (1942?) in nana's backyard. My sister Doni and I are with aunt Dolly, dad's youngest sibling, and her boyfriend Dan who is obviously home on leave. Doni, age 2, is proudly wearing Dan's army hat. Nana and Rose's husband, Jim Synnott, are sitting in the background. Dad brought us over to nana's house a lot during the war years undoubtedly to cheer her up and distract her. It just occurred to me that dad took these two wartime pictures and it made me smile.

Two of nana's sons found themselves in harm's way. Dad, as patriotic as his servicemen brothers and his "America-first" father had been, was doing his part on the home front. He was in demand as a speaker at local and county-wide service club meetings, bond rallies and other "war efforts."

The following excerpts are from a speech dad gave for the Ossining, N. Y. Rotary Club in May, 1941 months before the Japanese invasion of Pearl Harbor. The points he raises show how dad was always one step ahead of the game. I learned young, it pays to know history!

I'm sure of it. My father said so.

— 35 —

"LIVE FOR YOUR COUNTRY" SPEECH

HEADLINE:

Live for your country, speaker urges Rotarians.

> *With many people, patriotism begins and ends with the singing of the National Anthem. Too many words are used in the pledges of love for country when what we need is action.*

> *Mr Cribari continued, Every citizen regardless of his origin has an opportunity through individual action to aid in bolstering the national morale.*

His brother and father-in-law, Paul and Gustav Ankerson members of the Rotary Club, were in the audience that day. Of German descent, they certainly could relate.

Dad told a story to illustrate his point.

> *A young German singer is imprisoned in a concentration camp for having referred to Hitler as 'that actor' during a conversation in a private home. He is subjected to torture before he is finally released and banned forever from his native land.*

The article continues,

> *Mr. Cribari transposed the elements of the German case to our own country: "when during the last presidential election campaign countless Americans openly criticized and ridiculed acts of President Roosevelt. The process of law would take place if the young German man were to utter a treasonable or libelous statement against the Chief Executive. Various safeguards would protect his rights prior to and during the trial of his case."*

(In other words, the young German singer would never have been punished if he was living in America.)

> *Many of us are apt to take our individual liberties for granted, forgetting that it took centuries of time and oceans of blood to achieve them. If we lose these liberties, we will have the whole battle to fight over again. This is no time to take liberties for granted. The lesson of Europe is that man-made laws and institutions can be destroyed with one burst of lightening. Eternal vigilance is the price of victory.*

Powerful words!

Dad's growing reputation as an eloquent and entertaining speaker spread countywide pre, during and post World War II for obvious reasons. His oratorical skills, acting talent and Italian last name made him a popular attraction. He was proud of his avocation as an orator, a natural outgrowth of his acting talents. The fact that he chose to keep so many speeches highlights his love for speech making and the language with the world's most extensive vocabulary.

Here's one of dad's speeches which he recorded in 1941 just before America entered the European war. Its poetic images of America's land are lovingly described and wonderfully moving. It is miraculous for me to hear his voice again. I'm sure I never heard him make this record, I was only five.

Look at these great pictures of dad in the role of guest speaker while you listen to him speak. You can see the seriousness in the first and the enthusiasm and humor in the second. Dad knew how to engage his audiences, always!

— 36 —

STARS AND STRIPES SPOTLIGHTS CASE

AMONG DAD'S PAPERS WAS a copy of *Stars and Stripes*, the daily newspaper of the United States Army published for troops in Italy under the auspices of the government. Ironically, it was printed at the plant of Il Messaggero in Rome, Italy. The date: Thursday, December 28, 1944. I was about to reject it when I noticed the name Dr. G. It piqued my interest; what a strange story to include in a wartime army newspaper.

Before I saw Dr. G's name I thought Dad got the article from his brother Mario who was stationed in Europe for the duration. Both Mario and dad would have immediately recognized the name of the subject because Dr. G. was the family dentist and one of dad's good friends.

The dateline is White Plains, N.Y. Dec. 27, ANS. Here's the complete article.

> *A jury of nine men and three women, by a vote of ten to two today denied Dr. G., 35, a divorce from his wife after they inspected the front seat of a two-door sedan to determine whether it was "built for love."*

Mrs. G., 30, the defendant, requested the examination after her husband, a Mount Vernon dentist, charged that she and the car's owner, 36 year old heavyweight house painter Anthony M. had been guilty of misconduct in the car.

But the alleged unfaithfulness, Mrs. G. retorted, would have been physically impossible in the car. She asked the jurors to be allowed to look at the front seat and Justice P. agreed.

While the car was being inspected from all angles with the door open to permit a close look at the front seat, Judge P. observed one of the male jurors starting to measure the distance in the car's interior with a tape measure. "No, no, none of that," the jurist admonished.

Dad was Dr. G.'s lawyer. They lost because they couldn't prove the act of infidelity took place as Dr. G claimed. The only grounds for divorce in those days was proof of adultery. Dr. G. continued to use dad as his lawyer and was always dad's dentist. There were obviously no hard feelings. What an oddly titillating story to feature in *Stars and Stripes*. It probably made some G.I.'s worry about their sweethearts/wives at home.

— 37 —

ON THE HOMEFRONT

HERE'S A PERSONAL WARTIME memory that is typical of dad's persistent, unexplainable habit of being late.

Dad and I are sitting in our breakfast nook, he's reading the morning newspaper. Dad's in his navy blue corduroy bathrobe and pajamas. It's 8:00 in the morning. I'm dressed and ready for school.

"Camille, look at this. It's D-Day." Dad shows me the headline in his newspaper. I can read the newspaper now...two capital D's. D-DAY.

Daddy is really, really happy. But he isn't dressed for work; he's going to be late for the office and he won't be able to drive me to school on time.

"What's D-Day, daddy?"

"See, Camille, the paper says June 6, 1944. It's your birthday, sweetheart, but it's D-Day too. Look, June six."

"I know, daddy! I'm eight years old, almost ten."

I keep thinking. What **is** D-Day? What does D mean? "Maybe it's something about the war? Daddy's happy. Maybe it's an "all clear" like the siren after the air raids.

Dad folds the paper, gets up and dashes up the stairs to get dressed for work.

I look at the kitchen clock, 8:15. Oh no, I hope I won't be late for school again.

It's o.k. daddy's happy. About the war.

Good, maybe he won't worry so much about Uncle Mario.

Anyway, it's D-Day AND my birthday. I'm going to tell my teacher, Miss Kahler.

I'm sure of it. My father said so.

— 38 —

WAITING IN THE CAR AND OTHER FRUSTRATIONS

"WAITING IN THE CAR" was an almost daily childhood frustration. This picture is the epitome of how it felt to be a child of our two chronically late parents.

Two year old Bill is in the backseat, chin resting on the window frame. Doni, 5, in front, is eagerly watching for mom or dad to drive us to nana's Cribari or Nana Ankie's or to school, anywhere.

I don't know where I was but I remember that black Chrysler. It embarrassed me because I thought it was too big and too "rich" for our family.

I believe this was in 1945, at the end or after World War II. No seat belts in those days, but the windows were always rolled down in nice weather.

Since dad was always the driver, I assume that Carola was the one making us late. She could never make up her mind what to wear, if her hair looked right, whether she needed more lipstick, whether we all needed a wrap?

But if mom was the Queen of Late, dad was King. He was always late for dinner, late for his tee time at the club, late for church. I'm sure he was never late for a client, late for court, late for Thursday night spaghetti. I guess you might call his problem "selective lateness."

We all remember the time dad drove up the street, reversed gears and backed down the street, then kept driving up and down the street that way at least ten times. The three of us were in the back seat secretly enjoying the back and forth ride, listening to him yell **"Carola!"** and honking the horn. I wonder what the neighbors thought.

— 39 —

DAD SETTLES DOWN

BECAUSE OF MY HARD-TO-PLEASE, restless father, my parents moved many times in my early childhood; every house was near nana and Rose in the Fleetwood section of Mount Vernon. The first home I can remember is 395 Westchester Avenue. A three-story, colonial made of red brick with a charming portico entrance that had two white benches on either side of the front door. I drove by it not so long ago, it's serene and stately just as I remembered.

My baby sister, Carola Helen, "Bill," was born when we lived on Westchester Avenue. Dad's sugar cube on the windowsill theory was three for three. Dad gave boyish nicknames to Doni (Donna) and Bill (Carola). I never had a nickname until my first grandchild called me Mimi. I love it, thanks Chrissy!

Fast forward: six decades. Bill reminds me that she had to stay in the hospital for weeks after her birth because Doni and I had measles or was it chicken pox? It doesn't matter because newborns, even those as hardy as my nine pound baby sister, were kept in the hospital to avoid exposure to communicable diseases.

Since I'm writing this during the 2020-2021 Coronavirus pandemic I can finally connect to my sister's sequestration and relate to that feeling of isolation.

Fast forward again to this wonderful memory piece Bill wrote in 1977. Like our hyper-literate father, Bill writes poetry and song lyrics in English and German in addition to her varied musical opuses. Her range of talents always amazes me.

This was inspired by an e.e. Cummings poem.

And I thank you God
for sisters to have
who accept & encourage
& who give & who grow
and who love
in spite of
spin the bottle in a garage
or stolen "trolleys"
or pictures almost flung,
from a Parisian window
on high
or wet towel fights on the
deep blue sea
temperamental brats who
always tagged along!
yes, I thank you God for
Camille

Thank you, Bill, for your happy childhood images. They belong in this tribute to dad because every image, every word from his daughters evokes his expressive eyes smiling through those cherished shared memories.

Back to images of Westchester Avenue's red brick home with its welcoming portico. It now includes a group of women surrounding Bill, my two year old baby sister. There's my aunt Rose combing Bill's thick, brown hair. She examines the comb each time it passes from Bill's scalp, through the tangled brown strands, checking to make sure there are no more… bugs.

Bugs? What? My baby sister has bugs!

Yuck. Don't tell anybody, please.

Bugs! Not an inviting image to start with in describing my first childhood home, but I'm being led by memories, and that is a very powerful one. It was considered shameful in those days for anyone to have bugs. It only happened one time, but no one ever explained how Bill got them. She was too young for in-school contact with other children. Luckily, no one else got them.

Enough with the bugs! Let me take you on a house tour.

Walk inside the front door; to the right is a living room and off the living room is a nice big screened in porch. Now go back to the entrance and go to your left through the dining room. See, there's a small breakfast nook, that's where my father used to read his morning paper. Breakfast nooks and booths in restaurants still give me a sense of comfort and security.

Next to the nook, there's the kitchen with a back door. That door leads out to a hilly street, Grand Street, which I walked down every weekday morning when I was old enough to walk to school.

There were lots of bedrooms upstairs, three or four, I think. I know I had my own room. I spent many hours trying to get to sleep in that room, staring in fear as headlights from passing cars created ghost like monsters on the walls.

My two bedroom windows faced a street that was busy day and night.

There was also a really scary closet in my room, dark and forbidding. It was between me and the hall bathroom. I'd peek out from under my covers and yell, "Daddy!" "Daddy!"

"It's all right, Camille." he'd yell from his bedroom down the hall. **"It's just a closet. No monsters, just clothes. Go back to sleep now. Go-o-o... ba-a-a-k t o-o-o-...."**

My bedroom was scary. Maybe it's because I was sick so often with terrible ear-aches. I remember too well Doctor Cerchy sitting on my bed, his wife Mary by his side, and the pain of my infected ear before and after he was forced to "lance it" .I hated that word lance.

My persistent ear infections created a reason for dad's anxiety. He must have had flashbacks of the mastoidectomy he witnessed as a pre-med student; the one that caused him to change his career path. Now his oldest child was a potential candidate for that same surgery. What a relief when I "outgrew" those earaches.

Westchester Avenue was the scene of many bouts of tonsilitis for me and Doni. Dr. Cerchy finally recommended we "have our tonsils out." Since it was considered minor surgery, even in those days, dad was able to bring us to the hospital. I'm pretty sure mom stayed at home with Bill. Dad probably asked uncle Jim to go along with him and I'm sure Dr. Cerchy was there too.

This is the story I was told. Doni and I were taken into the pre-op part of the hospital. Dad and his "support team" were in the waiting area. I was scheduled to go first for the tonsillectomy. Doni and I were both wheeled into the operating waiting room out of dad's sight.

About five minutes later, Doni, still on the gurney, was wheeled back out into the waiting area. When he saw Doni still on the gurney, Dad's knees buckled and he slid to the floor. He fainted. He thought Doni was dead.

What happened in those out of sight minutes? I went into surgery, but when they took Doni's temperature they discovered she had a fever and immediately returned her to the waiting area. Poor dad, but what a story!

Our Westchester Avenue home had a happy place I thought was just for me; a lovely finished, carpeted playroom upstairs on the third floor. I spent hours there playing on the comfy floor with my beloved paper dolls of Shirley Temple, Rita Hayworth, Betty Grable; cutting out pages of their glamorous wardrobes.

I remember sneaking a "big" scissors into my hide-away to cut out my new paper dolls quicker and easier than my children's scissors could. To my chagrin, I cut off a piece of the tip of the middle finger on my left hand.

I ran down two flights of stairs holding my bleeding finger, crying for help. Who was watching me? I wasn't old enough to be on my own and I had two younger sisters. From my earliest memory, we always had a "maid." Where was the maid that day? I can show you the scar. The memory stops right there…

I wrote this for a "what I wanted to be when I grow up" memory piece years ago.

> *"I wanted to be a movie star who sings and dances. Everybody will want my autograph*
>
> *I'll sing and dance for everyone whenever they want me to. I'll have beautiful dancing costumes. The skirts will twirl around. There will be sparkles all over my dress and the sleeves will be like wings, long and flowy. Oh, how I'll dance! I'll be just like Rita Hayworth. Daddy knows the president of Columbia Pictures, he lives on California Road He knows Rita Hayworth. Someday I'll meet her. I'm going to be just like her. I know it!"*

So much of what I was wishing for had already come true. This picture proves it. I spent a lot of my childhood dancing and singing at least once a week in nana Cribari's *living room* surrounded by the most supportive and responsive audience any star could wish for, my adoring uncles and aunts.

Here I am and there they are: Hugo** (sitting in front of the fireplace), **Olga and Guido** (on the right sitting on the couch) **Dad definitely took this picture of little Rita Hayworth.

Another Westchester Avenue memory is of a childhood birthday party when I received a uniquely "romantic" birthday gift, a beautiful, beribboned bouquet of purple violets. To add to the unforgettable moment, the bouquet was presented to me with charming, elegant bow by Paddy, a young gentleman of eight.

Paddy (Pasquale?) Martinelli, arrived at my party with his mother, the wife of one of my father's friends or maybe clients. Paddy wasn't in my class at Pennington School so I didn't recognize him. And he wasn't dressed like the other third grade boys. Paddy was dressed in a child-sized-three piece formal suit. Mrs. Martinelli introduced me to her little prince whereupon he bowed and recited a birthday greeting. Paddy instantly became my first crush, and proved a hard act to follow. Thank you, Paddy, I will never forget you or that lovely bouquet of violets, ever.

It was during the same time and in the same place that my next door neighbor, Jimmy (*I'm omitting his last name to protect the innocent*), provided my first real exposure to the opposite sex.

It was a hot spring day and Jimmy decided to water the yellow daffodils that were growing between his house and ours in what I found to be a truly creative way. I'm sure I don't have to go into detail. Use your imagination. Let's put it this way, Jimmy watered the flowers with his own built-in watering apparatus.

I never told dad about that Jimmy moment. But I can still envision it.

Looking back, dad would have been the one to tell about my accidental "discovery" of the opposite sex. I'm not sure why I didn't tell him. I guess I didn't have the words. Or the nerve.

All I knew is that I would never be able to water those daffodils the way Jimmy did.

— 40 —

BUILDING BRIDGES

A MAJOR SOURCE OF DAD'S political, social and religious viewpoints had been silently staring me in the face in the content of the carefully selected speeches and memorabilia he kept. I didn't realize how deeply he felt about the topics he chose to speak on until I started to read every word.

I always suspected dad was "ahead of his time" but the following speech which he gave at a colored church congregation in the middle of World War II (1942) proves it. Here it is word for word. Please remember colored was a respectful term in those days.

> **I am happy to be among my colored friends and I greatly appreciate your invitation. My association with many of the members of this parish goes back many years to the time when during my summer vacation from college I used to deliver my dear father's delicious ice cream to this very church. I have cherished those friendships during the years and many of those old time friends have become loyal clients of mine.**
>
> **I have endeavored to show my appreciation of the friendship of the good people of this church by my efforts to assist them. I am proud to say that on many occasions both to the church itself and to the members, I have given of my time and services**

gratuitously. I am proud to say that the doors of my office have always been open to the poor of this parish who could not pay for services. But I have been repaid a hundred fold for they have returned to me a deep, loyal, warm friendship and support, a priceless possession.

I am very proud to participate in these glorious exercises for the boys of this parish who are fighting, side by side, with their white brothers in the far flung fronts of the world. These are the times that indeed try men's souls, but through the dark shape of the times certain things begin to show clear. The barbarian that has blotted out free nations from the map of Europe is not, as was first thought, an invincible fate to be written in the stars. It now is being fought.

It is now being resisted and it will, in God's time, be mastered.

This barbarian has become the fight of the white and the colored, the Jew, the Protestant, the Catholic, the Italian, the Irish alike. Today in America we are not white or colored or Jew or Gentile or Catholic or Protestant. We are all Americans, we intend to stay Americans.

The Negros are proud of their history in making America. At the same time they are endlessly grateful for the privilege of working and fighting alongside of other Americans no less brave, no less devoted to the high ideals of our democracy. Negroes have fought for America in every war of her history. They have been in every rating and rank, and today an endless stream of them join their white brothers in fighting and making the supreme sacrifice in the air and on the seas and on the land.

The colored boy and the white boy fight side by side for the same thing. What they fight for belongs equally to each of them. They fight for human rights, for democratic principles. And the greatest human right of all is that all men are created equal. There is no room for race prejudice in a foxhole or on a blazing desert or in a bombing plane. The colored boy and the white boy fighting side by side know what they fight for. But do we here at home?

I am afraid that sometimes we forget. For as long as we let race prejudice continue to spread like a treacherous disease we are forgetting what our boys are dying for. *Of all the alien enemies in our midst, the most alien to the democratic principles, the most destructive of national unity is race prejudice. Like other dangerous germs, it flourishes in darkness and only the sunlight of understanding and good will destroys it.*

And like other treachery it often wears a disguise. It is sometimes masked by a false patriotism or by mistaken pride. Those who are descended from the pioneers may fairly count that an honor, but if it causes any to discriminate against citizens of a different ancestry, a different color, then they dishonor their proud heritage. In combating race prejudice at home among ourselves we are waging the same war as our armed forces – the war for human rights, for democratic principles.

They have the front to hold and we have the rear. While they fire the guns and fly the planes and sail the ships, we here in safety must struggle as tirelessly, as dauntlessly to wipe out race prejudice, to prove that democracy works. And we have got to keep our thinking very straight these days if we are to make democracy work. We will remember, I know, the heroism of the little brown race that bled beside American boys at Bataan. We will keep in mind what excellent officers and fine combat fliers our Negro boys are making.

We will remember that America is a nation that is based on a practical political faith in the brotherhood of man. To uphold that faith is an essential part of the great war effort. Any unfairness or unfriendliness to good citizens among us of another color is a kind of sabotage. For race prejudice is one of the favorite weapons of the enemy. Any American who might be tempted to toy even carelessly with it had better look well at the blood stains on it and shudder away.

We are the people who once fought a bloody Civil War among ourselves to preserve a union in which all men of whatever color should be free. The glory of American democracy is that it welcomes men of every descent.

The color of the Negro and white blood that flows on the battlefield is the same – the full measure of their devotion is given for the same glory. Let us not forget this. So then, when American boys, colored and white are dying for that glory, let no one among us, here at home, taint it by act or word which might spread the pet poison gas of the axis – race prejudice.

Let us as Americans wipe from our hearts all hate, rancor, and prejudice and through good days or bad, let us try to serve our country as our boys at the front are serving.

For today we are all a great multitude of people on pilgrimage, common and ordinary people of every race and charged with the usual human feelings. Yet we are filled with such a hope as never caught the hearts and imaginations of any nation on earth before. The hope of liberty, the hope of justice, the hope of a land where man can stand straight without fear, without rancor.

Our land, our people, our flag. Our land, a continent; our people of all races, our flag, a symbol of what humanity may aspire to when the wars are over and the barriers down. To these let us be dedicated and consecrated anew, to die for, if need be, but above all in friendliness, in hope , in courage, to live for.

I'm sure of it, my father said so.

— 41 —

TRADITIONS CRIBARI STYLE

Thursday Night Family Dinners & Fraternal Fighting

For more than a decade my sisters, father and I never went to nana Cribari's house for dinner without becoming innocent participants in a family "fight!"

The first and best example that comes to mind: my father and his brothers' loud, endless, heated fights about which New York team was gonna win the pennant, the Yankees, Giants or Dodgers. These fights grew increasingly intense as the baseball season progressed and the three teams battled it out for the National and American League pennants. Although I never took sides, I became a real expert at identifying favorites like Joe DiMaggio, Yogi Berra, Ralph Branca and others. All Italians, wow!

My two sisters and I always looked forward to Thursday nights. Thursdays at nana's started after work, 5:50 or 6:00, and ended around 8:00. Just a few hours, but those hours were often the highlight of my week. I can still picture all of us gathered around the long table that dominated nana's dining room.

Each family member had his/her place at the table. The chair at the head was often empty, perhaps in honor of my grandfather Beniamino who passed away when I was six months old. Or maybe it stayed empty because no one felt right taking his place. That can't be right because nono Cribari never lived in that house; nana moved there two years after he died.

Maybe it was considered nana's chair but I don't remember nana ever sitting down. She walked back and forth between the kitchen and the dining room, serving her sons and her grandchildren. Doni, Bill and I were there with dad every week; my mother never came with us. Why? And the three of us were usually the only grandchildren. Nana had nine others. Where were they?

My father's place was to the right of the table's head, a place of honor. He wasn't the oldest, Victor was, but dad was the "star" of the family and everyone knew it. My youngest uncle, Guido, sat at the foot of the table. I loved watching him eat. I thought Guido was cool, a sports news reporter. He always kept his hat on while he ate. All reporters wear their hats indoors, Guido said. It's good my mother never saw Guido with his hat on at the dinner table, she would have been appalled. When Guido bent down to gobble up his huge plate of spaghetti, his hat sometimes slipped down over his forehead so he looked like an eating hat.

My sisters and I sat on the left side of the table because I distinctly remember looking across at my father and the line-up of his brothers.

Where did the Cribari women sit? My aunts? My uncle's wives? Did the two younger girls, Dolly and Olga, ever sit and eat with us? I remember they sometimes served us, but where were they during dinner? Thursday night was all about Nana and her sons. She was the weekly hostess of her one woman cooking show. Even when my aunts were around, they acted like waitresses, in and out of the kitchen. I do remember them being in the living room after dinner.

If nana had other culinary dishes in her repertoire, I never knew it, there was only one choice on the Thursday night menu: spaghetti with marinara sauce, nana's famous meatballs, a simple salad with oil and wine vinegar (*I never ate salad until I was 35 years old*) And for dessert chocolate pudding with "skin" on top. I keep trying to find chocolate pudding with skin in supermarkets. Not easy.

For a few hours we were transported to a world of delicious food, popular music: aunt Dolly playing the old player piano in the living room, Guido singing, my sisters and I singing. Then we were drowned out by loud, raised male voices with powerful loyalties to their different New York baseball teams.

By 8:00 that houseful of brothers was hoarse from their post digestion battles, but still comforted by nana's comfort food. No wonder dad was so good in the courtroom, he had lots of practice arguing every Thursday night.

Dad drove us back to our quiet, orderly home just a few blocks away, well fed, invigorated and yes, comforted by our Italian family traditions.

Speaking of Nana's Meatballs

You could always smell the meatballs being fried as you entered nana's house.

So when my sisters, cousins and I reached the age of reason, we followed the lead of our elders, snuck into nana's dinette and took a warm one from a big flowered plate on the dinette table. To this day, we have all tried to duplicate the taste and texture of those wonderful meatballs. I'm not sure any one succeeded, but we never gave up trying.

By a happy coincidence this year I found a notebook with a recipe written in dad's handwriting for **Meat balls and loaf;** I include it here. By the way I don't know if he ever followed the recipe and made his mother's meatballs from this recipe, I think he forgot about having it. I plan to try it soon.

Dad's recipe for meat balls or loaf

Mix meat, squeezed out bread and parsley and garlic chopped and add

- Oregano - teaspoon pressed between fingers
- Basil - teaspoon pressed between fingers
- Salt
- Black pepper
- 1 egg
- 1 small dish of parmesan

Fry with mixed oil about 1/8 inch at bottom of frying pan after heating oil. Fry over medium flame. If no bread, use bread crumbs, but must then add water, about one half can of water.

For meat loaf, place in Pyrex dish and cover in silver foil at 350 for one and ¼ hours. Grease dish first - margarine.

1 lb. meat = 1 egg + 1 saucer cheese

— 42 —

DINNER TIME BATTLEGROUND

I **HAVE NO MEMORY OF** dad cooking, none! I do have a recurring one in which he is "doing the dishes" which means "doing the pots." We had a dishwasher in the very early years of its invention. We never had to wash dishes, only "do the pots" after dinner.

Although our family was composed of three daughters, a mother and a father, the three of us girls were never asked to "do the dishes." Unless there was a maid in the house after dinner, that job was always mom's.

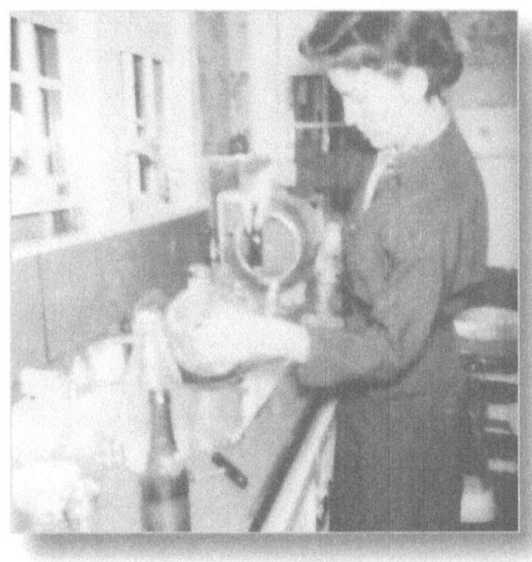

Here's mom doing her least favorite domestic chore, the after dinner dishes. This is the kitchen at 317 Claremont Avenue, the scene of mom and dad's most creative "battles."

Mom's appearance in her unlikely role as dishwasher can be described as elegant and even graceful. Incongruous for the work.

I wish I had a picture of dad doing the dishes, we wouldn't have dared take his picture performing that improbable chore.

I'm not sure why my sisters and I managed to avoid those nightly cleanups.

When a dinner time fight carried over into the evening, mom would leave the dining room with a provocative comment, run up the stairs to her bedroom and slam the door. This left my father in charge of the cleanup. Not a good thing.

I have dozens of memories of dad at this very kitchen sink: angry, reverberating sounds of banging, clanging metal, loud rushing water, louder, more abrasive banging and clanking, ear-splitting metallic crashes on tile counters, more rushing water to clean out the sink. Finally, a brief calm, then cabinet doors slamming as the dried pots and pans were stowed away.

— 43 —

DAD'S IN-LAWS–THE ANKERSONS

HERE'S THE ANKERSON SIDE of our family, dad's in-laws. They were the polar opposites of the Cribaris. Their Overlook Street home was peaceful and as Doni put it "a safe haven." Back row: dad, me, uncle Paul, cousin Bob, aunt Ginny, uncle Joe Barnett; Seated: mom, Nana Ankie, Nono Ankie, aunt Elfrieda. Seated in front Bill, Doni, and cousin Bill. This is in front of Uncle Paul's house on Thanksgiving Day, November 1948.

Nana Ankie and dad had a unique relationship. I felt their mutual respect, but I also felt a distance between them. My mother was nana Ankie's pet. Nana was a silent source of security and comfort for my sisters and me. Mom was in daily communication with her mother, her fashion adviser. Mom said she would call nana every morning and ask her what to wear. It's a little hard to believe, but my mother never, ever lied.

NANA ANKIE:
A FORMIDABLE PRESENCE

Here is Nana Ankie when she was young; she must be in her 20's. I see my sister Bill in her and in some ways, I also see myself.

She was a formidable presence. I always wanted to please her. I believe dad felt the same way. Nana encouraged me to play the piano and sing. I remember crawling under her piano while she played "The Erl King" with power and passion. That piece is so dramatic and frightening in both its tragic subject and its programmatic musical style.

My grandson Stephen learned to play it for me recently. I'm glad I didn't know what the subject was until later in life, it's not child-friendly.

I didn't really get to know my nono Ankie until I was a teenager. He was always a comforting, yet silent presence in his home. Dad was crazy about his father-in-law and treated him with respect and admiration. There was nothing "not to like" about Gus Ankerson. He seldom spoke, but when he did, we all listened.

Nono Ankie told me when we traveled home from Europe together that I looked like my mother. I was at an age when I didn't want to hear that. I didn't look like anybody, especially not my beautiful mother. I thought nono was just being nice. I didn't see my mother when I looked in the mirror. I saw a possible pimple, straggly hair, and thin lips. A long overdue thank you, nono, on behalf of my typically teenage self.

This is a picture of nana, nono and Carola on a Maine vacation. They had friends in Maine who they visited often. Dad mentions this place in a letter to mom which I've included. But this picture is before dad was in mom's life, she looks like a teenager. Nana's body language is exactly the way I remember her, confident and strong. She should have been a teacher, she taught me by allowing me to "do it." Although I do remember her teaching my cousin Bob and me how to paint by not so subtly guiding the paintbrush in our hands.

We visited nana Ankie at least once a week either in the company of my mother or on our own. I never felt I was being "babysat." Nana always had a "project" for us to do together: art, music, baking (*we could only watch her bake except for handing her the ingredients*) dressing in costume for mini-performances, dancing, walking in the garden and naming each flower. Visiting nana was always a new adventure.

Nana Ankie's was where my sisters and I learned to love the arts and to respect our elders. Not through rules and regulations, but through trial and error, childlike improvisation.

Here's another side of Nana Ankie as seen in the text of a "Dear Daddy" letter which Nana wrote on our behalf and which dad kept. It was for his August sixth birthday. I remember being at Nana Ankie's for VJ day, August 15,1945 so it was probably the first real vacation for our parents. We were 9, 6, and 3, quite a handful for our grandparents for those ten days. On the last day, VJ Day, nana let us parade up and down the street in celebration. It was probably the same day mom and dad came home. I remember showing them the crowns that we wore and the instruments we played.

Nana made the letter sound like I dictated it to her. Who knows? Maybe I did.

> ***Sunday afternoon (probably August 5,1945)***
>
> *Dear Daddy,*
>
> *Hope you will write a postal to me, going to make a collection of postals. We had a fine chicken dinner. Grandma bought some cake with chocolate frosting.*
>
> *When the Good Humor man comes along, we'll have some ice cream.*
>
> *Donny's taking her nap and Anne and Alberta are going out. Grandpa is reading Song of Bernadette. It's a beautiful day and we are glad Ginny has gone to the movies, it's so lovely and quiet.*
>
> *How are you feeling? Grandma sent your glasses and coat, be sure to let us know if they arrived safely, she had to send them from Polin's drugstore sub-station as the post office was closed Sat. P.M.*
>
> *Nana Cribari and Rose and Kathleen were here yesterday. I made a scrapbook. The noisy airplanes awoke me this morning. Donny was playing football with Joyanne and me.*
>
> *Thursday is your birthday; we all wish you a very happy one; we'll celebrate at Grandma Cribari's dinner and think of you and mommy having a good time too.*

Give our love to all of you there from all of us here.

Kisses from Donny and Carola and Camille X X X X X X

P.S. Hope you are having a good time and please write soon C. C. C.

P.S. Dear Mommy, This is Daddy' s birthday letter but he'll let you read it too.

Grandpa said he hoped it was placid in Lake Placid.

Love Camille

— 44 —

WAITING FOR HEAVEN

IT WAS MY DAD who guided me through my first experience with death. I was 13 years old and I remember it all as if it were yesterday. It was the unexpected death of nana Ankie.

I was sitting on the top of the stairs at Claremont Avenue waiting for my parents to get home from visiting nana in the hospital. Nana had been scheduled to have an operation that day and so far nobody told us how she was doing. It was probably five o'clock. Nobody had called. Where were mom and dad? It was almost dinnertime.

I had been listening to my after school programs on the radio, but decided to go downstairs when I heard the garage door open. They're home, I thought. Loud quick footsteps: they were rushing into the house. Mom was crying, really crying, very loud. Dad was trying to get her to sit down on the hall desk chair, but she kept walking back and forth between the kitchen and the hallway.

I leaned over the banister. "What happened, dad?" I asked. "What's the matter, mom?" Dad looked up, saw me and ran up the stairs.

Dad came up and sat next to me on the stairs. **"Nana Ankie is gone, sweetheart. I'm so sorry to tell you. She was very sick and she died."**

I stared at his unmoving features, looked down at my weeping mother, then back at dad and I laughed. I laughed!

Stunned and frightened, I looked at my mother below me. Silence.

Then mom cried out, "The doctor killed her," I looked at dad sitting next to me. He stood up and ran back downstairs.

"Carola, the doctor didn't kill her. No one killed her."

I was shaking with fear, shame and a growing sorrow. Sorrow for nana, shame for having laughed, LAUGHED. And fear. Fear that mom was going to hate me. I laughed. Nana died and I laughed. I never spoke about my horrible reaction to anyone. No one ever did in those days. Somehow my guilt was assuaged by the love and understanding of both my parents. But I want to go back, apologize and embrace them both.

A few days later, dad told me he was taking me to see nana Ankie at Burr Davis. Nana was laid out at the Burr Davis mortuary on Fourth Avenue, two stores down from Ankerson's, my grandfather's, her husband's drugstore. I knew what Burr Davis was because I once asked nono Ankie about Burr Davis's mysterious, dark windows. Even though nono tried to explain, I still wasn't sure what kind of business it was until dad took me inside that day.

Dad held my hand as we walked through the dimly lit front entrance and down a short hallway into a dark room. I searched the shadows for nana. My eyes were instantly drawn to a long narrow box with a white light above shining down onto the person lying inside. We walked a little closer.

"See how beautiful nana Ankie looks?" dad whispered.

"Nana Ankie? I asked.

"Yes, that's nana, sweetheart. She looks like she's sleeping, doesn't she?"

"Yeh, yeh, yes!" I stuttered, "she does"

"We'll look at her for one more minute. Then we can say goodbye."

"Goodbye? Where's she going, daddy? "

"Nana's going to heaven, sweetheart. To heaven."

"Oh."

Then we turned around, hand in hand, left the room, walked out the front door into the bright sunshine.

We left nana Ankie waiting for heaven.

I'm sure of it, my father said so.

— 45 —

SHARING CHILDHOOD MEMORIES

YEARS AGO I WROTE this 'epic' poem to encourage my ESL students to write about memories of their own childhood holiday celebrations. Christmas Eve at nana was a childhood family tradition. Dad's family **was** Christmas for us!

Christmas Eve Chaos

Twas the night before Christmas when all through the house
not a creature was stirring ...

Nana **was,** *she was* **stirring** *pudding, chocolate pudding*
She always made chocolate pudding for dessert
no matter what occasion.
You need time to really stir pudding,
I know Nana didn't have much time.
Nana's chocolate pudding always had that skin on top.
I know now that stirring is the secret to skinless pudding.
I like mine with skin.

Christmas Eve my aunts, uncles, parents **weren't** *stirring, they were…*
laughing at memories of Christmases past,
fighting about politics, sports, religion, anything,
crying over imagined or real family snubs,
eating baccala and spaghetti with anchovies
pulling out bows on every little girl's dress, hair ribbon
yelling out names on the many gift-tags.

My eleven girl cousins and I **were** *stirring up a holiday storm…*
tearing open gaudily wrapped presents,
laying claim to more than our share "that's mine!"
chasing each other round and round the four-room first floor,
singing Christmas carols…

Wait! That's it! That's the night before Christmas I want!

There we are…gathered around that old black upright player piano..
young hands on old, yellowed ivory piano keys
small fingers sinking into the broken stuck ones.

"Away in a manger, no crib for a bed!"
A Protestant hymn in three-part Catholic harmony.
Why do I remember it being Protestant?
We had three non-Catholic cousins, that's why.

Uncle Ray shouts out his request.
"We Three Kings of Orient Are"
"We don't know it" the sopranos whine.

Uncle Mario this time.
"I Saw Three Ships"
"We don't know it!"

Today, that dog-eared collection of carols is in my piano bench
silently reminding me of my innocent attempt
to create musical order out of chaos.
on each favorite carol, names written in my childish script
the assignments still there.

Sopranos: Idaehla, Virginia Ruth, Bill
Second Sopranos: Donna Marie, Kathy
Altos: Camille, Roberta

And how we sang!! All of us, six uncles, three aunts, eleven cousins,
"Angels we have heard on high, sweetly singing o'er the plains…
Glo-o-o-o-o-o-ria in excelsis Deo!"
I can hear us, all trying the obligati,
Tears well up. I can barely sing carols without
first having to swallow the lump
that always rises in my throat.

On the night before Christmas in my Nana's house
old world traditions were few…
meatless, once a year meals, baccala (ugh!)
midnight mass, Aunt Rose's **Italian** *Christmas song,*
"I'm old enough to go to midnight mass," I'd whine
"I want to hear Rose sing" That did it.

Why not more Italian traditions in this season?

We made new ones.

We needed lots of shopping bags to carry our gifts home

We argued about whose new Christmas dress was the prettiest.
Sorry, Jim, Stephen and Arnold,
Until I was ten years old, all my cousins were girls.

We marveled as cousin Joan piled up her unopened presents
to take home for a Christmas morning bonanza.

We hoped our Protestant cousins would be back at Nana's next year?

The Noise!

We laughed! We yelled ! We cried! We sang! We fought!

Chaos! Yes.

We were stirring up a storm at Nana's house on what should have been a "silent night"

Chaos! Yes.

But there was always music…

"O little town of Bethlehem, how still we see thee lie."

— 46 —

CHRISTMAS REVISITED

FAST FORWARD 40 YEARS: In December of 1987, I wrote the following holiday memory for Port Chester, N.Y.'s weekly newspaper, the Westmore News.

It provides another perspective on dad's favorite holiday and a madcap tradition he started for his family that shows his love for making home movies.

> *"My father, Wolfgang Cribari, was a prominent trial lawyer and a very ambitious person, He and my mother, Carola, were born in Mount Vernon, N.Y. He was really a frustrated actor and had a flair for the theater. He was also the reason Christmas was so special.*
>
> *When I was 16, dad decided to make a Christmas movie, "The Arrival of Christmas." The whole family, the three of us and our parents dressed up in identical red and white striped night shirts. Mom was the family shopper. I wonder where she found those shirts. As a full-blown teen constantly embarrassed by dad's fun-loving schemes, I wished he'd thought of this one when I was younger.*
>
> *The movie's scenario was simply the family getting up on Christmas morning and discovering the tree and presents that had appeared while we were sleeping. The first shot was us creeping down the stairs. For half of the movie, my sister Donna took charge of the camera and dad became the star of the show. He always was anyway. Dad was a great comic actor especially in his red and white striped nightshirt.*

This story is special to me not only because of Christmas, but because it symbolizes the strong influence my father had on all of us. He was a holiday nut – he loved Christmas and went all out for it. Perhaps part of the reason was because he came from a poor family, he was the third oldest of 10 children during the Depression.

His family put all their hopes in him – he didn't disappoint them and accomplished a great deal. He died at age 63 in December 1966, right before Christmas.

— 47 —

RADIO DAZE…1940'S

LET'S TIME TRAVEL BACK to the Golden Days of Radio. Through the ears of this child, radio was magical; I was addicted to the world of sound. Listening. still my keenest sense, was enhanced and heightened during those days. Ironically, it was also when I suffered from severe ear aches and infections. This is the first time I've connected those two aspects of my young life. Wow, writing this book is therapeutic. Maybe too much listening and ear problems are connected. Not!

Anyway, here's my list of favorite listening moments based in mostly on dad's choices which I readily adopted as THE BEST. Some of the programs were daily soap operas, some were weekly variety comedy shows, others what we now call sitcoms. We all lost a wonderful source of auditory pleasure when radio succumbed to the more powerful ears **and** eyes medium, television. Those of us who were lucky enough to be raised on both media are different in ways that are difficult to explain.

The down side for me, I loved when I could stay home sick from school. Why?

I could listen to **all** my soap operas. They were called soap operas because the shows' sponsors were different soap products – aimed at the show's listeners, housewives, of course. "Put that Oxydol sparkle in your clothes" Many of my favorites were on in the daytime, usually school hours for me.

My favorites? "The Romance of Helen Trent" Could a woman over 35 find love? "Our Gal Sunday," "Stella Dallas" To an innocent pre-adolescent girl growing up in the forties, those stories of love lost kept me glued to my little radio hoping the girl would find true love. They also put wartime fears on the back burner.

Since dad was rarely home in the daytime, I only knew his radio favorites from the nightly shows we listened to together every night. Here are a few of the shows and the dad memories they evoke.

"Life With Luigi" – Dad loved this show so much. Luigi was an Italian immigrant with a thick Italian accent, just like nana Cribari's. Dad enjoyed the clever ways Luigi was able to outsmart his obnoxious Italian-American sponsor and boss Pasquale. I was too young to understand why dad loved the stereotypical Italian characters, but I loved them too. Rosa was the best, "You calla me papa?" And the theme song, "America, I love you, you're like a papa to me."

Favorite radio characters were called into life: typical suburban teenager of the time, *"Henry, Henry Aldrich" "Coming, mother"*; Molly of "The Goldbergs" calling out her tenement window, *"Yoo Hoo, Mrs. Bloom" "Yoo. Hoo, Mrs. Goldberg"*

Then there's "Blondie" - *"Uh, uh, uh, don't touch that dial. Listen to BLONDIE!"* a favorite because dad and I both loved the comic strip too.

Then there was the "Jack Benny Show" We couldn't wait for Sunday night. Dad love, love, loved Jack Benny and his diverse cast of supporting players: Rochester, a black houseman who could do just about anything his boss asked of him; Mary, Jack's smart independent girlfriend/wife, Phil Harris, Jack's friend, a rebellious Southern band leader; Dennis Day, a young Irish-American gullible golden-throated tenor. Such diversity for that time. Someone for everyone.

Right after "Jack Benny" there was "The Burns and Allen show." George Burns, Burns: "Say goodnight, Gracie." Allen:" Good night, Gracie." Supposedly they were Jack's next door neighbors. We believed it.

Then there were the weekly adult shows I occasionally had nightmares about: "Suspense" and especially "Inner Sanctum" with its familiar squeaking door. Having dad by my side always made the scary parts less scary. Dad also loved "Mr Keen, Tracer of Lost Persons " but that was definitely "over my head."

Here's the theme song/commercial for a cowboy favorite, Tom Mix:

> *"Shredded Ralston for your breakfast starts the day off shining bright*
>
> *Gives you lots of cowboy energy and a flavor that's just right...*
>
> *Take a tip from Tom, go and tell your mom: Shredded Ralston can't be beat.*

There was one after school radio show dad used to try to get home in time for. Here's another 1940's after school radio classic:

> *"Faster than a speeding bullet.*
>
> *More powerful than a locomotive.*
>
> *Able to leap tall buildings in a single bound.*
>
> *Look, look, up in the sky!*
>
> *It's a bird. It's a plane.* *It's Superman!!*

The outside door to our kitchen opens, it's almost 6:00 P.M.

"You missed Superman, daddy."

Dad sits down next to me in the breakfast nook,

"I'm sorry, sweetheart, I had a client, I couldn't get rid of him.

Tell me what happened."

"You can find out tomorrow, daddy, tomorrow."

Finally, every Saturday morning "It's time for 'Let's Pretend.'"

My favorite fairy tales as one hour radio plays, early morning enchantment every week.

Right after "Let's Pretend" there was…

"Grand Central Station," crossroads of a million private lives.

Gigantic stage on which is played a thousand dramas daily."

No pretending now, real life stories for grown-ups. I was enthralled.

Thus in the first decade of my life, I was subtly led into a lifelong love affair with theater! One I shared with my actor-lawyer father.

— 48 —

CUTTING RECORDS–DAD'S FORTIES OBSESSION

IT WAS ALSO DURING the early 1940's that dad became obsessed with a new invention that took the place of his live stage performances: recording.

In those days home recorders were few and far between. I remembered ours so I googled 1940 recording devices and found a picture that looked like it.

This picture is closest to my memory of that 1940's vintage recorder. The name Victrola also rang a bell. I do remember it had a turntable and looked more like a record player.

My husband converted dad's records into audio recordings. Lou's help has given me a truly unique feature for dad's story, his voice.

Dad served as performer and sound engineer with his new "toy." I think of this aspect of this book as a collaboration of my two favorite men.

Over a two day period, I listened to all dad's 1941-1945 recordings. I was inspired to use some. Here's why…

First, hearing dad's voice again, it's even more vital, engaging and higher pitched than I remember. He was in his late 30's, early 40's at the top of his game and psyched by this new way to express himself. Dad's diction is impeccable; it stands out among the other adult voices he recorded.

Second, hearing and feeling the freedom with which dad used the new medium to express himself. His singing voice is effortless, soaring; he brings new life to his Italian culture with his beautiful "Vicino Mare" and "Ti Voglio Bene."

At the end of one particular recording session dad is speaking Italian. While I was listening I realized this was in the middle of World War II fighting against Italy.

Then I found another recording of Doni and me singing and speaking in Italian.

In 1941 we had an Italian expatriate nanny/ nurse for Doni named Tina so Doni learned to speak Italian before she learned English; at two she sounds like a native. I join in and try to recite an Italian nursery rhyme.

Third, hearing mom in the background harmonizing, accompanying dad on the piano, connecting on the same artistic level that first brought them together. Mom sings one song alone, "Why Was I Born." Doni tells me she used it as an audition piece when she tried out for Broadway shows. I never heard her sing any other song by herself. Mom had perfect pitch and was a talented, sensitive musician, but she didn't consider herself a singer or actor. In her eyes, dad was both. Mom didn't compete. During the 1941 recordings mom was pregnant with my sister Bill who became an opera singer/pianist. Bill certainly had a fitting in utero introduction to her life as a professional musician.

Fourth, reciting "Twas the Night Before Christmas" (1941) First dad, then me. Doni calls "daddy" in the background. This is two months before Bill was born. I must have memorized it because I was only five. I have tried to bring that Christmas tradition into my grandchildren's generation with unenthusiastic results. I'll try again this year. I still know it by heart!

Fourth, dad encouraging us children to express ourselves: to Joane, "Very good, Joane. Go on." (*she was playing a difficult piece on the piano*) to me, "Your turn, Camille." (*I tried to play like Joane, I couldn't, so I sang the "Trolley Song")* to Doni, "C'mon, Doni. Sing." (*she was 3-4 years old singing some wordy songs*) and to Bill (*not even two, singing the "Hot Ralston" commercial.)*

Finally, bringing his large family together; a typical Cribari activity like nana's Christmas Eve. No surprise, nana Cribari is recorded twice; her recognizable, Italian accent hard-to-understand. I remember the sound of her voice, but it was her laugh that brought her back, hearty, raucous, dominating. Dad's sister Dolly harmonizes with brother Guido in popular '40's songs. Finally, a familiar sound reborn, Guido playing harmonica; his and dad's lifelong signature artistic gift.

I'm sure of it, my father said so.

— 49 —

WORLD WAR II AT HOME & ABROAD

THIS IS OUR DECEMBER 1940 Christmas card, the first of our yearly holiday family portrait cards. We sent this the year before America entered World War II. Everyone except baby Doni looks a little worried.

America's entry into World War II created an atmosphere of hatred and feelings of resentment for German, Italian and Japanese Americans. I've read a lot of books and seen many movies from the perspective of interned Japanese-Americans, but little about Germans and Italians.

My parents must have done a wonderful job of protecting us from their wartime fears. I was aware that my uncle Mario might be in danger, but was also sure no one could hurt him because he wasn't fighting, he was driving the general. We learned in school to identify enemy aircraft by the markings on the planes that flew overhead. We had regular air raid drills as part of our daily lives. I confess I was afraid of "Japs" who I only knew as frightening images in political cartoons.

— 50 —

SINGING PATRIOTIC SONGS OF WORLD WAR II

I WISHED MY UNCLE MARIO'S branch of the service, the Signal Corps, had a song like Anchors Aweigh, The Caissons or The Marine's Hymn. My classmates and I proudly learned all those popular service songs by heart and sang them in school, on the playgrounds, in our backyards, everywhere.

What American over 65 doesn't know these lyrics and their catchy melodies?

Anchors aweigh, my boys, anchors aweigh,
Farewell to college joys, we sail at break of day-ay-ay-ay.

Over hill, over dale, we will hit the dusty trail
As the caissons go rolling along.

From the halls of Montezume, to the shores of Tripoli
We will fight our country's battles on the land and on the sea.

Even though I have 'protested' every war we've been involved in since the 1960's, I still love to sing those 1940's wartime songs. Back then they made us feel pride in our country's servicemen who were sacrificing for us all.

While we were proudly singing those wartime songs at home, our Italian cousins overseas were singing another catchy tune called "Giovinezza"

Giovinezza, giovinezza, primavera di belleza.
nel fascismo et la salvezza de la nostra liberta
Per Benito Mussolini, e-ya e-ya, a-lala!

It translates:

Young people, young people, springtime of beauty.
Fascism is the salvation of our liberty.
For Benito Mussolini, yeah, yeah, yeah! (Let's cheer!)

Ironically it's the first Italian song I ever learned, it was during our European vacation, summer 1953. Our Italian driver, Alfredo, taught my sisters and I that fascist song; we never heard at nana Cribari's house, that's for sure. Alfredo taught us "Giovinezza" only when dad wasn't around. We had no idea of its political significance until we sang it for dad after we left Italy and Alfredo. Dad laughed it off, but I'll bet he was mad.

I have no first hand information from the Ankersons, my German side, or the Cribaris, my Italian side, as to how their families were affected by World War II. I can only surmise they both had feelings of alienation and anxiety from speeches dad gave during and after the war.

In this speech dad gave for the Mount Vernon war bond drive he reveals his passion for the subject "Red-Blooded Americans." He gave it in May 1942, five months after Pearl Harbor.

> *"Red-blooded Americans, December 7, 1941, in every corner of the world, were shocked and rudely aroused by that unprovoked and savage attack on Pearl Harbor. That attack, following the pattern set by the dark wave of totalitarianism in Europe was the beginning of the most formidable and brutal menace to our fundamental freedoms and our precious way of life in the history of our democracy.*
>
> *Five months have elapsed since that fateful day in December. In this short space of time we have seen the American people undergo fantastic*

changes. From a gullible, disinterested, and completely unprepared nation, we have seen, almost overnight, Americans everywhere spring to the nation's defense and gird for the death-struggle with the ruthless invader of our liberty.

Tremendous strides have been in the mobilization of our armed forces, of our industries and our defense. But the greatest of all accomplishments is the awakening of the American people at home, the men and women in the home line of defense. I speak of men like you, the volunteer fireman, the mail carrier, the school teacher, the citizen, the police auxiliary section chief and the air raid warden. You have labored as only men can who are inspired with overwhelming love for our great nation; and for the freedom for which it stands.

The efforts you have put forth in the last few months organizing, enlightening and preparing your co-workers have brought pride to us at home and great consternation among our enemies who had been advised by their spies and saboteurs that the American people were permanently locked in the grip of lethargy and indifference to their peril.

(Several paragraphs are omitted in order to focus on his rationale to involve his listeners on a personal level. His oratorical skills help make his audience feel empowered.)

On June 15, 1942, there will commence in this nation a great America-wide campaign to give every American an opportunity to help his country by signing a pledge for the regular purchase of Defense Bonds and Stamps. This pledge is not an order for the purchase of bonds but a promise and it is confidential and entirely voluntary.

Every pledger will take upon himself the responsibility of buying the amount of bonds he has promised to buy. The campaign is based on faith in Americans – faith that our citizens are eager for a chance to help defend our freedom – faith that they will not shirk. And because the campaign is based on faith, the American people will not fail for it is for this very type of thing that we fight –a government by the people.

Posterity will record the role you play in this campaign. You will be the modern prototype of the Minute Men of Concord and Lexington. In the conduct of this great campaign your special obligation will be to demonstrate that the method of friendly appeal and voluntary response is not only the American way it is also the most efficient way to enlist the billions of dollars upon which our final and certain triumph will depend.

Today, patriotic devotion and pride of government are surging over the land. Americans everywhere are ready to do their utmost to bring Victory. This pledge will offer millions of our people the opportunity and the privilege to help save America and to help secure their own future at the same time.

UPON YOUR SUCCESS MUCH DEPENDS --- *Our lives, our liberty, our sacred honor, not alone for America, but for the world.*

Dad's passionate war-bond appeal speech brought back a memory of the books of stamps I bought in my elementary school. I was always so proud to have a dime or a quarter to buy stamps and especially proud when I collected enough to fill up a book. The idea was that a certain number of filled stamp books earned you a war bond. It was a unique, exciting school activity I looked forward to.

Here are excerpts from another one of dad's dynamic speeches: **post-war**.

"We are now facing one of the saddest effects of war. In the face of the problems of the peace, we will long to relax – to run away from them. War is a heart attack. The shock, the pain and the fear of death may be so great that the patient on his survival may rush to enjoy all the pleasures of the life that was threatened. When that happens to the individual, he can expect another attack. If it happens to an entire nation, it can expect another war.

Our duty as Americans in this critical post war period is three fold:

1. *to face with realism and courage all of the problems that will confront us.*

2. *to appreciate and tackle with all our vigor the problem of the returning veteran*

3. *to not bicker and quarrel among ourselves.*

We will say to ourselves that today in America we are not Italians, Germans, Irish, Jews and Americans. We are all Americans and we intend to stay Americans. A pure-blooded American is an impossibility. And there is no such thing unless it is an American Indian.

The last 100 years of American history have seen an eager influx of recruits from every corner of Europe flocking to join this great pageant of the common man marching so confidently under its banner of democracy toward an ever brightening future.

We will preach that here in America there is no room for race distinction. We will cite the fact that Americans of Italian descent are proud of their history in the making of America.

Italians were among the first settlers of this great country. Scores of them helped win the War of Independence. Since then Americans of Italian stock have fought for America in every war of her history. They have been in every rank from buck privates and seamen to generals and admirals.

Today an endless stream of them, many more than any other nationality that makes up this great country, are fighting and making the supreme sacrifice in the air, and on the seas and on the land.

In New York harbor, with her face toward Europe stands the Statue of Liberty, enlightening the world. But liberty can die in the light as well as in the dark. The task of young America today is not only to enlighten the world, but to set it free.

How I wish I could hear words like dad's coming from the mouths of America's 21st century political leaders. He had such love and respect not only for country, but for the English language, a respect and love I share.

Dad's pride in his Italian heritage seemed to diminish in the years following World War II. Since I never discussed it with him, I can only guess why he occasionally sounded like a self-hating Italian. Indicative of dad's mixed feelings was his obsessive, yet unfulfilled, desire to change his name. He periodically "modified" his given name, Volfango to Wolfango, then to Wolfgang before World War II.By mid-century, it was finally consistent -Wolfe.

I'm sure he never considered changing his decidedly Latin/ Italian appearance.

The same name "obsession" also effected dad's younger brother, Guido. I often heard Guido tell how he was ruthlessly teased about his name by his bosses, colleagues and readers alike. It never diminished the popularity and success of his entertaining sports columns, "Cribari Says."Then again, it wasn't "Guido Says."

Dad's sister Cornelia must have also had a problem with her Roman-Latin-based name. I never once heard her called anything but Dolly. She had a wide circle of friends from her hometown including Ralph Branca and Art Carney who never heard her called Cornelia.

Dolly's wedding in the 1940's is the scene for the most inclusive family pictures I have, only two of the ten Cribari siblings are missing. Mario was serving in the Army but where Hugo was I have no idea; that was Hugo.

I'm not sure who gave the bride away but I have a memory of dad wearing a formal outfit like the groom's and changing into regular clothes, so maybe he gave Dolly away.

— 51 —

EIGHT OUT OF TEN: CRIBARI FAMILY AT DOLLY'S WEDDING

Back row L. to R: Guido, Ray, Rose, Nana, Dad, Olga, Arnold, Victor
Bride and groom: Dolly and Jim Di Marzo. Eight out of ten siblings.

I can't resist this picture, it's my substitute for a Christmas Eve one. In the 1940's there were 11 granddaughters: here are six of us: Roberta, Virginia Ruth, Bill *(little one in front)* Kathy, Doni, and Camille, on Dolly's left.

Dolly first born, James Wolfe DiMarzo, was the first Cribari grandson. He has dad's name. Later two more grandsons joined us: Stephen Wolfe and Arnold Jr.,

— 52 —

SPORTS ENTHUSIAST & ARDENT FAN

I **FIRST BECAME AWARE OF** dad's passion for two of the three sports he always followed, golf, tennis and baseball, when I was ten years old. His Saturday golf games often became the cause of my parents' frequent quarrels. The two to three hours it took to play golf Saturday mornings evolved into day-long outings. He blamed the extended hours on the need to entertain clients or a late tee-off.

Post World War II, dad was one of the first Italian-Americans to apply for and be accepted as a member in the prestigious Westchester Country Club. He spent lots of time in and around the popular Sports House and on the world class south and west courses. One of dad's home movies is set at the club during a foursome round that included two of his brothers, Guido and Arnold. Guido was a sports writer, then sports editor of Gannett newspapers, Arnold, a construction company executive. Arnold was reputed to be the best golfer in the family, I'm not sure Guido or dad would agree.

Here's dad with two other golf buddies at The Club.

In addition to dad's weekly golf outings, my mother, sisters and I looked forward each summer to going to The Club for dinners on the elegant terrace, the Fourth of July fireworks, the children's and teen-age shows in which the three Cribari sisters often starred. The Club offered wonderful experiences for the whole family.

Dad's played golf as often as he could until he had a heart attack and was advised to give it up. I'm not sure if his golf partners/competitors weren't somehow responsible for dad's heart attack. According to dad's stories, he and his fellow golfers fought over everything, someone was standing too close to the pin when the other guy was putting, someone picked up the ball when it was in the way of a putt and moved an inch closer to the cup when he replaced it. I never wanted to play golf, too stressful.

Another sport that dad really enjoyed as spectator and ardent fan was baseball, especially during the late forties, early fifties. He looked forward to watching his friend Brooklyn Dodger pitcher Ralph Branca pitch. Although dad was 20 years older than Ralph they struck up a real friendship in the late 1940's I believe through dad's younger brother Guido, a sportswriter who knew Ralph.

Ralph and dad had a lot in common. Both were from very large Italian-American families, Ralph was the 15th born of 17 children, mostly brothers; dad the third of ten with six brothers. Both men were the "chosen ones" of their respective working class Mount Vernon families.

Ralph wrote about his friendship with dad in his autobiography, "A Moment in Time" which was published in 2011. Ralph's wonderful memoir also revealed his close relationship with Jackie Robinson, the first Negro to play on a Major League professional baseball team. Ralph was already one of the Dodgers starting pitchers on April 15, 1947 when Robinson "broke the color line." I discovered how close Ralph was to Jackie Robinson from reading Ralph's book. He had a lifelong friendship with Robinson through the ups and downs of both their careers and was asked by the Robinson family to be a pallbearer at his funeral.

In 1947, not too long after Robinson was in the starting lineup playing second base, dad took us to a game at Ebbets Field. I remember the day clearly. We were sitting downstairs underneath the first tier, several rows behind the Dodger dugout. Our seats were in shadow, but we looked out at a sunny playing field. Jackie Robinson came up to bat. The crowd booed. They booed their own second baseman as he stood at the plate. I looked at dad.

Fans in the upper decks started throwing bottles and cans onto the field as Robinson stood waiting for the first pitch. Then the plate umpire turned to the unruly fans above his head and motioned for them to stop. Robinson waited for s few seconds and resumed his batting stance. The pitcher threw the ball, Robinson swung and missed. Strike one! The stadium erupted in boos and catcalls. I'm sure there were racial epithets, but I didn't hear them.

Bottles, cans, debris of all kinds rained from above onto the field. Robinson backed out of the batting box once again and looked to the Dodger dugout. Since we were right behind it, he seemed to be looking at us. Dad stood up, **"We're going home,"** he said. **"C'mon, let's go."** He took my hand and led me out of Ebbets Field.

I never asked why, I just followed dad to the parking garage. We drove home in silence. I felt terrible; embarrassed and angry at the Dodger fans, at the people throwing things at one from their home team.

A few months later dad invited Ralph's teammates, Duke Snider, Pee Wee Reese, and Gil Hodges to the house and to play golf at the Westchester Country Club. I noticed Jackie Robinson's absence. I never asked why. Dad told me years later why he couldn't invite Jackie to join them: Negros weren't allowed at the club. He didn't want Jackie exposed to more rejection. Dad never used the word "racism." Times have changed.

During the years after dad's death I had several opportunities to sit down and talk with Ralph about dad at a mutual friend's home. His eyes always misted up when he spoke about Wolfe, there was real love there. Ralph's palpable warmth always brought me back to our shared Dodger days experiences. I cherish them.

Another related memory: One memorable spring weekend dad arranged for our family to travel to Philadelphia to watch Ralph pitch in an away game against the Philadelphia Phillies. I can't remember much about the game, but I do remember the train ride back to New York City because we were scheduled to travel on the same train as the Dodgers, all of them. Was I ever excited.

As we waited on the station platform for Ralph and the team to join us, a group of fans began milling about looking for recognizable Dodgers. We were right in the middle of the crowd. A young fan walked up to dad and asked, "Can I have your autograph, Mr. Furillo? " Dad took the paper and pencil and wrote Carl Furillo for the happy fan.

"Oh no, dad, what did you do?" I cried once the fan was out of hearing. I knew the answer without seeing what was on that piece of paper. **"I signed an autograph for the guy."** dad laughed.

"But you're **not** Carl Furillo."

"He thinks I am. C'mon kids, let's get on board." I worried all the way home on the train that Carl Furillo, or some other person in authority, was going to find out what dad did and have him arrested.

Another memorable image is of dad reclining in front of the black and white television in his den with the fingers on both his hands and the toes on his bare feet crossed. *(Not easy, don't try it.)* Dad was putting a "hex" on the pitcher from whatever opposing team the Dodgers were playing. When he did that hex position, we knew Ralph was the Dodgers starting pitcher that day. He even put the "hex" on any Dodger pitcher who had a better win/loss record than Ralph's. Dad was sure his hexes worked. We never questioned his blind loyalty to Ralph or his blatant disloyalty to the team.

I'm sure of this, my father said so.

Ralph Branca, Number 13 on the Brooklyn Dodgers in 1947. He wrote "To Camille, One of my most loyal and cutest fans, Love Ralph."

It was one of his best years, he won 21 games. He was like a member of our family. Ralph played 12 seasons of Major League Baseball, 10 with the Brooklyn Dodgers

Ebbets Field, Brooklyn in the 1940's. I remember taking this picture when I was 10 years old. We obviously had a friend on the team (Ralph) to have had such good seats over the dugout.

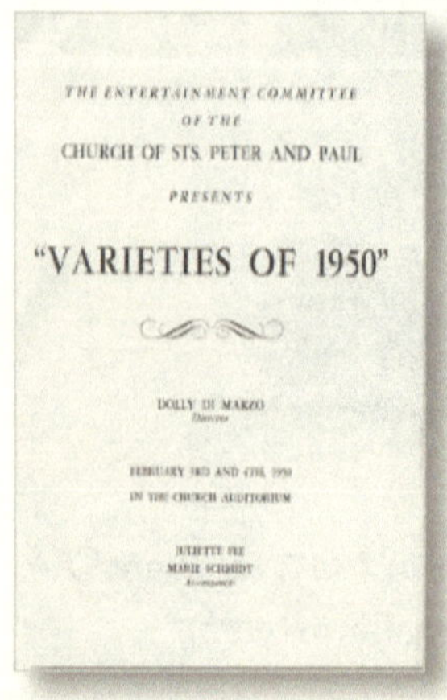

THE ENTERTAINMENT COMMITTEE
OF THE
CHURCH OF STS. PETER AND PAUL
PRESENTS

"VARIETIES OF 1950"

DOLLY DI MARZO
Director

IN THE CHURCH AUDITORIUM

Ralph Branca and The Cribari Sisters even sang together in a 1950 show at Sts. Peter and Paul Church in Mount Vernon. We sang, "I Wanna Go Home with You." My sisters and I had been singing together in local shows and at the Westchester Country Club since 1946. To sing with baseball idol, Ralph Branca, was a different story. All three of us had major crushes on Ralph and his Dodger teammates. Singing with Ralph made us feel like Hollywood stars. We were the only children ages 13, 10 and 8 in the cast.

BALL 'N JACK CHORUS

Marguerite Smith	*May La Sala*
Jane Mennis	*Rosemarie La Sala*
Dorothy Leland	*Joan Conboy*
Marion Baker	*Joan Synnott*
Grace Bloom	*Joan Frisch*
Anna Marie Ferry	*Elsie Kiely*
Christine De Lazzero	*Gloria De Lazzero*

NEOPOLITAN SONGSTER .... *Carmen*

SONGS .... *Ralph Branca*
(Assisted by Cribari Sisters)

SONG STYLIST .... *Marie Pope*

"ATS'A MATTA WALYO"

PLACE—*Courtyard of Sts. Peter and Paul*
TIME—*Present*
CORNACCHIO—*Tony Tizzarello*
OFFICER—*Harry "Van" Leggat*
BACIGALUPO—*W. E. Cribari*

TEA FOR TWO .... *Chris De Lazzero and Chorus*

A REPORT .... *Frank Ansbro*

MINSTREL

INTERLOCUTER, *Mark Keefe*
ENDMEN

Jay "Shortcake" O'Brien
Ed "Nicodemus" Borza
Ray "Honeychile" Cribari
Fred "Hambone" Herr
Don "Rastus" Nugent
Ernie "Dewdrop" Whittle
Charlie "Satchmo" Pastorino
George "Hot Lips" Scapolito
Walter "Sambo" Moran
Jimmy "Lijah" Capparelli
Ray "Joshua" Casey

SOLOISTS

LET'S HARMONIZE .... *"Honeychile" Cribari*
DARKTOWN STRUTTER'S BALL .... *"Sambo" Moran*
GALWAY BAY .... *"Joshua" Casey*
ROBERT E. LEE .... *"Satchmo" Pastorino*

FINALE .... *Entire Company*

The Committee gratefully acknowledges

the valuable assistance of

FRANK ANSBRO
CHRIS DE LAZZERO
ED BORZA
VINCENT NATELLA
CAROLA CRIBARI
MANLIO SEVERINO

STAGING AND DIRECTING

BETTY SULLIVAN AND COMMITTEE .... *TICKETS*

ANTHONY JERAMIAH .... *MAKE UP*

RICHARD EDGAR AND COMMITTEE .... *LIGHTS*

JAMES DI MARZO AND COMMITTEE .... *STAGE*

ART CARNEY .... *Radio and Television Star*

RALPH BRANCA .... *Star Brooklyn Dodger Hurler*

The committee's special thanks to FRANK ANSBRO and BETTY SULLIVAN for their general assistance.

Lots of Cribaris were involved in "Varieties of 1950." It was the annual fund-raiser for Sts. Peter and Paul parish. Dad was in a skit called "Atsa Matta Wallyo?" which he wrote and played Bacigalupo. He loved to play comedic Italian characters. Besides acting in a skit and two choruses, W.E. Cribari was Master of Ceremonies. Where did he find time to rehearse?

Dad's brothers, Ray (Raven) and Mario (Marion) joined him (Gypsy Wolfie) and 13 other men in the Aloha Chorus as Hawaiian hula dancers, complete with grass skirts. They brought the house down. My mother who had learned the hula in Hawaii choreographed it. Mom also played a violin solo. Talk about variety.

Dad's sister, Dolly Di Marzo, directed the show. Mount Vernon native Art Carney, at the beginning of his highly successful radio/television career, is acknowledged in the program. Artie was another close family friend.

— 53 —

WHAT WE DID FOR SUMMER VACATION

WHEN I WAS GROWING up the timeless question, "What did you do on your summer vacation" always greeted us on our return to school in September.

For many years, we never took a vacation, dad didn't have time, so we spent summers either in our neighborhoods playing ball or bike riding. Sometimes we put on shows which involved neighborhood friends and family. But not everyone was like our family, eager to be onstage.

My first boyfriend, blond, blue-eyed fifth grader Donald Miles, had willingly been cast in the role of Prince Charming in the Summer 1945 Camille Cribari Players production of *Cinderella*. Of course, I not only directed but cast myself in the title role. Doni was the Fairy Godmother, my cousin Roberta was one of the stepsisters and my three year old baby sister Bill was the Page.

We did the show outdoors that summer in our Claremont Avenue backyard. We enjoyed ourselves so much that we decided to schedule a repeat performance for our friends and families who couldn't attend the daytime performance. We made plans for a Saturday night, December 1 performance at 7 P.M. in our house.

Here's the ticket dad had printed for my first original production.

Camille Cribari Players
Present
CINDERELLA
at 317 CLAREMONT AVENUE
December 1, 1945 - 7 P. M.
Admission Twenty-five Cents

Two days before the scheduled performance, mom received a call from Donald Miles' mother. Donald was sick and wouldn't be able to be in the show that Saturday. Oh no, how can we do Cinderella without a prince? When dad got home from the office that night I was in tears.

You guessed it. Dad to the rescue.

He wore mom's blue velvet bed jacket, a pair of skinny legged snow pants, and ad-libbed the part of Prince Charming. Our family, friends and cast members loved it. We did the play in our front hall/stage for about 25 friends and family who could barely fit in the living room/audience.

But Bill stole the show, as she always did in those days, with her celebrated line: "It fits perfectly, your Majesty!"

Back to summer vacations…

When we were between Country Club activities, we were trapped in the pre-central air house's hot, humid atmosphere. We could play just so many "cutthroat" games of gin rummy, Go Fish and Canasta. So we improvised…

During those hazy, lazy, crazy days of summer, dad and his four girls often played a game I'll call the 3 C's (*Candid Cribari Conversation*) .I don't know who thought it up but it provides verbal snapshots of our family during the late 1940's-early 1950's. Part-improvisation, part playwriting, this game evolved from "busy doing nothing" summer boredom. One of us, usually Doni or me, copied down whole family conversations in real time. Something like what a court stenographer does. I just realized how that relates to dad.

Here are a few examples which Doni actually kept all these years.

Bill: (*starts dancing)*

Camille: Wrong, wrong! (*shows her how*)

Bill: (*imitates Camille, starts talking to dog)* I must get an Amazon costume

Camille: You don't need a costume.

Dad: (*reads an engagement announcement out of the paper and says what it means in Italian)*

Camille: Bill loves to hear about herself. If she saw in the paper Bill Cribari is a moron, she'd frame it.

Dad: Let that poor dog in.

Bill: (*opens the door, the dog won't come in)*

Dad: That dog is just like the rest of us, nuts.

Camille: Le chien, that's dog in French.

Bill: Oh, like Sean and Roebuck?

Dad: *(hears a cricket, recites in French)* **La cigale ayant chante..**

Bill: (*starts dancing in dad's shoes*)

Camille: What size shoe do you wear?

Dad: About 11 and ½

Camille: Ronnie wears size 13.

Dad: *(hears the cricket again)* **La cigale ayant chante tout l'ete**

Camille: *(to Bill)* Look at the bottom of your feet.

Dad: That shows how often you clean the porch

Camille: That shows how often you wash your feet.

Dad: *(goes outside to turn on sprinklers which make a loud sound)*

Bill: (*gets scared at the sound*)

Camille: I hope Bob comes now so he'll get wet. (*starts singing*)

Bill: (*is outside, she starts making up a new dance. The man in back looks at her so she runs inside*)

Dad: (*makes a face at Bill*)

Bill: (*growls at dad*)

Mom: (*comes in with a hair dryer to dry Camille's hair*)

Dad: Oh, god, take that thing away.

Camille: If you come near me, I'll throw this at you.

Mom: (*goes out)*

Bill: (*reads out loud from a magazine)*

Camille: (*struts back in, says to Bill*) I wish someone would learn to speak Spanish instead of mumbling. If you talk to Felicia that way she'd put you away in the kitchen somewhere.

Dad: *(asks Bill for a stick)*

Bill: What?

Camille: A stick. What do you want a little booklet on the subject. I'm turning on the television.

Dad: La cigalle ayant chante

Another day. Family is watching the Democratic convention on television

At this point, dad was an avid Republican.

Camille: Why should the Democrats be on television. Why? Just why? I don't think they should be allowed in this country. I just think that's awful about Ronnie going in the frog men.

Mom: Maybe you can talk him out of it.

Camille: Maybe we can drown him.

Dad: The rest of the lemonade-iced tea is in the ice box.

Bill: This stuff is horrible

Dad: The best place to sleep is outside.

Mom: It's too damp

Dad: Is there anything I ever say that you agree with?

Camille: *(talks about calling Roberta)*

Dad: Just a minute. Did you feel that?

Camille: What? A breeze? That's Senator Moody. Would you please turn it louder.

Bill: Boy, you're sure Moody.

Camille: Morbid.

Mom: My little chicken wants to go to bed.

Bill: Your little chicken does not want to go to bed because she'll have to wash her feet.

Camille: You won't have to wash em, you'll have to soak em for a week.

(*Phone rings for Camille*)

Bill: Can't I listen?

Dad: No, that's a terrible thing.

Bill: But you listen to mom's conversations.

Dad: Well, that's different.

Mom: (*watching the convention)* Look at that man.

Bill: He's a big fat slob.

Dad: (*repeats Joe Martin's talk about the Blackstone Hotel)*

Mom: (*sings Deep in the Heart of Texas*) Speaking of nutty. I haven't had nuts in a long time. I like nuts.

Camille: Yeah, I know.

Mom: (*listening to speech*) You're a rat. I hope you forget your speech.

Dad: That's a speech? How can he forget, he hasn't anything in his head.

Mom: (*in middle of speech*) There is too much dust around here.

The next morning

Mom: Drink every drop.

Bill: Ugh..

Mom: I'd better take that bird for his toenails.

Bill: I'd better write to Mother Mary Joan...I haven't written to her in a long time.

Doni: I love cake. I like angel-food and devil's food the best.

Bill: I like angel-food better. (*She starts singing "You Go to My Head")* What does intoxicate mean?

Camille: Drunk.

Bill: Lies like in liar?

Doni: Yeah.

Bill: It does not mean drunk. I'll splash you.

Mom: (*at the piano, playing "You Go to My Head"*) I can't play the darn thing. It's in five flats.

Bill: *(To dad)* What's a good book around here?

Dad: I don't know.

Bill: Camille, do you know a good book?

Camille: *(reading "A Tale of Two Cities")* This is so confusing. Don't make it more confusing.

Bill: Camille, is *"Wake of the Red Witch"* good?

Camille: If you ask me one more question...

Dad: Tell her to make me an egg.

Mom: She's not here. Where can I find her?

Bill: (*she found a book)* Is this all right?

Dad: You picked the right one.

Bill: Aren't I smart? Did you read *"Kidnapped,"* Camille?

Camille: No and I'll never read this one if you don't shut up.

Bill: All you do is pick on me. Gee, this is good. I'm glad I have such good taste. I'm going to Villain Forest and read this.

Mom: Carola, come drink your Bosco, and here's a piece of rye toast that daddy didn't eat.

Bill: I don't like rye toast.

Mom: That bird ought to go and have his toenails cut. Bill, you look like a mop. I think I'll call you Rag Mop.

Bill: Tell her to leave me alone.

Dad: *(to mom)* **Leave her alone.**

A different time:

Mom: Do you like my nail polish?

Dad: It looks like fingernails to me. Hey, Camille, we might be able to see something now.

Camille: Yeah, we might.

Dad: *(looking at the t.v.)* **Hey, Dick Tracy's on.**

Bill: Isn't that funny. I'm so proud.

Dad: Turn on Dick Tracy. Hey, is that the guy who flies like Superman?

Bill: No, that's Captain Marvel.

Camille: No.

Dad: Hey, that's Dick Tracy and Prune Face. *(To Bill)* **Call B.R.2-9163 for me, will you please.**

Bill: *(dials phone for dad)*

Camille: Oomph, you can't even put the phone down.

Bill: Is that Prune Face?

Camille: No, you are.

The last one, I promise:

Mom: One of you were almost called Christine.

Bill: Which one?

Mom: Oh, one of you two.

Bill: I was the only one born with curly hair.

Camille: I wouldn't brag about it. Look at it now, rag mop. She can go by the initials R.M. Cribari.

Mom: I love you, but I wish you'd get your hair cut. Good night, this is enough. You can't even talk around here. I'm going down to get the dry underwear.

Camille: Is that Chris Van Cyke?

Dad: Mmm

Camille: I got the hiccups.

Bill: Hic, hic, cackle, cackle, cackle

Camille: You and Beulah Witch. You don't need anything except a nose. You look like her, hair and all. Oooo, my finger hoits.

Bill: Cackle. Hello, little girl.

Camille: Go away and leave me alone.

Dad: Bill!

Bill: (growls at daddy) Now the infield is tightened.

Camille: Tight, you mean tight, get it? get it? get it? Oh you stupid, dopey, jerky bum.

— 54 —

DAD'S TRIAL SKILLS ATTRACT MEDIA ATTENTION

HIS EXPERIENCE AS A grandfather helped Supreme Court Justice Frederick G. Schmidt of Port Chester last week to make a quick settlement of litigation over visitation rights of a Bronx man to his children living with their mother in North Pelham.

11/4/45

John R. Paolello, represented by Wolfgang Cribari, asked that he be allowed to take his son, John R. Paolello, Jr. 10 months old, to visit his parents at the above address weekly and that he be allowed to take his infant son so his parents can see him.

His wife, Doris Cummings Paolello, who lives with her parents, Mr. and Mrs. John A. Cummings at 18 Second Avene, North Pelham, at first contended that her husband should visit the children at her home, but at Judge Schmidt's suggestion agreed to the weekly trips for the older boy. Thomas F. Croake represented Mrs. Paolello, who has brought a separation suit against her husband.

In the separation action Mrs. Paolello contends her husband does not support her or the children. Paolello who is now a GI student, asserted he will give her $30 a month as soon as he starts receiving the $90 government allowance.

Dad must have chosen to take this case pro bono. I have no proof of that statement, but I often heard mom say dad let his feelings interfere with how much he would charge his clients. Dad's client was obviously a war veteran; he was receiving a government allowance in the days following World War II (1945).

Like so many returning military personnel, dad's client was not financially or educationally prepared for civilian life. His two infant children were living with their mother and her family. Dad could relate. His brother Mario took years to readjust to civilian life, he lived with nana Cribari until she died, but he never married or had children. The headline reinforces how dad's client benefited not only from his compassionate lawyer, but from the judge being a grandfather.

That my father was a local celebrity cannot be denied, not just for his professional skills, but for the unique character he was. These two news articles show his fabulous sense of humor and unpredictability in the courtroom.

Justice Schmidt's Experience Helps

WHITE PLAINS — His experience as a grandfather helped Supreme Court Justice Frederick G. Schmidt of Port Chester last week to make a quick settlement of litigation over visitation rights of a Bronx man to his children living with their mother in North Pelham.

John R. Paolello represented by Wolfgang Cribari asked that he be allowed to take his son, John R. Paolello, Jr., 19 months old, to visit his parents at the above address once weekly, and he be allowed also to take his infant son, Lawrence once so that his parents can see him.

His wife, Doris Cumming Paolello, who lives with her parents, Mr. and Mrs. John A. Cumming at 18 Second Avenue, North Pelham, at first contended that her husband should visit the children at her home, but at Justice Schmidt's suggestion agreed to the weekly trips for the older boy. Thomas F. Croake represented Mrs. Paolello, who has brought a separation suit against her husband.

In the separation action Mrs. Paolello contends her husband does not support her or the children. Paolello, who is now a GI student, asserted he will give her $30 a month as soon as he starts receiving the $90 government allowance.

ford Hills High.

cil honors the same day at the Ryewood Country Club—Leon Kahan, a real civic standout! . . . Wolfgang Cribari, Mount Vernon's Barrymorish mouthpiece, surprised one of the county's town attorneys one Sunday afternoon at how adept he also was with a basketball. On a bet, both wandered into a Y gym and Wolfgang surprised his tormentor by dropping in shots from midcourt—and so long after his high school days, too.

* * *

Wolfgang Cribari, Mount Vernon's Barrymorish mouthpiece, surprised one of the county's town attorneys one Sunday afternoon at how adept he also was with a basketball.

On a bet, both wandered into a Y gym and Wolfgang surprised his tormentor by dropping in shots from midcourt…and so long after his high school days too. 2/20/55

> Denny Donovan of Harrison marries Joan Gannon of Bronxville Dec. 14. He's son of Harrison Police Chief Bill Donovan. . . . That raucous shouting emanating from Bronxville's Special Sessions the result of a hot verbal duel between Mount Vernon lawyer Wolfgang Cribari and Assistant DA Doug McGuire. Cribari demanded a 12-man jury to try one of his defendants, a drunken driving suspect. McGuire held out for a six-man panel. The case ended up in the lap of the grand jury.

That raucous shouting emanating from Bronxville's Special Sessions (Court) the result of a hot verbal duel between Mount Vernon lawyer Wolfgang Cribari and Assistant DA Doug McGuire. Cribari demanded a 12-man jury to try one of his defendants, a drunken driving suspect. McGuire held out for a six-man panel. The case ended up in the lap of the grand jury. 11/21/54

For me this was shocking. Dad defending a drunken driver? There must have been extenuating circumstances because Dad was a fanatic about our not driving if we had even one drink. He told the most frightening tales of the horrible accidents that had happened to his clients when they drove drunk.

The issue the news article deals with is not whether the client was a drunk driver but whether or not there should be a 12 man or six man jury to decide. A question crossed my mind: "When did breathalyzer tests become legal in NY State? The answer: *In 1953 New York became the first state to pass an implied consent law mandating that all drivers gave their implicit consent to chemical tests if they were suspected of drunk driving.* Thank you, Google.

This review of a few of dad's publicized cases, as opposed to his own saved transcripts, gave me new insight into the wide spectrum of dad's professional expertise.

— 55 —

WHEN WE WEREN'T FIGHTING, WE WERE SINGING

When we weren't fighting, my sisters and I were singing, no matter which house we found ourselves.in, nana Cribari's, nana Ankie's, 395 Westchester, or 317 Claremont. Although dad was our most supportive fan, it was Dolly and mom who taught us the songs and encouraged us to first sing in harmony and then to learn choreographed routines to fit the singing. Our early experience in the performing arts was a harbinger of our future career choices.

Donna (Doni) became a musical performer, learned to play piano, clarinet, guitar and majored in music. She is also an experienced and gifted composer who taught and directed music in Florida, Pennsylvania and Canada. Doni still music-directs shows in New York City, Westchester County and Nantucket.

My sister Carola (Bill) majored in classical music in college, performed in operas in New York City, moved with her opera singer husband, Edoardo Assali, to Germany for work as an opera singer. She continues to compose and direct groundbreaking musicals and concerts in Heidelberg, Germany.

Like mom and dad, Bill met her husband Edoardo Assali onstage. Their connection was through opera; Ed was an established professional when Bill met him. I saw them perform together in a production of "Tosca" in New York City and they were electric. Their mutual passion for music and acting led them to successful careers in Germany where every major city has an opera house.

The Assali family: my sister Bill, her husband Edoardo & daughter Carla at home in Heidelberg, Germany.

It's my favorite picture of all three of them

Bill and Ed went to live in Germany in the late 1970's where they established careers in German opera companies.

Carla, born in the U.S., lived and went to school in Germany. She now lives in Michigan where she teaches at the local university.

Sadly, neither Ed nor Carla ever knew dad.

My contribution to our Sister Act? I was the oldest, the first to learn to sing harmony like the Andrews Sisters, our role models for our almost professional trio. I say "almost" because the same year we had our first professional offer (*the McGuire Sisters were popular at the time, we sounded like them*) Doni chose to enter the convent. I was already married and had my first daughter Denise. The Cribari Sisters career as the new Maguires wasn't to be.

Singing together had defined our identity since 1946 when dad joined the Westchester Country Club. The Club produced two shows every summer under the direction of Dorothy Fine, an incredible advocate of the performing arts, and a mentor for me personally. We had our first taste of stardom on the terrace of The Club in the summer of 1946 where The Cribari Sisters made their debut singing "Sentimental Journey" in two-part harmony. Bill was just four years old.

The picture at left appeared in The Club magazine our debut year. I'm 10, Doni is 7 and Bill, 4. The one on the right of is of our second year when we performed "Clancy Lowered the Boom," that one appeared in newspapers county-wide.

Singers In "Big Little Show"—

THE SINGING CRIBARI
TERS, of Mount Vernon, al-
s a favorite of "Big Little
ow," are pictured while
ing rehearsal of their
"Clancy" routine which will be
included in this year's show tomorrow night at the Westchester Country Club. Left to right
are Camilla, Donna and
Staff Pho

The Cribari Sisters performed at the WCC summer shows for years. When anniversary shows were planned, we were always invited back for guest appearances . I remember the year Miss Fine asked me to direct The Big Little Show as one of my life's full circle moments. Even better, years later she hired my daughter, Denise Colangelo, as director.

— 56 —

DAD'S AUTOGRAPHS

MANY OF THE MEMORIES of dad I've been able to access are based on pictures of the people we loved, the houses we lived in, the places we went, and the things we liked to do. Another source of memories is my two autograph books. I loved to collect autographs, especially when I was a teeny bopper.

I looked up synonyms for "teeny bopper" just in case. Here are a few that define a young girl ages 9-13: missy (*thank you, John Wayne*) maiden, girly, nymphet, schoolgirl, patootie (*as in "sweet patootie"*) bobby-soxer (*1940's choice*) lass, baby doll, wench, and the most common 2000 version, tween.

Dad would have loved this dictionary excerpt. According to mom, he used to read the dictionary for entertainment. Why doesn't that surprise me?

Here are two autographs that dad wrote in my autograph books, one from sixth grade (*elementary school*) and the other from junior high (*grades 7-9*) It took me years to be able to look at my father's distinctive handwriting without crying.

> *June 12, 1947*
>
> *May God shower all of his blessings upon my talented and lovable daughter Camille.*
>
> *Dad*

June 20, 1950

To Camille,

You're gentle and kind and talented too.
So I'm sure life has in store for you
nothing but happiness and great joy.
So here's to you, my sweet.
I'm glad you weren't a boy!

All my love, Dad

The last line of the second autograph "I'm glad you weren't a boy" is no accident. Dad used to say that all the time. It made me want to say, "o.k., o.k., enough!" But when I saw the words in my autograph book it was different somehow. It was in his handwriting!

I'm sure of it, my father said so.

One thing I do know for sure about dad as a parent, he never said no to any of us, giving us many an opportunity to misbehave without fear of punishment.

See the innocent look on Bill's face? Just a few hours before this picture was taken she accidentally hit Doni in the eye with dad's golf club which she was not supposed to be playing with. Doni's shiner is clearly visible in this photo of us singing the Andrew Sisters hit, "Big Brass Band from Brazil" in the Big Little Show. Doni had a black eye for the show. She's giving Bill a "look," dad didn't.

Dad and mom's reactions to their daughters youthful "career paths?" Mom helped us "stay on pitch" and dad whistled his approval while we took our bows!! Of course our parents must have been delighted by our love of performing; it was how they met. It also kept us from fighting in the backseat of the car on family road trips.

We were raised in both mom and dad's unique artistic styles which encouraged three creative personalities to take their respective, diverse paths: acting, musical theater, opera, dancing, directing and composing.

All three have been teachers; dad's unrealized retirement-career goal.

— 57 —

POST WAR PROSPERITY

THE 50'S BROUGHT DRAMATIC changes to the lives of each member of the W.E. Cribari family. Dad's career as a much sought after defense attorney was getting to be more than he could handle so he took on partners and became Cribari, Scapolito and Solinger. Mom spent more time away from our spacious new home on Claremont Avenue learning to play the organ, taking sewing and design classes, joining friends for weekly Broadway matinees. Within just a few years Bill was the only one of us girls living home.

I was a boarding student at Marymount Academy for my last three years of high school. Doni joined me there as a boarder in eighth grade. We both missed being home but became completely immersed in Marymount's variety of learning experiences and social activities.

This picture of dad and me at the annual Father-Daughter dance shows how Marymount tried to include family members in our lives away from home. We had a great time that night. At one of those later dances, dad and I both got to meet Jackie Gleason who was his daughter Gerry's date that evening.

I found a movie/video that was taken at a 1950's Marymount Father Daughter dance when Doni was a student. There are quite a few scenes in the video where dad is seen "in his element," dancing with his daughter, a few of her friends and even with their fathers in a mad-cap series of improvised dance steps. Dad even brought along his brother Mario as a substitute father for one of Doni's classmates. Our Marymount friends and teachers loved dad's free spirit.

At this point in dad's story, I would like to include word for word this wonderful English composition Doni wrote in April 1953 when she was a freshman at Marymount Academy. It's entitled:

"The most unforgettable character I have ever met."

There is a very distinct difference between my subject and other characters that I have met. When I finish my story you will know why I chose this man instead of another.

One morning, quite a while ago I was introduced to him. I was very young and would never remember exactly what he looked like, but he couldn't have been much different than he is now. Probably he was a little thinner. But now, he is by no means fat.

As I came to understand things better, I noticed some things that really attached me to him. I guess the first one was how he loved me when I was little. When I realized how much he was doing for me, I guess I loved him all the more. It was probably because of the natural selfishness in such a little child that I wanted more and more. He always gave me what I needed, and very often just what I wanted, but he didn't spoil me then by any means.

When I grew older I noticed how deep his devotion was to his home and family. He did little things, big things, and, I am told, he even helped mother around the house after a hard day at the office.

He doesn't like going out, he'd rather stay home and watch the television set, but when he does go, he can usually adjust himself to his surroundings and feel right at home.

Another one of his abilities is law. He has great talent for arguing (that was not meant as it sounded, but legally) and is quick to respond to any type question you put to him. He can be either very funny and entertaining or as gentle and serious as anyone. He loves singing and the piano and even though he does not play, he will often sit down and try.

He is very fond of sports, especially golf, which, during the summer months he plays on Saturday. He also has a great talent for acting although he doesn't do much anymore. Some say he's a bit "hammy." He loves to see plays and entertain by singing, comedy and straight acting.

When he is helping people, he is happy. From what I have seen and heard he loves to give when he can, and is especially generous with anyone who asks advice. I think it is hard for him to refuse anyone, and that is why he chose law as a profession.

I don't think I need to go any further to tell you about my subject. I can only tell you, I may have been prejudice in my writing. You see, he is my father.

This adorable picture of eight year old Doni pushing dad on the tree swing illustrates Doni and dad's playful connection. It has a history of its own

FAST FORWARD: Doni recalls an incident about the loss of the picture.

> *During the first and second years of training to become a Catholic nun, all incoming mail written to the postulants and novices was censored. Apparently our mistress of novices did not notice that this little photo had slipped out of one of dad's heartfelt and emotional letters to me. It had fallen on the floor of the crypt where the nuns went to pray every day. The wonderful coincidence that occurred was that in the next group of nuns that went to the crypt to pray there was a classmate of mine who had entered the convent three years earlier. She just happened to notice the little picture on the floor and recognized me and my dad. Somehow, she surreptitiously slipped the picture to me knowing how much it would mean to me. I had no idea what the letter said until years later when I found a copy, but I kept this picture with me in my wallet all this time until Camille started writing this book.*

— 58 —

FAMILY VACATION/ BUSINESS TRIP TO ITALY SUMMER 1953

Summertime was family time. Since 1946 we had enjoyed the diverse activities offered at Westchester Country Club. At the club the three of us could swim, meet new friends, sing, dance every single day; it was Utopia. Dad and mom enjoyed separate but equal time at the club: dad as weekend golfer, gin rummy player; mom preferred catching up on her magazines and sitting under the umbrella with her legs outstretched in the sunshine trying to "*get my legs tan.*"

Believe it or not, when dad told us we were all going to Europe that summer, we balked; even mom. I had just graduated from Marymount Academy and looked forward to taking part in Sky High Varieties at the Club with my summertime friends. It wasn't to be.

One of dad's clients wanted him to represent him in a lawsuit against an Italian businessman. Dad's hypercritical attitude towards Italians always bothered me. It was sometimes apparent even in in his casual conversations. How was he going to act in Italy? Would he slip and call someone there a wop?

Let me sidebar for a moment. I recently discovered the etymology of "wop" *its origin dates from 1908 and comes from the southern Italian dialect "guappo" which means a swaggerer, a worthless fellow.* I thought it was worse than that. I guess it was the way dad, the son of southern Italians, said it.

My inherited love of words, their meaning and derivation made me read on. *One false etymology of wop is that it is an acronym for "without passport" or "without papers" implying that Italians entered the U.S. as undocumented or illegal immigrants. Wop has nothing to do with immigration documents as they were not required by U.S. immigration officers until 1924, after the slur had already come into use.*

After I wrote about dad's ambiguous feelings of being Italian, I discovered a speech he made to an Italian American club right after World War II. Here is a section from that speech that made me think twice and see his unique ambiguity.

> **I consider it a privilege to address a group not ashamed of its Italian parentage. Like your selves, I am the son of an immigrant who often told of great happiness in the chances America offered his children for education and profession and who had great love for America as all immigrants do.**
>
> **Are we less American because we cherish and honor our fathers and their birth land and our heritage? There is a growing feeling that those who bellow most about their Americanism are those who practice racial discrimination the most.**
>
> **By being proud of our ancestry we are much better Americans by far than those who conceal it. I hope I never see the day when I am ashamed to meet as you do here with others of Italian ancestry.**
>
> **When people claim they have ancestors who came over on the Mayflower, tell them ours came on the Santa Maria with Columbus.**
>
> **Remind them… Columbus was the first European to land on American soil.**

Verrazano was the first to navigate the Hudson River.

Amerigo Vespucci gave his name to America.

Filippo Mazzei, friend of Jefferson, is the original author of the words "All men are created equal"

GuillermoPacewasasigneroftheDeclarationofIndependence.

Italians fought for Washington in the Revolution and Lincoln in the Civil war, in fact all wars in America's history.

Garibaldi, father of Italian democracy, worked in Long Island.

Enrico Fermi, an immigrant, discoverer of atomic energy, gave his findings to America.

Back to 1953 and our family trip to Italy. I only have one reference in My Trip Diary as to why dad had to go that summer so I'll never know the whole story. I know Dad was offered an all expense paid six week European (Italy, Switzerland and France) vacation for all of us as an incentive to take the case.

We weren't booked to go by plane, dad never flew, but to travel on two luxurious cruise ships, the SS *Constitution* and the RMS *Queen Mary*. These four pictures are of the SS *Constitution* in the Mediterannean; dad on board the day we sailed; our family passport photo; Bill, Doni, mom and dad on board the day we sailed.

I love this passport photo, it has really good likenesses of all of us. Dad insisted we were going to love Europe and could be in shows next summer.

I'm sure of it, my father said so.

That first ocean cruise was life changing for me and as a result for the whole family because on that cruise to Italy I met my future husband and father of my children. Warren Voigt was in his sophomore year at the U.S. Merchant Marine Academy and assigned to the *Constitution* as a Cadet Officer for the exact same time I was a passenger.

My sister Doni spent most of the ten day cruise either in our cabin seasick or up on deck trying to forget about it and breathe the **"nice healthy sea air"** dad promised. She started to come out of it when we sighted the Azores, but she didn't look like herself until we debarked in Naples.

I was so involved with the new friends I met on board, which included Warren, that I have no idea what dad and mom enjoyed most on their second European cruise. We always met for meals at our table in the ship's dining room where dad would remark how calm and stable the ship felt. **"Look, the water in the glass isn't moving."** Doni's cue to get up and run back to our cabin.

Dad was a teenage girl's ideal father, loving, protective and flexible. That summer I'm sure his flexibility was challenged. The first night in Italy I stayed out until 4:00 a.m. partying with my college age friends, Warren and his fellow cadet officers. When we got back to Naples' Hotel Excelsior, the front door was locked. After banging on the door and screaming for what seemed like an hour, someone let us in. I expected a lecture from dad the next day. It didn't happen.

There were many incidents on this trip that reveal why dad's social skills were so effective: he was a consummate actor. Our first night on board we met the Goodmans of Bergdorf Goodman fame who knew us as fellow members of the Club. Oozing charm, dad acted thrilled to see them. As soon as they were out of earshot, he said, **"Thank Goodman the goodnesses are gone."** We couldn't help but laugh, he'd totally charmed them then deliberately avoided them the rest of the trip.

In Rome, dad met his cousin Ortensio Manes for the first time. Ortensio was mayor of Rome and had arranged to host a family party for us during our week long stay in Rome. For the next few days before the party, dad complained about having to go. Of course, he was the life of the party.

I'll never forget that jam packed nana Cribari style, Roman family party. We all sat at a very long table placed outside the ristorante; the table was on a hill so we slid dishes and food downhill to each other. *"Io sono nato in Brazil" (I was born in Brasil)* is the only Italian I remember a cousin saying to me. I realized much later she wanted me to know that her family had fled Italy before Mussolini so she was born in Brazil. It was an Italian-English gabfest. We laughed a lot!

Our English speaking Italian tour guides in the Eternal City led us through churches, galleries, catacombs and places like Scala Santa (*Holy Stairway*) where we saw the staircase from Pontius Pilate's palace which Jesus walked on. My sister Doni was the only one of us who made the pilgrimage by climbing the sacred stairs on her knees.

Shades of a future nun.

As soon as our well-meaning guides were out of hearing range, dad whispered to his credulous daughters: **"they're lying," "that's impossible," "don't believe a word they say."** Not sure why dad felt he had to mock the traditional Roman Catholic mythos, but he always got a laugh from us.

On the other hand, dad was appropriately respectful during an audience with Pope Pius XII which dad's client arranged. I remember the slight, fragile pontiff as being sweet and gentle with each person who approached to kiss his ring. He was the epitome of the title Holy Father. Dad was on his best behavior and I believe as moved and comforted by him as we were.

Another of my memories of Rome involves dad and Michelangelo's Pieta in St. Peter's Cathedral in Vatican City. We were waiting on a long line to see the Pieta up close when dad started to subtly move ahead of the people in front of us. He had an interesting line-crashing technique that seldom failed.

It did this time. The people ahead of us said something in Italian and gave dad a nasty look. Dad moved out of and to the side of the line while continuing to inch his way up into the nave in which the Pieta stood. He motioned for us to join him, but we stayed in line.

When we got as close as you were allowed, everyone gazed adoringly at the extraordinary sculpture, mesmerized by its beauty and power. The lifelike marble figures of Mary holding her dead son were heartbreaking. I could see dad standing engrossed off to the side in what must have been the longest time he ever stood gazing at any work of art. Bravo Michelangelo.

I fell in love with Rome in July 1953 and have been back twice since then.

Here are pictures from our memorable Roman holiday.

Mom, Bill, dad and Doni in front of the Coliseum.

Dad always had his movie camera strap over his shoulder, he loved taking movies, not snapshots. The only snapshots I took are these tiny ones.

Dad was our documentarian in Europe that summer recording every new sight and our immediate reactions.

Me at the Bocca di Verita (Mouth of Truth) which is featured in the movie "Roman Holiday." I watch it every chance I get.

There he goes again, getting me on camera while I'm taking my snapshots.

I'll always connect dad to two of my favorite Roman sites: the Coliseum which he circled around in record time and the Catacombs where he walked in, took a quick look inside, turned around and walked out. He was a tour guide's nightmare. Mom, the three of us and the guide were always six feet behind him. But we loved his irreverent approach and laughed a lot.

Ortensio Manes, a composer of popular music and a career politician was a cousin from the Manes side of the family (*Nana Cribari's*). He and dad had a lot in common. Both were successful, artistic and charismatic leaders in their respective communities.

In Florence, our next stop, we visited churches, museums and saw the greatest artwork of the Renaissance. One day we had lunch in a piazza overlooking the city where a replica of Michelangelo's David stood. For years I used to argue with friends that the piazza statue was the real thing not the one they had seen in a museum. I eventually found out dad *let us believe* (he never actually told us) that we had seen the iconic David in that piazza because when he tried to get tickets to the museum that housed the **real** David, it was closed.

I'm sure of it, my father said so.

Within the city of Venice we visited the traditional tourist attractions like St. Mark's where I took this picture of the family. It was right after we walked in and out of that opulent cathedral that dad said "it's falling apart" I recorded his memorably sarcastic artistic opinion in my diary.

We didn't stay in Venice proper, we stayed on Lido beach where dad could relax, sun bathe and run in and out of the Adriatic surf. Since he wasn't a strong swimmer, he chose instead to stare intently at the waves lapping up on shore in the same way he used to stare at a fire.

Both water and fire undoubtedly relaxed him.

Most of our time in northern Italy and Switzerland was spent shopping for watches, Venetian glass, leather pocketbooks, belts and shoes. This is still typical of most tourists who visit there. I'm sure dad and my sisters were bored, but mom and I weren't. Milan was just another big city for me until our guide took us to see daVinci's Last Supper. I was amazed at the artistic detail and the diverse faces and forms of the men around Jesus, but the faded colors were being restored and they looked washed out, didn't they, dad?

Look what I wrote in my diary on August 6, 1953 while we were in Lake Como, Italy:

> *Today is dad's birthday.* (He was 50) *and we stayed here all day long. In the morning Doni went swimming but no one else did. Too many fish. This afternoon we also stayed here for lunch. The spaghetti was just fabulous, the food here is really the greatest. After lunch we rested for a while and then* ***Doni and I went in swimming****. Giorgio and his cousin were there and we all swam out to the raft. It was wonderful out there. We sat and talked a combination of English and Italian…*
>
> *Had a lot of fun swimming today. It was not too bad with the fish. Ate here at hotel tonight and before going up to pack I went outside a while and danced with Giorgio and a boy from Belgium. Giorgio really handed out a line and said he was going to write to me in Cannes* (our next stop). *This place has been great. Very sorry to leave it!*

Mom and dad must have finally had a chance to be alone together on dad's birthday. Reading this diary entry helps me remember the many warm and affectionate moments I saw my parents share on this trip. I have always associated our stay in Lake Como with togetherness and relaxation. Their roles as parents were put on hold and their romantic natures nourished by their stay at the beautiful Villa D'Este. It was time to leave Italy and travel to Cannes, Paris, Cherbourg and finally to the ship home all within the next ten days. The itinerary was well planned and each night's hotel reservations made.

Then the unexpected: A national strike in France happened the day we arrived at the celebrated Hotel Carlton in Cannes. I remember the Duke and Duchess of Windsor were staying right down the hall from our room which overlooked the Mediterranean. Dad was not impressed and even more irreverent than he had been in Rome. Though he loved reciting "Cyrano" in French, he was definitely not a Francophile. The strike really angered him.

The strike angered him and he started cursing the French.

Here's dad with Doni on a balcony of the Carlton Hotel in Cannes just before we were caught in the strike. Bill is peeking out the balcony door.

We ran into several snags in our travels from the French Riviera to Paris. On our way home from a movie our first night in Cannes there was a national blackout.

As newcomers to the city, we had no idea where we were or how to get back to our hotel. It was so dark in the streets we couldn't see two feet in front of us. Dad did nothing but curse: **"these crazy French," "these nuts."**

To add insult to injury our train reservations from Cannes to Paris were cancelled because the railroads were on strike. We had to rent a car and drive to Paris with no place to stay overnight. We drove and drove until we finally found a really cheap hotel in Valence which we feared was " buggy." It wasn't, but we talked more about that one restless, anxious night in Valence than we did the luxurious, peaceful high-priced hotels we'd been staying in.

Next stop, the world famous Hotel George V in Paris where we found a letter from Marcello and nono Ankie, mom's father, waiting for us. Nono, age 84, had flown transatlantic for the first time to join us in Paris; a real feat in those days. Nono was an amazing man who dad loved and admired; we all did. He was the best traveling companion you could ask for.

We visited all the Parisian landmarks, churches, museums together including a night at the Follies Bergeres. That's a night I won't forget; especially the part when Doni turned her back on the stage to avoid seeing a stage filled with naked Parisian chorus girls.

Nono Ankie's presence set the tone; dad was on his best "tourist" behavior, no racing through ancient marbled hallways. Here are mom, Doni, Nono Ankie, dad and Bill at the Castle at Fontainbleau, It was a homecoming for mom who had been a music student there when she was 22. Nono Ankie is peeking over dad's shoulder.

The last days of our Parisian venture pulled it all together. Dad, Doni, Bill and I visited Marymount's Paris school. Mom and Nono shopped.

I wrote *"We walked down the Champs Elysees at night for the last time. On to Cherbourg, then home on the Queen Mary"*

This was our regular family grouping every night on both the *Constitution* on the way over and the *Queen Mary* on the way back. Mom used to join us just before it was time to go into the dining room, not one second sooner. She was usually in her stateroom making last minute adjustments to her hair or her wardrobe or at the bar having a champagne cocktail to avoid sea sickness. She was off doing one of the above when the ship's photographer asked us to pose for this portrait.

The one exception to our nightly dinner ritual happened the night we sailed through an Atlantic hurricane on the *Queen Mary*. The only person who made it to the dining room that night was octogenarian nono Ankie. He was an amazing man, as unforgettable in his own quiet way as his histrionic son-in-law!

— 59 —

BACK TO NORMAL

A DAY OR TWO AFTER we returned from our trip to Europe, Dad went right back to his Mount Vernon law practice and court trials in White Plains. This picture shows him and his fellow legal thespians at his favorite yearly event, the Westchester Bar Association's annual golf outing and dinner.

This appeared in the Reporter Dispatch newspaper sometime in either spring or fall of 1953, before or after we were in Europe.

> *"Loud enough even if the microphone was off – rough-rider quartet gleefully goes through its airs in entertainment at the Westchester Bar Association's annual beefsteak frolic last night at Schmidt's Farm, Greenville. Quartet members are: John J. Dillon of White Plains,* ***W. Edward Cribari*** *of Mount Vernon, Robert Trainor of Eastchester and Francis J. McNulty of White Plains."*

Here are the lyrics of a song Doni remembers from when the judges came to our house to rehearse with dad for this event. He wrote this parody to the tune of "Marching through Georgia"

> *"Hooray, hooray, we're thorough buccaneers.*
>
> *Hooray, hooray, we're in for fourteen years (probably their judicial term)*
>
> *We know you think we're lousy, but*
>
> *We've banished all our fears.*
>
> *For we have the power of appointment"*

Dad loved each and every opportunity he had to perform and his exuberance is evident in both pictures. In the first one he obviously upstages the others. One of his colleagues in that picture, Robert Trainor, became a New York Supreme Court judge. In the second one, dad also "takes stage." Second to becoming an actor, dad's unfulfilled dream was to become a judge. Neither were to be, but he combined those two passions, the law and acting, into a notable, successful career as a defense attorney until…

Dad attracted the attention of a corporate insurance company he had often opposed in court. Dad's legal objectives were always aimed at achieving the best possible outcomes for his clients. In the majority of his trials the client was more than willing to rely on dad's legal judgment and advice. But in one of his most interesting cases, dad's client didn't listen to him. Since he kept the article which appeared in the Reporter Dispatch, December 27, 1954. I believe the situation was unique in dad's career. It bears including in his story.

I have a personal recollection of this particular client because during our family's Christmas dinner on December 25, 1954 that client rang our doorbell and brought dad a Christmas gift. When I found this article among dad's memorabilia I finally understood the reason for that uniquely timed visit. I'm including excerpts from the article within my narrative.

The article begins: *"An attorney's perseverance in seeking executive clemency for a client who gambled and lost on a jury verdict brought the first Christmas not behind bars since 1937 for the convicted man."*

Dad's client had been charged with striking a drunken man during a robbery attempt in August 1936. The robbery victim toppled down an outdoor staircase, struck his head and died. The prosecution offered to let dad's client plead guilty to second degree manslaughter which carried a maximum 15 year term and the possibility of much earlier parole. Dad's client decided to take his chances with the jury and face first degree felony charges against dad's advice.

The client "*had expected to spend Christmas in prison* (he had been in prison for 17 years*). Instead he arrived in Mount Vernon on Christmas Eve and was welcomed by his parents, four sisters and two brothers."*

"The Governor acted on the fifth clemency petition prepared yearly by attorney ***W.E. Cribari*** *who represented him when he was convicted of first-degree felony murder.*

The ex-convict, his hair now gray and his face lined, has a job waiting for him with a construction company."

"New York Governor Thomas Dewey, exercising traditional yuletide clemency, commuted on Christmas Eve the non-parole-able life imprisonment sentence of the now forty-two year old client."

No wonder he couldn't wait to thank his compassionate lawyer.

— 60 —

"BLESSED ART THOU AMONGST WOMEN" (1930-1966)

GROWING UP WITH A man like dad as my father was having it all. I always felt he was a futuristic version of parent, a mom-dad fusion. Mom was mom and saw to our basic needs, but she also took lots of opportunities to pursue her own artistic and social interests. She was definitely not Donna Reed. Dad was.

Bill explained her feelings about dad's maternal qualities: *"One thing I always said my father was more my mother. When I was sick to my stomach he held my head. When I hallucinated with a high fever once and thought my hands and my pillow were shrinking, I remember him holding up his hand to my hand saying* ***"your hand is perfectly normal"*** *He was such a caring, loving father."*

The only drawback for dad was he didn't have enough hours in the day to be available as a mom. Today I think he would have loved being a stay-at-home dad, working through the Internet and/or out of an in-house office. Today's flexible work schedules would have allowed him more time to enjoy his children.

Dad encouraged me to be the next Shirley Temple, a performer like he was. He sang along with me, recorded every song I learned on a primitive phonograph that had a needle which cut into the waxed surface of a record and literally made sound "bites." (*Re-read the section called "Cutting Records")* He also provided dancing lessons for me when I was 3 or 4, improvised scenes from favorite stories, dressed up in silly outfits. A one man production team.

When Doni and Bill came along, they joined the troupe. But dad went one step further and engaged both girls in his love of sports, especially baseball. We all played kick ball on the quiet street in front of our home. I played if my friends were around, but I never cared about team sports the way my younger sisters did. I wanted to be a star.

Mom was there for us, accompanying our singing on the piano, calling out "you're flat" from the kitchen when we sang off key, but she was in a creative world of her own. I seldom heard her playing the violin in those days. I was surprised to see a home movie of her playing for friends at a party at Claremont Avenue. She bought a Hammond organ and learned to play it in record time. She also took weekly trips into NYC to attend Wednesday Broadway matinees.

By the mid-50's dad and mom were becoming empty nesters. I was away at Marymount College, Doni was a boarding student "down the hill" at Marymount Academy. Bill was the only one living home. All three of us were active in various arts activities throughout our high school and college years.

Continuing our family's roots in theater, I majored in Drama and performed in every single show I auditioned for. Dad and mom never missed one. Dad's "reviews" were always the ones I looked for after curtain call. Here's one he scrawled across the program for Marymount College's production of "Charley's Aunt," my first try at classic comedy.

> *"Camille – You gave a splendid performance. You are really an outstanding actress." Love Dad.*

One blip on the 1950-60 radar, dad wasn't very good at sending us "away to school." That is probably one of the biggest understatements I've ever written.

Every Sunday night before we got in the car for the ride back to school/ college in Tarrytown, dad would hug us so tight you'd think we were never going to see him again. If we started back a little late for our 8:00 deadline (we usually did), dad drove like a maniac. He wouldn't let mom or me drive; we tried. It was impossible to convince him that being upset at our departure made him a tense, keyed up driver. I learned to shut my eyes and pray.

His goodbye behavior never made sense to me because my parents made the decision to send us to Marymount and live away from home. They believed Marymount would give us a better education than local public schools. I never asked why, but I trusted both of them and never questioned their decision.

Dad always wanted me to be a teacher. I wanted to be an actress. It was the main source of our occasional arguments. I wanted to go to the American Academy of Dramatic Art in New York City. In spite of his lifelong love for theater, my career plans were unacceptable; he insisted a career in theater was too dependent on a "lucky break"

I'm sure of it, my father said so.

I went to college.

— 61 —

BREAKING AWAY

BACK TO MARYMOUNT ACADEMY/COLLEGE. Doni and I were off to a good start. The school was only a half hour away. It didn't matter, we still dreaded Sunday nights hugging a tearful father goodbye, the same dramatic exit. I wish we had known the cheerful goodbye song "So Long Farewell" from the Sound of Music in those days. We could have sung it to him. It might have lightened the mood.

Dad was great at lightening the mood when he chose to as this letter he wrote to Doni reveals. Dad wrote this eloquent witty four page letter because Doni got an 80 in Biology, a grade that kept her off the honor roll and rescinded her privilege of returning to school at 8:00 on Sundays instead of the regular 6:30 deadline.

February 3, 1955.

Dearest Donna,

How the mighty have fallen! So finally in your perennial combat with the honor roll you have been toppled from its distinguished lists. Calamity!

How you must have wailed and gnashed your teeth! But all in vain, eh. And by the margin of one point, too! Needless to say our household was plunged into the deepest gloom. None of us have eaten a morsel since the terrible news arrived. Long faces, profound silences, broken only by occasional recriminatory remarks uttered in the bitterest of invective.

Sporadically too, when the silence has become unbearable, each of us looking into the piteous features of the other, a sudden frenetic, simultaneous chorus of denunciation of the cruel fates, the school and the teachers that brought about this catastrophe.

How can you face life with this ignominy staring you constantly in the face? How can we go on with a daughter that has brought such obloquy upon us? Biology, of all things!

When you walk to your betrothed who awaits you with breathless disbelief at the picture of supernal beauty and charm he sees before him, will you be able to keep from him the dread news – 80 in Biology?

We must try to forget – but how can we with the ever constant reminder – the cruel punishment we must suffer for your dereliction! You must return at 6:30 instead of 8:00. Could anything be more harsh and severe?

I frankly feel the penalty is unconstitutional in that it violates the guaranty against cruel and unusual punishment. I am confident, dear one, that I can obtain your release until 8:00 on a writ of Habeas Corpus. But then that would involve publicity and we can ill afford to have the public share our dread secret – 80 in Biology.

I am intrigued by the suggested panacea of Mother Luke. She says: "Donna is a very good student. We are more than pleased with her. However, with a little more continuous effort, she could be on the honor roll."

Ah, my beloved, how true. You must expend a little more continuous effort. Now listen to your dad who loves you so! Instead of getting up at 4 a.m. as you have so selfishly done, arise at 2 a.m. Do you think it fair to luxuriate in your warm and comfortable bed every morning until 4 a.m.?

Think of the myriad of wonderful things you can learn in the extra two hours from 2 to 4 a.m. and such a splendid time of the day to delve into the mysteries of the life of the tadpole and the protozoa.

Before saying ciao, I feel impelled as your guardian to lay down for you certain directives and interdictions which you must adhere to meticulously if you want to salvage something of your wrecked career.

Increase your study hours from 4 A.M. to 12 midnight each day.

Every waking hour you have, drive yourself to keep constantly in your mind

> *the tadpole*
> *the protozoa*
> *the shark*
> *the frog*
> *the swamps they live in*

If you must play the piano, (and I don't recommend it) have before you a glass jar with a lot of floating parasites and study their habits.

Wear a dead tadpole on your uniform this will serve two purposes: it will be your badge of dishonor (remember 80 in Biology) and also serve to constantly remind you of the subject that has brought about this cataclysm.

If you must partake of food once in a while, touch nothing but fish, in fact I recommend that you that you limit your recreational lapses to the pastime of fish swallowing (you know the little ones) and before you gulp each one, study it closely.

If you will follow the foregoing, I have no doubt you will go a long way towards redeeming yourself. In fact, it is not beyond possibility that you may get to look like a tadpole. Wouldn't that be wonderful!

Then you will be biology personified and your fellow students can study ***you*** *instead of the book. Think what that will mean. From an 80 in Biology to the very exemplification, nay, the very personification of the subject.*

Herewith my real thoughts –

As usual I continue to be proud of you!

'Io sono contento' come never before with you.

I hope you flunk everything so you can come home to live where you belong. I think you have already studied and learned thrice as much as most college graduates.

In my humble judgment you will always be on the honor roll of loving, affectionate, dutiful, sensible, kindly and appreciative youngsters, the only important true honor roll there is.

You are an all-American daughter to me and

FINALLY. TO HELL WITH BIOLOGY!

All my love,

Dad

I 'd like to ask dad two questions about his classically clever letter to Doni:

Who typed it? Dad never learned to type; he just hunted and pecked like I do. Was it his secretary? It looks like he wrote it in his office because he used business stationery.

Did he use a thesaurus? Or did he really know how to use all those incredible words. Dad used to read the dictionary, but how did he learn to **use** the words with such facility?

Here is dad in his law office. His secretary, Miss Perone, worked for dad 25+ years.

Did he dictate the "biology letter" to her?

I'm including this picture so you can get an idea of how incongruous it would be for any lawyer or business man to write that Biology letter in his office. Not so for dad.

It was during this first empty nester phase that our family acquired a sweet little black cocker spaniel named Lori who became a welcome stand-in for Bill's two absent sisters, mom and dad's daughters. Here are two pictures from the mid-to-late 1950s.that exemplify the changes.

Warren Voigt, my first husband and father of my three daughters. He's in the entry to our kitchen at 317 Claremont Avenue with Lori, our favorite pet.

Warren was an outdoorsman and an animal lover who became a regular weekend guest at our home while we were both in college. He was a cadet at King's Point Merchant Marine Academy in Great Neck. Remember our 1953 trip to Europe? That's when Warren and I met, on the *Constitution.*

We went steady until our 1956 marriage.

Mom and Warren either coming home or going out. They're in our spacious, unique coat closet which was also the entryway to the powder room. Mom is wearing her signature mink coat which both she and dad were so proud of. We still have it. Dad was proud that he could afford such a gift. During the 1950's it wasn't ecologically offensive to own a mink coat; it was a status symbol for the successful businessman and his wife.

My sister Doni entered the convent two years after she graduated from high school. It took every ounce of dad's love and admiration for Doni to accept her life choice. Three years before Doni entered I married Warren. When Doni entered I already had a child, dad's first granddaughter Denise. Dad had a difficult time with my getting married so young; I was nineteen, the same age Doni was when she became a nun. I could sympathize with Doni's choice which, like mine, caused dad what we would call today "separation anxiety" heartache.

Here's a letter dad wrote Doni right before she took her vows. He used his incredible skills for verbal argument to try and persuade her to reconsider her chosen vocation. Remember he was a gifted trial lawyer.

> *My dearest sweetheart,*
>
> *I miss you so much my Donnie that I seem to have a constant ache deep inside of me. Couldn't you possibly come home for a few days? If they want and need you so badly up there, I'm sure they would relax a rule for you. Sweetheart, it's bad enough during the year but these holidays without you really get me down. I wish they were over with.*
>
> *I'm sorry, sweetheart, I don't want to make you unhappy. I just can't help telling you how I feel. It would be so utterly hypocritical to say we are happy when you are away from us.*
>
> *Please be sure you are doing the right thing – the thing you want to do. Please don't let pride interfere if you have the slightest doubt. I will never be able to understand why you can't live at home, perform your religious obligations and pursue the career that you desire and be near to all of us who love you and miss you so much.*
>
> *There must be some reason why Denise keeps talking about you and asking why you don't come home. Whenever she mentions Camille and Bill, whenever she sees a photo of either of them, she invariably mentions Donnie too. I just can't help but wonder why.*

I wonder what would have happened if Doni had received dad's masterful piece of persuasive writing. *The fact is she never did.* Doni's superiors at the convent censored the postulants' and novices' mail. *(Remember 'the lost picture' page 259.)*

I don't know if dad knew about that policy. If he had known, he would have been livid, stormed up to the convent with an armed guard and tried to rescue his "imprisoned" daughter. On the other hand one must question the mistress of novices belief that correspondence between home and the convent's new recruits might out-*indoctrinate* their own indoctrination. (*I think I just made up that word.)*

In one section of this revealing, unique *eleven* page, legal sized missive, dad compares his daughter's emotional characteristics to his own. A self-portrait!

> *I'm very much afraid you inherited a lot of my temperament – hypersensitivity, emotionalism, moodiness, overpowering pride, restless striving for perfection, constant preoccupation with the problems of others and indecision. These are not mere words, sweetheart.*
>
> *We older folks don't know much but we are at least able to see with the wisdom of the event why we have never attained that perfect state of serenity and happiness that we strive so mightily for throughout our lives.*
>
> *When I was your age, my darling, I was a completely lost, unhappy and mercurial personality. I too entertained thoughts of great self-sacrifice, getting away from people and being to myself and puzzlement as to what my role in life really was destined to be.*
>
> *Had I had your religious training it is quite possible I would have sought out the religious life as a simple answer to all the problems that beset me. But looking back now I realize that my decision would have been prompted by selfish personal reasons rather than a true vocation. But at the time I would undoubtedly have believed that a calling or a special destiny was influencing my judgment.*
>
> *I do not say that the above necessarily applies to you. But I have a right to ask you to weigh carefully and honestly just what factors have motivated you. And to be careful and honest you ought to review as much of your life as you have a clear and total recall of, both prior to and after your entering the convent.*
>
> *If you do this, sweetheart, can you honestly tell me that you didn't possess a number of the unfortunate facets of character and personality which have beset your old lonesome daddy all his life?*
>
> *For you to suggest, sweetheart, that if you didn't have the vocation those in authority would know and would not permit you to continue*

is tantamount to saying that those in authority know you better than you – better than your parents,

I often feel that I failed you badly. I saw mirrored in you these self same traits of mine. I failed to take time out of that darn inexorable pursuit of material security for my loved ones to try to give you, sweetheart, directions (as I was learning them) toward the road of stability and security of temperament.

I may be completely wrong (I hope I am if your decision to stay is approaching definitiveness) when I suggest …to a very large degree your emotions and the impact of your surroundings for many years (the tender and formative years when your parents should have been giving you more than love) are responsible for your decision. You probably do not realize this now anymore than I did the things I referred to above when I was your age. ***But in time the cloud will lift and realization will dawn upon you.***

I'm sure of it. My father said so.

You were right, dad. Doni was a nun for 12 years, but eventually left the order. Thank you, Doni, for sharing dad's letter and this glimpse into his struggles to raise independent women, then stand back and calmly watch them follow their separate paths. It wasn't easy for him, but he tried.

— 62 —

MARITAL MILESTONES

THE PEOPLE AND THEIR relative positions in this picture of mom and dad's 25th wedding anniversary celebration at Vernon Hills Country Club, Eastchester, N.Y. June 1955, inspired me to describe the event and its attendees in the dramatic terms dad and mom's marital milestone deserves.

Close your eyes, then take a second look at this picture.

Your eyes immediately focus center on dad, dressed in his favorite navy blue blazer, a white flower in his lapel, a cigarette in his left hand. It was just before he gave up smoking. (Dad's smoking is a topic I want to avoid in this happy setting) Mom is looking up at dad with a smile and a quizzical expression. Is she thinking, are you o.k. with this?

Mom might be concerned about dad's reaction, she knew he wasn't good at surprises. But she didn't plan the party.

My conclusion: this was **not** a surprise!

Dad's youngest sister, Dolly, in the white dress on dad's left, is the only one of his family next to him. I wonder what part she had in planning this party. My guess, she just wanted to be the first to greet dad. On mom's right is the country club's owner, Bernie Grey, and his wife. He was one of dad's clients and undoubtedly helped to arrange this party.

The three women standing on the left side are my sister Bill, Mary Asselta, mom's best friend, and dad's older sister Rose. All three are leaning in to get a better view of the guests of honor. There is a warmth between Mary and Rose, they were obviously friends. Dad's business partner, George Scapolito is cheering his colleague on as seen on the right side of the picture.

Dad had surprise phobia, but maybe it only applied to surprise *birthday* parties, not anniversaries. Someone probably told him about this surprise or maybe he felt more comfortable with mom by his side. I have one vivid memory of dad being "surprised" and it isn't pretty.

Evoking memories can lead you to your desired destination, but some memories also distract you by evoking other related memories. Here's a related distraction about dad and surprise parties.

I am sitting at the top of the stairs. Dad's friends and family are gathered in our living room waiting for dad to get home from work. He was late, of course. Then all of a sudden, dad was home. They all heard the garage door open and shut. Everyone shushed.

He was walking toward where they were hiding on the opposite side of the house. When dad got to the front hallway, everyone jumped out and yelled surprise! There was a moment of complete silence…

Then dad stomped up the stairs right past where I was sitting, went into his bedroom and slammed the door. My distracted memory stops right there.

Back to when dad obviously wasn't surprised, the 25th anniversary party.

Watching my parents' ease and grace as they danced together always made me want to learn to dance the way they did.

This picture shows the feeling in dad's expressive brown eyes, tears of joy.

His leading posture and their mutual comfort in an art form his talented wife used to teach was a tough act to follow.

A wonderful photo!

Here's the invitation 50+ people received for mom and dad's party. I have no idea who created it, but it's really clever.

Mom is the judge, Doni, Bill and I are the jury. And of course, dad is the "star of the show" Lori the dog is wearing #25. This party was the first time my boyfriend Warren was introduced to my father's large, spirited family.

Five of dad's six brothers and two of his three sisters were there. Nana Cribari and nono Ankie weren't there.

Some of dad's siblings are pictured below at other family get-togethers.

Dorothy, Guido's wife,* Guido *and dad.

Victor, *mom and* Arnold.

Mario *and me.*

The picture below is of five Cribaris together at a family celebration 20 years later for Bill's commitment ceremony (1975).

This picture has nothing to do with my parent's 25th anniversary party, but it does show five of my father's nine siblings in one place: Left to right: Dolly, Ray (with glasses), Olga, Guido and Mario.

They are all in my mom's backyard in Port Chester. This was several years after dad passed away; mom moved to Port Chester to be closer to me and my family.

The same group of relatives 19 years earlier gathered with 250+ others at Saints Peter and Paul Church and the Westchester Country Club for the marriage and wedding reception of Camille Cribari and Warren Voigt.

The role of Father of the Bride was not my dad's best performance. From the moment he slid out of the backseat of the bridal limo to walk me down the aisle until the reception's end when my new husband and I left in my brand new car, dad was on the verge of tears.

At one point we had to send someone to find him so we could take the traditional family pictures. I thought he approved of my choice of a husband so his behavior on my wedding day surprised me. To put it kindly, dad was not typical "father of the bride." He was a reluctant, even remote, participant.

Dad managed to get it together for the Father of the Bride dance. Warren's mother and father are at the edge of the dance floor. I'm sure I was more aware of dad's offbeat behavior than the others. Pictures don't lie: dad has the same stoic, unexpressive face in both pictures. He managed to summon up his acting skills as the day progressed, but as we left for the honeymoon, he went home.

My marriage was typical for my generation. Warren was the first young man I met who was different from those I grew up with. He was from another state, a different culture, a merchant marine cadet, "worldly and movie star handsome." Like me, he was a leader, but not a demanding one. He was ambitious and willing to work to "get ahead." Dad never said one word to criticize Warren until I went to him and asked him to help me get a separation.

I was and still am a Romantic; idealistic about men in general. The fact that I'm writing this book about my dad will tell you exactly where my role model came from. This phrase sums up my lifelong goal: *To find someone who loves* ***me*** *as much as I loved my dad.*

I finally did. *Grazie Luigi*

— 63 —

EMPTY NESTERS

DAD AND MOM WERE getting a chance to recast themselves as "empty nesters." That term wasn't in use until the late 1950's so no one would have described them that way then. But it certainly describes 317 Claremont Avenue as "*a home from which the grown children have moved out, leaving some unoccupied bedrooms: also the parents in such a home*"

During the 1950's, dad watched as his three daughters left their comfortable, loving home on Claremont Avenue to take on new roles.

Marriage to Warren Voigt cast me in the role of Navy wife; Doni became Sister Regina, a religious of the Sacred Heart of Mary, and Bill, a music major at nearby Manhattanville College was on her path to becoming an opera singer.

Challenges didn't frighten dad's daughters.

How did this new phase affect their marriage and dad's career? It was "back to the future." Dad and mom were once again the leading players, Wolfe and Carola, artistically and emotionally connected. Their supporting players were moving on, starting their own separate lives.

One of the first stumbling blocks in their way was dad's heart attack in 1958. It was considered a "warning" as he explained to me over the long distant phone call to Charleston, South Carolina where Warren, Denise, his beloved baby granddaughter, and I were living at the time. I remember fighting back the tears.

Dad recovered well and resumed his law practice and court trials. But he had to make several changes in his diet especially reducing his intake of high cholesterol food. This was a real challenge for dad who loved eggs in all their many culinary forms. Mom was a diligent watchdog over his daily temptation to cheat.

Another of dad's passions was taken away to protect him from too much stress: driving. Mom became his chauffeur for his frequent trips to White Plains courtrooms. Mom's new role as elegant mink-coated chauffeur became the talk of Westchester's lawyers and judges. Dad loved it.

Bill was the only one living home, here's a picture of her and dad around that time. When Bill graduated from college, she told mom and dad she wanted to pursue her dream and become an opera singer. I'm sure dad was tempted to repeat the doubts he had for my actress dreams, but he didn't. He made sure she had the best teachers and encouraged her artistic vision.

As Bill tells it…

> *When I got a scholarship to Marymount he took me aside and asked me if that is what I wanted to do. I said actually the music department at Manhattanville was really the best and I already knew about my future superlative teacher Bill Harms. He told me* ***"don't worry about having a scholarship. Go where you want to."***

On another topic, Bill recalls dad's advice on a very touchy teen age right of passage:

> *Learning how to drive. He took me out to teach me. I still use his advice to keep my foot over the brake pedal when giving gas. He said it saved time in case of a fast threat you were ready to brake. He also rigged the driver's test. He told me I would pass because I was ready. He would tell the motor vehicle's guy I was ready and to pass me.*

— 64 —

"THE LAW" THROUGH DAD'S EYES

DAD'S LAW PRACTICE WAS busier than ever. His reputation as defense attorney was attracting the attention of insurance company executives. Idealist and legal scholar that he was, dad started to question the future of the law as is seen in this 1950's speech he made to members of the Westchester County Bar Association.

The title:
There's Too Much Law

It is difficult for a trial lawyer of 33 years to know what to say to an erudite group like this without boring them to distraction. I'm staying clear of a drab, humdrum type of address like: how to be a good witness, how to be a good juror, our laws and their effectiveness, the usual pedestrian stuff.

I thought maybe you might be interested for a change in the layman's complaints about the law and the courts and a lawyer's analysis of their validity rather than hear the slanted view of the lawyer.

"There's too much law."

The people who make this complaint really haven't the vaguest notion of how much law there really is. The Library of Congress justifies an estimate of over 600,000 new state laws passed by our 48 states since the turn of the century. Think of it, 600,000 new laws in 50 years."

Dad cited this example 60+ years ago, I shudder to think of what the numbers might be today.

By the time much of the unneeded legislation becomes law, it is no longer even wanted or needed yet it remains on the books for it is rarely, if ever, repealed.

We still have unrepealed laws passed to protect communities from marauding Indians.

Statutes are still effective to regulate dueling.

Ancient traffic laws are still on our books regulating the speed of vehicles according to the horse and buggy era.

New England communities still have blue laws prohibiting work or play on Sundays.

The law is uncertain. Another complaint of the layman.

Here dad tells a story, one of his most effective oratorical techniques. I'm including it word for word.

Mary H. murdered her husband. She was convicted and her conviction was affirmed by the highest court of the state.

Between the date of her conviction and a date of the hearing for her appeal, a careless legislature in N.Y. State had repealed the existing law which imposed the death penalty and passed a new statute.

But it forgot to include in the new statute the usual provision that murders previously committed should be punished under the old law.

Consequently, Mary's lawyer argued that she could not be hung under the old statute since it was no longer in force, and she could not be punished under the new one since it was not in force when she murdered her husband. As a result, after hemming and hawing about the matter for five years, the judges turned the woman out of the death house and let her go scot free.

At the bottom of uncertainty in many of our laws is an inability *to say what we* mean.

How can legislators use the simple word *person* in a statute without risk of relegating the word to the purgatory of uncertain law?

They may understand it to mean *person* as "*a being having life, intelligence, will and separate individual existence as distinguished from an irrational brute, an inanimate thing*" as Webster defines it.

Having used it did they intend to include a dead person?

A lunatic?

A man sentenced to life imprisonment, an army officer, a druggist?

A slave? A woman? A stillborn child?

Every term I used represents an actual controversy in which the question of whether *person* could apply. Thousands of other dilemmas arise from the legislative use of the simple word *person* and have engaged courts for years.

As a matter of fact, it is almost impossible to select a phrase or a practice in our laws that a lawyer cannot confuse or confound, misconstrue or challenge.

Commercial corporations such as those that insure against accident, sickness and death are skilled in employing evasions to avoid liability.

An even more striking phase of uncertainty of law is illustrated by conflict in decisions of different courts, of the same court and even of different judges in the same case.

In spite of efforts to make the law uniform , they differ mightily. In all there are 33 grounds for divorce. The residence requirements all differ. Result is that one need but cross a state line after divorce to remarry; to create legal confusion men and women legally married in one state become bigamists and adulterers in another state.

***The law is too* technical.**

The law says a man who breaks into a building is guilty of burglary. The statement seems simple enough. But when a man broke into a railroad car, his lawyer argued that it was not a building and he could not be convicted for breaking into a building. An Arkansas judge frees the defendant and a Nebraska judge convicts him.

Homicide committed by a person engaged in felony is murder first and punishable by death unless jury recommends leniency. No criminal design or intent to effect death needs to be proved.

(The last sentence relates to a 1940's case of dad's which I wrote about previously.)

In the very nature of things we cannot avoid technicalities and legalisms. Since the year 4000 B.C. we have had approximately 16 different legal systems of which about half still survive. Of

these our own is about 400 years old as against the Chinese which has survived, in one form or another, for some 5000 years.

None of these systems have been able to avoid technicalities or to work out an effective method of administering exact justice between man and man.

There are many justifiable complaints about the law and its processes. What can be done about them?

Throughout the ages we have been told and are still being told what to do about the law.

The law is little else than the temporary command of our rulers.

In a democracy the rulers are the majority.

Assuming that the majority truly makes the law it would necessarily mirror their defects, their selfishness and greed, their vanities, their hypocrisies, their emotions. From all these as we have seen, the law suffers.

The fault in the last analysis lies not with lawyers and judges but with the people; the remedies, of necessity, must be with them.

I'm sure of it, my father said so.

— 65 —

MEDICAL & LEGAL PROFESSIONALS CLASH IN COURT

DAD WAS A LAWYER in the purest sense of the word, *"one versed in law, one whose profession is suits in court or client advice on legal rights."* In this 1959 case, one of the few he chose to keep a transcript of, he represents the plaintiff in a negligence suit against Mount Vernon Hospital Doctors.

Dad knew both defendant-doctors. His client, plaintiff Marie Gaspar, was suing the hospital and the two doctors named. Here is the Plaintiff's side.

SUPREME COURT OF THE STATE OF NEW YORK
COUNTY OF WESTCHESTER
MARIE GASPAR, An infant by her Guardian
AD LITUM, Leslie Gaspar, and LESLIE GASPAR individually.
Plaintiffs,

Against

MOUNT VERNON HOSPITAL, DR. CHARLES YAVELOW
And DR. WILMER WILSON
Defendants

PLAINTIFFS' MEMORANDUM OF LAW

(Written by dad)

This is an action on behalf of the infant, Marie Gaspar, against the Mount Vernon Hospital and Drs. Charles Yavelow and Wilmer Wilson.

This action is based upon the negligence, carelessness and recklessness of the defendants, their agents, servants or employees who failed to prevent the plaintiff from falling off an operating table while under anesthesia and unconscious, giving rise to the injuries mentioned below.

On February 3, 1959, Marie Gaspar, then fourteen years of age, had been operated upon at the Mount Vernon Hospital by Dr. Charles Yavelow for nose polyps under general anesthesia.

The anesthesiologist was Dr. Wilmer Wilson.

Immediately after the operation and while still under the effect of the anesthesia, and while awaiting transfer from the operating table to a recovery room stretcher, the infant fell to the floor and suffered a fractured skull, severe cerebral concussion, gran mal epilepsy, and related injuries.

The operation herein was performed between 8:00 and 8:30 A.M. on February 3, 1959. Attending the two doctors was a nurse employed by the defendant, Mount Vernon Hospital, Louise Davenport.

Her examination before trial revealed that she left the operating room within minutes after the operation to secure the recovery room stretcher.

At the time she left, the patient was strapped on the table in a prone position. Both the defendants, Drs. Yavelow and Wilson were in the room. Dr. Wilson being at the head of the operating table. When the nurse returned she noted the patient on the floor and the two doctors assisting in picking up the patient from the floor. She noticed that the patient had a large hematoma on the forehead. The two doctors placed the patient, thereafter, on the recovery room stretcher.

Dr. Wilson in his examination before trial in regards to the instant situation stated that Dr. Yavelow had removed the strap after Dr. Wilson had cleaned up immediately after the operation. He affirmed that the nurse had left after the strap had been removed to secure the stretcher. He further stated that Dr. Yavelow had walked over to a window to write up his chart.

At that point he stated that ***"the patient's legs went up in the air and to the left. I grabbed the patient by the head, but I couldn't hold her and she went off onto the floor on the left side of the operating table."***

The operation ended at about 8:30 A.M. and it took 2–3 minutes for Dr. Wilson to clean up and the patient fell to the floor approximately two minutes afterward.

The patient had been at that time in a medium level of unconsciousness and he stated that the patient ***"would wake up in maybe an hour or so"*** *from that time. Dr. Yavelow had been near a window about a minute or two before the patient fell.*

Dr. Wilson revealed that two nurses should have been in the operating room, one to clean up, called the scrub nurse, and a circulating nurse. Her responsibility was to help with the care of the patient and assist in moving the patient off the operating table with the aid of an orderly. He admitted that he, the anesthetist, is not supposed to be left alone after an operation.

A nurse was supposed to be standing by the patient while on the operating table until the patient was removed from the operating table. Dr. Yavelow admitted that after the operation he instructed Miss Davenport to secure a stretcher, at which time he turned his back on the table and walked over to write up his chart.

He stated that neither the nurse nor Dr. Wilson removed the strap holding the patient onto the operating table, but he was uncertain as to whether he had removed same.

After the patient fell he observed a hematoma the size of a lemon on the right side of the forehead and a bump about a quarter to a half inch high.

He admitted that after removal to the recovery room plaintiff was still under the anesthesia.

During the operation the plaintiff had been in almost a sitting position but immediately after was placed in a prone position on the operating table.

POINT ONE; THE DEFENDANT HOSPITAL IS LIABLE FOR THE NEGLIGENT ACTS OF ITS NURSE AND OTHER AGENTS.

The sole questions regarding the liability of the hospital vis a vis the nurse are: (1) whether the nurse was an employee of the hospital;

(2) whether she performed a negligent act. She was an employee of the hospital and if she was guilty of negligence, then the hospital must respond to the plaintiff in damages. Three precedents are cited for the point.

POINT TWO: THE FACTS OF THE CASE AT BAR PRESENT QUESTIONS FOR CONSIDERATION OF THE JURY AS TO THE NEGLIGENCE OF ALL DEFENDANTS.

Even if the strap had not been removed when Miss Davenport left the operating room, the hospital's liability is still a question of fact for the jury. Dr. Wilson has testified that there should be, and the hospital normally does have, two nurses present during and after an operation. If this was the normal precaution taken by the hospital, then in the instant case, the failure to take such precaution was an act of negligence. The fact that the nurse in the case at bar may have been acting at the direction of the attending physician does not relieve the hospital of liability. There was a breach of duty to the unconscious.

In the case at bar, Dr. Wilson has admitted that he is one of a group of anesthesiologists which services the Mount Vernon Hospital and that he was ***"booked for that operation that morning"*** *by a hospital nurse.*

The negligence of Dr. Wilson, therefore, raises a further question of the hospital's liability therefore to be determined by the jury.

That Dr. Wilson's acts immediately prior to the plaintiff's fall raises a question of fact is too basic to require additional argument. The facts speak for themselves. Dr. Wilson admits he saw Dr. Yavelow remove the strap and walk away. He admits he saw the nurse leave the room.

As a physician treating a patient, he had a duty in those circumstances to do all in his power to protect the plaintiff from a foreseeable injury. Whether or not he did so is a question only the jury can decide.

Dr. Yavelow, as chief of the operating team, had if anything, a greater duty than the others. His was the prime responsibility of the safeguarding of his patient. Dr. Wilson's testimony that Dr. Yavelow removed the strap, then told Miss Davenport to get the stretcher, then walked away from the operating table, must be negligence as a matter of law. On Dr. Yavelow's own admission, he was the one who removed the strap, told the nurse to go for a stretcher and then walked away from his patient.

My conclusion: I'm sure Marie Gaspar, the plaintiff, was awarded damages, but I have no details. The two doctors named were obviously found guilty of negligence.

Dr. Wilson admitted he saw Dr.Yavelow remove the strap and walk away. He had a duty under these circumstances, to do all in his power to protect the plaintiff from a foreseeable injury. Dr. Yavelow, as chief of the operating team, had a greater duty than the others. His was the prime responsibility for the safeguarding of his patient.

I'm sure of it, my father said so.

Another twist of fate.

Doni found a program dad kept from the Mount Vernon Medical Society's November 20, 1952 meeting . We wondered why he kept it. Then I read it over carefully.

MOUNT VERNON
MEDICAL SOCIETY

FOUR HUNDRED AND SEVENTIETH

THURSDAY, NOVEMBER 20TH, 1952

8:45 P. M.

at

THE WALKER LABORATORIES

Bradford Road, Mount Vernon, N. Y.

(Opposite Wilson Woods Pool)

Tel. MOunt Vernon 4-5000

BUSINESS SESSION

PROGRAM

All members of the profession
cordially invited

"Medicine and the Law"

by

MR. WOLFGANG CRIBARI

Attorney at Law

COLLATION

COMMITTEES

PROGRAM
Dr. Frank Rogliano, *Chairman*
Dr. Nelson Cornell   Dr. Henry W. Kaessler
Dr. Lucille M. Bond   Dr. Bernard Scholder

MEMBERSHIP
Dr. E. Moskowitz, *Chairman*
Dr. H. L. Carideo   Dr. George Sirignano

NOMINATING
Dr. Camillo Cerchiara, *Chairman*
Dr. Louis Lobes   Dr. H. Belsky

BIOGRAPHIC
Dr. A. E. Emmel, *Chairman*
Dr. J. H. Tallman   Dr. C. W. Johnson

ENTERTAINMENT
Dr. Samuel Fairstein, *Chairman*
Dr. Francis X. Morrone   Dr. C. Yavelow
Dr. A. R. Walsh   Dr. A. F. Angello

PUBLIC RELATIONS
Dr. W. A. Kelly, *Chairman*
Dr. E. B. Sullivan   Dr. W. J. Van Wie
Dr. N. F. Fiegoli   Dr. S. R. Breen

AUDITING
Dr. E. Bolgar, *Chairman*
Dr. Joseph Lombardi   Dr. L. R. Rosen

PARLIAMENTARIAN
Dr. K. R. Bush

Dad delivered a speech "Medicine and the Law" at their meeting. I couldn't find a copy of that speech in his files, but I recognized the name of Doctor Yavelow who was sued in the above 1959 Gaspar case. He was on the Entertainment Committee, one of those who invited dad to speak.

The two men, doctor and lawyer, were destined to meet 7 years later in a Westchester County courtroom where dad represented a plaintiff against the Mount Vernon Hospital doctors of which Dr. Yavelow was the primary defendant. Dad won the case. Both doctors were convicted of negligence.

I wonder if Mount Vernon Medical Society ever asked dad to speak again.

— 66 —

PROFOUND LOSSES, HEARTENING GAINS

DAD CONTINUED TO TRY cases in court throughout the late 1950's into the early 1960's despite undergoing major surgery. His battle with cancer dominated the last five years of his life. No matter what he was going through health-wise, dad was always there for his family and clients.

There were two significant losses to our family during this time, the first nono Ankie. Dad loved his gentle, kindly, stalwart father-in-law. The feeling was mutual. Gustav Ankerson was of Western pioneer stock and a community leader in his own humble way.

His passing merited an editorial in the Mount Vernon Daily Argus. Headline: "He Was An Asset to Mount Vernon."

GUSTAV HERMAN ANKERSON 1873-1959

Gustav Ankerson, 86, Dies, Druggist, Civic Leader

Gustav Ankerson, eighty-six, long one of Mount Vernon's best known businessmen and civic leaders, died yesterday at the home of his daughter, Mrs. Joseph Barnett, 70 Dogwood Lane, Rye, where he had been living for several years after leaving Mount Vernon.

Funeral services will be conducted tomorrow at 2 p.m. at Burr Davis Funeral Home by the Rev. John Chequer, a long-time friend of Mr. Ankerson. Interment will be at Ferncliff.

For a half century, Mr. Ankerson owned and operated a drug store in Mount Vernon which bore his name. He sold the business in 1945 and a year later sold the building at 11 Fourth Ave.

Mr. Ankerson was born Oct. 10, 1873 in Davenport, Iowa, the son of the late Mr. and Mrs. George Peter Ankerson. His parents had come to this country from Germany. For many years his father was a merchant in Davenport.

Graduated In 1894

After attending schools in Daven-

GUSTAV ANKERSON

The lead paragraph in this news story reads

> *Gustav Ankerson, eighty six, long one of Mount Vernon's best known businessmen and civic leaders, died yesterday at the home of his daughter, Mrs. Joseph Barnett, 70 Dogwood Lane, Rye, where he had been living for several years after leaving Mount Vernon.*

Nono Ankie's Editorial Obituary:

> *News of the death Sunday in Rye of Gustav H. Ankerson, who for a half century conducted the drug store that still bears his name, has brought sadness to the legion of friends who knew him in Mount Vernon.*
>
> *Mr. Ankerson was one of the enterprising businessmen who made Mount Vernon an outstanding center for retail stores. He was sound in advertising and merchandising; he brought to the task of satisfying the public needs in his own field of retailing a personalized human touch that all too often is being lost in the buying and selling of commodities today.*
>
> *A member of numerous Mount Vernon organizations, Mr. Ankerson carried his share of supporting community activities and not the least valuable of his labors was the part he played in the organization of the Mount Vernon Rotary Club. He was its first president as well as a leading spirit in bringing it into being as the first service club in Westchester County.*
>
> *Mr. Ankerson helped to make Mount Vernon a good city, a friendly city. Those who knew him will treasure his memory.*

Nono Ankie's strong presence always made us feel like family, even though we only got together as a family twice a year. Thanksgiving was the Ankerson family holiday, a peaceful, comforting day that always ended with dad, Doni, Bill, my uncle Paul and cousins Bob and Bill outside playing football.

In his later years I'm sure nono Ankie wished he could join the game, but he was definitely happy to be with "the ladies."

Here's nono Ankie with four of his five grandchildren: Camille, Bill, Doni and Bob.

Bill Barnett is absent from the picture, but his portrait is behind nono.

Mid 1950's

Denise has a poignant memory of her great grandfather. It's from the last month of his life. We were at Elfrieda's house in Rye. Nono lived the last decade of his life at his eldest daughter's home. It is also the site of this Thanksgiving day picture . Denise remembers Nono in a wheelchair being pushed out of the elevator by his nurse. Elfrieda had an elevator installed for nono. Denise remembers standing by his wheelchair and seeing nono with her baby sister Diane in his arms. She also remembers tbe elevator in great detail: *it looked like a cage.*

I have a memory that must be the same year as Denise's. It was the day I brought my newborn daughter, Diane, and Denise to see Nono. He was in his bedroom and not feeling up to going downstairs. I put Diane on his bed so he could see her. Nono looked down at her, smiled up at me and played with her little fingers. No words, just his gentle smile and unspoken approval.

Mom was the apple of her father's eye. She called him pop. My mother's acceptance of pop's death foretold the inner strength and courage she was to show in the later years of her life. When nono passed she told me she would always think of him as "*being away on a long journey.*" Bravo, mom, that's as close as any one I know has come to describing death without using religious imagery.

EUGENIA MANES CRIBARI 1876-1961

Nana Cribari's death also merited a featured obituary in the Daily Argus; she would have been proud of that and the two sons who were undoubtedly responsible. Her last name was familiar to readers through the sport columns of her youngest son, Guido, and the many accounts of legal trials headlining her son, Wolfe.

Mrs. Cribari Dies At 84

Mrs. Eugenia Manes Cribari, a Mount Vernon resident for 60 years died this morning at 8:40 o'clock at her home, 468 North Fulton Ave., after a long period of failing health. She was 84 years of age and the widow of Benjamin Salvatore Cribari, who died in 1938. Mr. Cribari, an ice cream manufacturer, was for many years active in Republican party affairs in this city.

Mrs. Cribari was one of the founders of the Ladies' Guild at the Church of Sts. Peter and Paul and long active in the affairs of that parish.

Surviving Mrs. Cribari are six sons Victor Cribari; W. E. Cribari, attorney; Raymond Cribari, Arnold Cribari, and Mario Cribari all of Mount Vernon; and Guido Cribari of Eastchester, sports editor of the Westchester County Publishers; and three daughters, Mrs. James Boyd Synnott, Miss Olga Cribari and Mrs. James DiMarzo, all of this city.

Funeral services will be held at 10 a.m. Friday at the Church of Sts. Peter and Paul. Mrs. Cribari is reposing at the Fred H. McGrath & Son funeral home in Bronxville.

A SOLEMN Requiem Mass will be celebrated Friday at 10 a.m. for Mrs. Eugenia M. Cribari at the Church of Sts. Peter and Paul, in which she had been active since its founding. Mrs. Cribari, a resident of Mount Vernon for more than 60 years, and the widow of Benjamin S. Cribari, died at her home, 468 N. Fulton Ave. yesterday morning. In lieu of flowers, friends may contribute to the Heart Fund.

Nana's news story obituary reads:

> *Mrs. Eugenia Manes Cribari, a Mount Vernon resident for 60 years died this morning at 8:40 o'clock at her home, 468 North Fulton Avenue, after a long period of failing health. She was 84 years of age and the widow of Benjamino Salvatore Cribari who died in 1938. Mr. Cribari, an ice cream manufacturer, was for many years active in the Republican party affairs in this city.*

Mrs. Cribari was one of the founders of the Ladies Guild at the Church of Sts. Peter and Paul and long active in the affairs of that parish.

Surviving Mrs Cribari are six sons: Victor Cribari; W.E. Cribari, attorney; Raymond Cribari, Arnold Cribari and Mario Cribari, all of Mount Vernon; and Guido Cribari of Eastchester, sports editor of the Westchester County Publishers; and three daughters, Mrs. James Boyd Synnott, Miss Olga Cribari and Mrs. James DiMarzo, all of this city.

Funeral services will be held at 10 A.M. Friday at the Church of Sts. Peter and Paul. Mrs. Cribari is reposing at the Fred McGrath & Sons funeral home in Bronxville.

Nana was treated with reverence by all of her children. The one exception I remember is uncle Ray's predictably playful greeting, *"How ya doin, ya old bag?"* Nana ignored him. I couldn't. I wanted to burst out laughing. I didn't!

We were expected to stop by nana's house "after church" every Sunday but I never saw nana in church even though she lived right across the street. The parish priests visited her on a regular basis. Maybe their pastoral visits counted for her obligatory attendance at Sunday Mass.

Maybe she fooled us all. Was she unable to cross the street? Maybe she was agoraphobic. Nobody thought about that then. For whatever reason Nana Cribari was house bound for most of the 25 years I knew her. Nevertheless, she was in charge, of that I'm sure; independent and strong!

The last time I visited her was right before she passed in early 1961 to introduce her to her youngest great granddaughter, Dana, 6 weeks old. I placed baby Dana on nana's bed, nana sat up, looked down at Dana and said, "The most beautiful of all." I felt like we were in a fairy tale.

For years after nana's death I dreamt about her. It was always Sunday in the dream and I had forgotten to visit her. Nana was in the house waiting, waiting for me. It was so realistic, powerful and recurred for years. When Bill read this she told me she had the same recurring dream. I wouldn't put anything past the powerful spirit of our unforgettable grandmother.

Here's a short biography my cousin, Virginia Ruth, Arnold's oldest daughter, wrote about our grandmother:

> *"My paternal grandmother, Nana, lived to be eighty-five years old and confined to a wheelchair with crippling arthritis as well as the after effects of rearing ten healthy children and surviving countless miscarriages and stillbirths*
>
> *I know little of her as a young woman. Her husband, my grandfather, died before I was born. I do know that their first child, Victor, was born in Italy, but I believe that the rest of them were born in New York. The family business was an ice cream store, reputed to serve the richest, creamiest Italian ice cream in the area. I never tasted this treat, but this part of my heritage must have affected my genes in some mysterious way. Ice cream has always been and will always be my favorite food and my source of comfort in times of stress. I can always find room for a tartufo.*
>
> *Nana lived until I was in my early twenties, and I always saw her as an old, but strong willed and dominating force. She insisted that all of her children live in or near Mount Vernon and visit regularly. Two of her younger children, Olga and Mario, never married and lived with her until her death. The others took turns visiting to give these two some freedom. My father's night was every Thursday.*
>
> *Nana never accepted my father's civil marriage to a non-Italian, and even worse, a non-Catholic. She saw my siblings and myself as illegitimate children of an unsanctioned marriage, and while we visited her on Christmas and Easter, I never felt like I really belonged in the same way my cousins were bonded to each other.*
>
> *I loved those big family gatherings – the smell of the meatless spaghetti that was served to all of the children on Christmas Eve, the sense of a huge extended family. At the same time I was very aware of the strain that these visits brought to my parents' relationship and could sense the tension between them whenever we were at my grandmother's home.*

She was a true Italian matriarch who ruled her sons and daughters with an iron fist, stood for no-nonsense and commanded total allegiance to her last day."

I never felt nana showed preference among her 12 granddaughters, five of whom are in this picture: Kathy, Doni and Bill seated, Camille and Roberta standing. Others would surely disagree and say we were the favored ones. But nana communicated through action, not words.

The all girl cousins changed with the arrival of those two little boys, James Wolfe & Stephen.

Stephen Cribari, Guido's son and dad's godchild, wrote the following in a story that is wonderfully in synch with our cousin Virginia's portrait

> *"My grandmother ruled until she died in her eighties. Nonna was not liked, but either loved or hated. She was resented but obeyed.*
>
> *I remember visiting her and sitting for hours, fanning her slowly with a spade-shaped bamboo fan. She seldom spoke. Mostly she just stared straight ahead. Occasionally her eyes seemed to focus on something which was not there. I was still in grammar school when she died."*

Nana Cribari was an Italian immigrant who lived sixty years of her life in a country with traditions and lifestyles she constantly had to adjust to. She did it, "her way." Remember it was nana Cribari who accompanied dad and mom on their "honeymoon" to Europe in 1933. She was a fearless matriarch who demanded her children's and grandchildren's attendance at family gatherings.

Silent in her old age; always a woman of convictions, like them or not.

— 67 —

FAMILY LOYALTIES ARE CHALLENGED

FOUR YEARS AFTER NANA Cribari's death, dad decided to buy nana's house from my aunt Olga and uncle Mario so my young family and I could live there. Olga and Mario had been living their whole adult lives in the house which dad bought for his (*their*) mother a few years after nono Cribari's death in 1937. The fact is Olga and Mario never owned the house, dad was the buyer and owner,

This peculiar arrangement is typical of the way dad always bent over backwards for his birth family. He eventually bought nana's house twice: first **for** my grandmother and then thirty years later for me **from** my uncle and aunt. Mind you, both his siblings held steady jobs and could afford their own apartments.

Dad's plan created serious tension between me and Olga who badmouthed my father for *kicking her out of her home*. I remember that day at nana's house right before she was scheduled to move out. I'll never forget our heated exchange.

I already had a house key so I unlocked the front door and walked upstairs to see if anyone was home. I wanted to start bringing clothes over; we were supposed to move in the following week. Olga didn't hear me come in; she was upstairs in her bedroom. I stood for a moment at the door of her bedroom and looked in. There were piles of clothes on the floor and on every piece of furniture; dresser drawers were wide open.

Olga looked up and saw me at her bedroom door. "I won't be ready to move out," she said, "your father didn't give me enough time. Look at this mess."

"You knew about this weeks ago, Olga."

"A lot of thanks I get for taking care of his mother all these years. Kicked out of my own house."

I could feel my blood pressure rise, I tried to control myself. "What do you mean, his mother? Nana's your mother too."

"How am I ever going to get all my things packed? I'm being kicked out of my house by my own brother."

That did it! " It's not your house. It never was. It's nana's house. Dad bought it for **her**."

"I took care of his mother all these years and that's the thanks…"

"His mother, his mother? Nana's your mother. Dad bought it for her. You lived in **her** house."

"I took care of nana, he should thank me for taking care of his mother all these years."

"**You** took care of her? You lived here, that's it."

"I took care of her."

"Dad got nana a maid and a cleaning woman, years ago, whatever she needed. You lived with her. You had the cleaning woman…"

"Your father is kicking me out of my own house."

"It's not your house, but he's paying you for it. You ungrateful bitch!"

"What did you say?"

Silence.

"I'm going over to Rose's. I'm going to tell her what you just called me. Stay here as long as you want." She stomped out the door and down the stairs.

My poor father, he was so hurt when he heard about our "fight." Not from me.

I don't think Olga or Mario ever realized how much they hurt dad until he finally found the courage to write them a letter expressing his real feelings and his disappointment in the awful stories they were telling others.

Not only did dad pay them for a house they didn't own, he found each of them a nearby apartment and paid for their moving expenses. I discovered a copy of the letter he wrote to them in his papers after his death. In his own inimitable way, dad writes: ***"after hearing the way they were bad-mouthing me, I considered moving out of town."***

This serious family rift undoubtedly opened his eyes about how dependent his siblings had been on their mother on the one hand, and on their generous, naïve brother on the other. That letter, which dad never showed me *(mom did)* made me proud of him. It was long overdue and took courage for dad to write.

My confrontation with Olga also opened my eyes to mom's spot-on instincts to stay out of Cribari family issues. Unlike me, she always stayed in the background. She and dad must have made some kind of an agreement. I realized how well mom "handled" dad's family when I was in therapy many years later.

Nana's house, our weekly meeting place in the '40's, became home to my family twenty years later. My husband Warren had completed his two years in the Navy and returned to civilian life. Dad bought nana's house for us after Warren got a sales job with a New York City engineering firm.

Sales was a perfect fit for Warren's outgoing personality, it required lots of schmoozing with potential clients. But Warren was used to a predictable work schedule under the strict regulations of the military. He couldn't handle the "freedom" of working in the city and spent less and less time with his family.

Dad and mom were unaware of most of the problems Warren's absentee parenting caused because I didn't want them involved. Let me just say, our problems multiplied and 3-4 years later I went over to talk to dad while Warren was home with the girls to ask him what I had to do to get a separation or a divorce. Dad's answer to my question involved a complicated, yet legally airtight solution.

Dad arranged for me to fly to El Paso, Texas, cross the border into Juarez, Mexico where my divorce papers would be reviewed and approved. I was scared, scared to fly alone, scared to leave my kids, but dad convinced me that it was the least stressful and most efficient way. In those days the only grounds for divorce in N.Y. State was proof of adultery and years of waiting.

The following letter dad wrote me during my separation shows how his legal expertise was always a benchmark in helping family and friends with their varied problems. No wonder everybody sought his advice. He clearly explains divorce and the situations I might have to negotiate for my three little girls. Neither Warren nor I wanted to drag out a potentially contentious settlement.

> *Dearest Camille,*
>
> *I want you to know that you as well as the children are constantly in my thoughts these days. I of course do trust you completely. My only concern is that forces over which you have no control may precipitate serious problems for you.*
>
> *But please do not worry – if problems do arise you must talk them out with me and mommy. And please (and you have extreme*

provocation I know during these trying days to do otherwise) try not to be impatient with the children particularly Denise. Time will ease your problems, I'm sure. Finally you have our complete support in any decision you may make for I am secure in the conviction that you will do what is best for all.

I enclose a check for $500. You must religiously follow these instructions as they will become of major importance as time passes.

Keep an itemized account of every cent your husband gives you and insofar as you are able to ascertain all monies he spends on the home for you and for the children – dates and amounts.

Keep a separate account of all monies reserved from us, mommy and me, for any purposes. Dates and amounts.

Start a separate checking account with the $500. enclosed and henceforth deposit all your funds therein – account in your name alone.

Under no circumstances are you to pay any bills whatsoever incurred prior to the date your husband left the house. And do not pay any bills other than current day by day house expenses unless you check with me first.

Mr. S. is going to change all locks on your doors and check your first floor windows. Please see to it that you keep you doors locked at all times and your first floor windows as well at night. Give no keys out to anyone other than us and perhaps Rose. Let me know when the grass needs cutting or any other repairs or problem or need is encountered in the home. Use whatever of the $500 is needed for Spring Lake, the balance for yours and the children's requirements.

Let me know when you need more. We should get together soon and talk over your financial needs perhaps then I can work out a monthly stipend for you to supplement whatever you may receive from your husband.

We love you very much and don't blame you for anything whatsoever. All our children are equally dear to us.

May God bless you.

Love,

Dad

I'm sure of it, my father said so.

— 68 —

THIRD TIME FATHER OF THE BRIDE

A **MORE POSITIVE FAMILY OBLIGATION** for dad happened in 1965. Dad's niece Joane asked him to take on the role of Father of the Bride for her upcoming marriage to Gene Fitzpatrick. It would be his third time: first for his sister Dolly, second for daughter Camille and third for niece Joane.

Joane's father, Jim Synnott, had passed away the year before. Jim had always been dad's go to person when he needed help. Whether it was exterminating squirrels from the chimney of our Claremont Avenue home, driving two year old me and mom to a NYC hospital for my split palate surgery, fixing any and everything that broke in our home, dad could always count on Jim. In fact "call Jim Synnott!" was our family's SOS.

A recent conversation I had with my cousin Kathy told the same story from her father's perspective. She too remembers dad calling Jim to ask for his help on a regular basis. Every time Jim got off the phone with dad he'd say, "I'm going to Wolfe's" and they knew what was up...Jim to the rescue! What a great relationship dad and Jim had, a mutual admiration society.

On this occasion dad was given a rare opportunity to pay back the many kindnesses Jim had shown him over the years and act as "father of the bride" for Jim's daughter's wedding.

Here are dad and Joane in the background. My daughter Denise is the flower girl. On my left is Joane's sister, Kathy.

Joane married late, she was ten years older than me, we used to go to NYC together when I was in my teens. We both loved movies, shows and being in The City.

Dad's third time as "Father of the Bride" was much easier for him than my 1956 wedding. Unfortunately he was already ill and looks it in the photo. He had the weight of two families on his frail shoulders, but tried not to let it show.

Joane always looked to dad for inspiration. They shared a love of learning, especially reading, and the arts. Joane was often included in our family's activities: movies and shows in NYC, summers at the Westchester Country Club, and summer trips to The Monmouth Hotel in Spring Lake, N.J., where she met her husband Gene,

My daughter Denise remembers a trip to Spring Lake that also spotlights mom and dad's dramatically charged relationship.

> *We were on the way to Spring Lake. We left early. I was in the car with nono, Carola and Joane. Mom, dad and the girls were in the other car. They left an hour after we did.*
>
> *Carola would only drive on roads with "no trucks," so she chose to take the Tappan Zee instead of the George Washington Bridge, driving north when they should have veered south. Remember, Carola had become dad's chauffeur after his heart attack to avoid his being stressed. Not this time.*
>
> *Joane was in front with Carola, I was in the back with nono. He was slumped in the back seat corner of the car yelling* ***"Caro-la!"*** *because at every toll booth she would ask for directions, ignoring the traffic and the beeping horns behind her.*
>
> *Joane laughed every time nono yelled. Carola got mad at Joane for laughing. Nono was screaming,* ***Carola, I can't believe you're asking for directions! Again*?!** *We never stopped for a bathroom break.*
>
> *We got to Spring Lake an hour after the others. Dad (Warren) was standing on the front steps of the Monmouth waiting and worried. Nono got out of the car, stomped up the steps right past him and went inside, without a word.*

— 69 —

CRIBARI FAMILY 2021: "UNCLE" WOLFE

DAD'S NIECES AND NEPHEWS responded to my request to share dad memories.

When Wolfe had dinner at our house, he always covered the spots he made on the white tablecloth with suitably sized coins. Who could care about the spots?

My all-time favorite – He and Carola took us all to see the movie – "King Solomon's Mines" – at the Parkway Theater and stopped at Auriemma's little store on the way home. We were all in the car and he signaled waving his arms to open the car window, ***Do we need anything?*** *"No, thank you," we responded. Back in he went. Well, this scenario was repeated until we were all hysterical.* ***Do we need?*** *"No we don't" Each time he came out the arms went violently into a motion to roll down the window.*

Christmas Eve... Wolfe arriving at Nana's with a handful of envelopes containing $10. bills for each of us... our own Santa Claus.

Wolfe in the back seat of the Cadillac being driven away from some wake in Mount Vernon. He saw me walking nearby, had the car stop, rolled down his window and said, **don't smoke**. *I quit soon after.*

I wish someone or something had convinced dad not to smoke because he was a chain smoker for at least two decades. This popular post war habit was eventually the cause for his premature death. Kathy's memory evoked images of two yellowed cigarette fingers on dad's right hand, frequent attempts to quit like constantly sucking on hard candies even occasional lollipops. He tried, like so many others who didn't know until it was too late.

> *I remember feeling so much love for him after my father's funeral. He sat by me quietly, talking about my father whom he loved,* **Poor Jim, poor Jim.** *Little did we know he too would be dead within the next few years.*
>
> **Kathy DePasquale,**
> **niece, daughter of Rose, dad's older sister**

> *When I was quite young, for a bunch of years we celebrated my birthday at your parents' home. We always had a bocce match – your dad and I against dad and Jim. We always won – your dad always won*
>
> *One year I rolled the pollina into a hole that was cut in a big rock under a big tree. It was atop a bit of a slope. My dad launched his ball perfectly, fitting into the hole with the pollina. They won.*
>
> *Your dad informed us all not to move as my father's ball was rolling. It wasn't.*
>
> *He made us stand there for what seemed like forever. Of course, we all did.*
>
> *Your mother went into the kitchen to get us all drinks while we waited. And waited.*
>
> *All of a sudden, my father's ball rolled out of the hole in the rock and down the hill. Your dad's ball was the closest. We won.*
>
> *My father, a man with no temper, kicked his ball. It hit the rock and bounced into your dad's ankle on the rebound.*

The next day, we received papers informing us that your dad was suing my dad. Of course, that happened frequently. He even had us quarantined once. But, I divert.

I thought then and still do your dad had powers that were not of this world.

Maryanne DiMarzo,
niece, daughter of dad's youngest sister Dolly.

Two (memories) stand out – out of so many.

We had the flu. Your dad (Wolfe) sent the health department to post a quarantine notice on our front door.

And my personal favorite:

Uncle Wolfe handed me an envelope for my 16th birthday the contents of which were the answers to the New York State driver's exam. He was careful to tell me that he didn't consider that I needed the help, but that his gift was more one of convenience.

I am so proud to carry his name.

James Wolfe DiMarzo,
nephew, son of dad's youngest sister Dolly.

This may be just a coincidence and nothing more, but the founder of Cribari wine out in Fresno, California, I believe was named Salvatore Beniamino. If he came from nearby the same town (San Fili?), there would have been reason that they both used both names.

I remember Wolfe's presence. I remember him singing "Oi Marie" at Dolly's apartment on Gramatan Avenue when I asked him to and he really didn't want to. Pedestrian Neapolitan stuff.

I remember him saying nice things to me after Bill's Brigadoon, *and I once visited him in court in White Plains where he asked for a continuance on account of the court date previously set was the anniversary of my (meaning Wolfe's) "natal day."*

"You mean your birthday?" asked the judge.

Years after he died I was summoned to jury duty in White Plains and when my name was called in court both lawyers and the judge asked, "are you related to Wolfe Cribari?

My yes resulted in instant dismissal from the jury pool…which is too bad as sitting on a jury as a lawyer I've never done.

I would have liked Wolfe to know me as a lawyer. I, as they say. "took no prisoners" in court, went head to head with some judges, and took, and still take the sixth amendment right to be confrontational literally. Got two men off of death row; got some prisoners released on habeas corpus motions; asked (in court) an FBI Special Agent what was so special about her; had the U.S. Marshall for Maryland threatened with contempt of court; got a probation officer fired; and once got a federal judge to give ME, a defense attorney, a search and seizure warrant to seize evidence so the government didn't get it; and stood up pretty well before the U.S. Supreme Court on a couple of occasions. Rehnquist told my boss that I gave one of the best arguments of the term.

So what I remember most about Wolfe is that he did not know me as a lawyer

Stephen Cribari,
nephew, son of dad's youngest brother Guido.

As a child visiting Nanna's house with my parents, Uncle Wolfe seemed very serious and not as playful as Uncle Mario, Uncle Guido and Uncle Ray. I suspect, however, that Wolfe could be very playful, especially with children because my father was that way with me when I was a boy and I think my father was more like Wolfe than their other siblings.

The most vivid memory I have of Uncle Wolfe was one evening at Nanna's house when everyone gathered around him in the living room, including me. I must have been between 5 and 10 years old. Wolfe started singing. I don't remember what he sang except I think it was opera, and I was stunned. His singing voice was very passionate and beautiful. To me it sounded like God was singing.

I wish I had gotten to know Wolfe more. I think I was born too late. Wolfe died too young and my nuclear family did not get together with the Cribari relatives (all fascinating to me in different ways) so I missed out on getting to know Wolfe as well as others did. All of the stories about him are very interesting to me. Steve and I became lawyers so we might have had a lot of things in common with Wolfe if we were lawyers when Wolfe was alive.

As a young attorney in Westchester County (I was admitted to the New York State Bar in 1977) Wolfe's earthly life had long ended, but not the memory of him among his attorney colleagues and the judges. I benefited from the extraordinary respect everyone had of Wolfe as a lawyer and a man, and I derived significant benefits from that as a young lawyer.

What I am about to say is very strange. Although I had very little interaction with Uncle Wolfe, no one had a more powerful impact on me subconsciously than Wolfe Cribari except for my parents.

Arnold Cribari,
nephew, son of dad's brother Arnold

Dad was equally loved by Carola's side of the family.

This bizarre comic character shot was taken of dad during Thanksgiving at his sister in law Elfrieda's house.

There's the deadly cigarette again.

One of dad's two Ankerson nephews, Bill, is in the portrait behind dad.

Mom and dad's Ankerson-Barnett nephews enjoyed dad's silly antics, but also respected his status in the legal profession.

Both nephews were definitely influenced by him: Bob chose to be a writer and Bill, a lawyer.

— 70 —

ONCE UPON A TIME THERE WAS…THE SIXTIES!

DAD WAS THE QUINTESSENTIAL first generation Italian, the chosen one in a large immigrant family of twelve people. His struggle to improve his family's status in a new land dominated his short 63 years on this planet. He was the first "professional" in the family and always used his hard-won reputation to help his brothers, sisters and in-laws in any and all ways possible. Guido expresses his love and respect for his brother in this beautiful letter following nana's death.

Dear Wolfe,

Strange, isn't it, how death awakens us to the reality of life; Up until a few days ago, I had remembered little of my childhood. But with Mom's passing, countless incidents and episodes of my childhood leaped suddenly into focus. It was like viewing a film of my life for the first time. These, I guess, are the memories the Good Lord provides us with at particular times of life; the memorable moments one cherishes forever.

Laced throughout these memories, Wolfe, is the bond of love, and devotion you and Mom shared. How proud you must be; how comforting it must be to you to have been THE son who showered so many blessings upon her. I took so much for granted so long. I've always appreciated your devotion to Mom, but like so many selfish sons, kept this appreciation within myself, instead of telling the world, and most of all you, how deeply grateful I am.

I'd like you now to know of these feelings, and of the thousands of kind, appreciative words Mom had to say about you over the years. Even as late as the Sunday afternoon before her passing she spoke of you and your thoughtfulness, just as she did every time I was in her company. I guess I was one of her best listeners.

Yes, Wolfe, it must be a great source of comfort to you when you recall all the kind things you did for Mom. I only wish I could have done more than I did. Oh, how I wish I had. Every mother should have a son like you.

I didn't mean to get mushy about this, Wolfe, but I did want you to know. At 4 A.M. it's a little difficult to find the right words, but all words are inadequate at a time like this. It's impossible to describe my love and admiration for you, except to say the nicest thing that ever happened to me was to become your brother.

Love always, Guido

Guido shared dad's love of language and storytelling, skills that served both of them well in their chosen professions. In the beginning of Guido's writing career, he asked for dad's help. Dad was more than willing to give it and wrote several of Guido's newspaper articles for him. In the first few years of Guido's career he and his brother had a secret collaboration.

But Guido was a diligent student, worked hard to improve his skills and rapidly rose to the top of his field. He became Sports Editor of Rockland Westchester newspapers in the'60s. He told everyone his brother helped "make his career."

The following playful exchange illustrates Dad and Guido's adolescent sense of humor, love of language and affection for each other. I don't have a copy of Guido's letter but the picture he sent dad tells his side for him.

-2-

moments that he was struck with the inspiration which later led to his writing his immortal "Ode to a Freezing Ball."

Well, I guess that about sums it up except for a parting interdiction to you, my well loved brother --

"If castagnas you must eat,
Let not Sicilians apply the heat."

Affectionately,

Incoronato Wolfgang Cornacchio

The letter is hard to read. Here's the transcript.

Guido Cribari

72 Stebbins Avenue

Tuckahoe, N.,Y. *December 1, 1961*

Dear Guido,

Many thanks for the photo. If you think the man in the background looks like Dulles and the chestnut vendor is not a dead ringer for me, you definitely have arrived at that stage of pre-senility when the constantly changing ocular mechanisms and structure of the body demands attention. Get glasses, boy!

I am intrigued by the fact that the photo brought back poignant memories of and the desire for the "gastagna" of your youth. I don't know whether the pun was intentional or coincidental but the gas part is well put, especially when you tackle this gastronomical delight at my advanced age. It's "castagna," boy!

Albeit I have already indulged in my favorite fruit this season: just a few days ago, in fact. However, I would gladly sit with you and partake of a "castagna" feast on short notice, even though the preparation of the "nuts" by a Sicilian does violence to our Calabrian heritage.

Parenthetically, your insistence on the anonymity of the nut roaster causes me some concern. In the context written, I am irresistibly led to the conclusion ***(illusion shattering though it may be)*** *that your interest in the Sicilian is more than mere "castagna."*

My concern stems in the main from the fact that the Sicilians and Calabrese have been feuding for many generations and many Calabrese have been found in strange marital beds with stilettos neatly and firmly wedged between their shoulder blades. Is the castagna really worth the price?

I challenge your statement: respecting the author of the words, ***"Keep your nuts warm, brother: it's colder than you think,"*** *In the first place no frenchman would use the word nuts when a beautiful euphemism like "cugliones" is available to him.*

Secondly, the author of the words was Thoreau and they were uttered at Walden's pond when, during one of his well-known moments of abstraction, he fell in, broke the ice and was submerged in the frozen waters. It was during those uncomforable moments that he was struck with the inspiration which later led to his writing his immortal "Ode to a Freezing Ball."

Well, I guess that about sums it up except for a parting interdiction to you, my well-loved brother,

"If castagnas you must eat

Let not Sicilians apply the heat"

Affectionately,

Incoronato Wolfgang Cornacchia

Dad, a golf nut, would have been so proud of the following tribute to his youngest brother who was honored on his 90th birthday as Westchester County's pioneer golf promoter. I have chosen excerpts from the column written by Jim McLoughlin in Golf Course News, January 2006.

It all started in the 1940's when William F. Fanning, the publisher of Gannett Suburban News decided to promote golf at a time when no other outlet in the country was giving golf the time of day. Guido picked up the baton on golf's behalf and carried it forward.

Without question, the (Westchester) "Classic" was born from the 1959 Thunderbird Classic, at Westchester Country Club, grew, flourished and served as a constantly evolving PGA Tour model because it was cultivated within a fertile, unprecedented local media environment – thanks to Guido Cribari.

I remember dad going to the first Classic.

Patty Berg generously and publicly credits Guido for his counsel and support for helping create the initial and sustaining atmosphere that would allow the LPGA (Ladies Professional Golf Association) to be born in 1951 in Westchester County at the Knollwood Country Club. Patty and Guido remained lifelong friends.

Guido is more than an institution. He is the essence of what unselfish human behavior is all about. No one has brought more meaning and dignity to the game of golf in a lifetime than Guido Cribari. Thank you Guido for so much.

In addition to writing, another artistic talent Guido shared with his brother Wolfe is music: both men were naturally gifted singers and harmonica players. Neither ever took a lesson. Music was always a major part of every Cribari holiday celebration.

In his 90's, Guido brought his harmonica whenever he came to visit, especially if he knew his niece Doni was going to be there. He knew she would ask him to play. I remember how passionately both dad and Guido played that simple mouth-harp spreading their love and warmth to all.

Here's Guido in the magic of the moment probably playing "The Shadow of your Smile"

Yes, the Cribaris were musical people. I never heard nana sing, but I know she listened to opera on the radio every Saturday afternoon. Not until my sister Bill became obsessed with soprano Renata Tebaldi did anyone of the Cribaris try for a musical career. Without question, the Cribaris were all music lovers. Aren't all Italians?

Rose was our first diva. She had an operatic sound and warmth to her voice which we heard every Christmas midnight mass. Rose never sought the spotlight in any other performing venue.

Here she is with Guido. It's a favorite: oldest sister + youngest brother. Love!

Rose's daughter Kathy de Pasquale wrote lovingly and eloquently about her mother, Rose Cribari Synnott in a lengthy obituary that was published in Gannett newspapers June 27, 1996. Rose lived well into her nineties.

> *"My mother was an absolutely supreme family woman. She was the matriarch of a very large Italian family. Oldest daughter among 10 children (She) helped raise the younger children then raised two of her own. .*
>
> *She was just a wonderful, nurturing, loving human being. Her sisters and brothers, her children and grandchildren, her nieces and nephews – there were a tremendous number of people who thought of my mother as a nurturer in their life. My mother was kind of the center of the family in nurturing and giving."*

Her concern extended to strangers. When I was young and my mother was driving in the car and an elderly person was trying to cross the street, my mother would pull the car over, jump out and help the person across the street.

The church (Saints Peter and Paul) was the center of her whole life. From the 1930s through the 1950s she was a soloist in the church choir. You could hear a pin drop every Christmas when she sang "Adeste Fidelis' She was absolutely a dynamic soprano. But in those days a career as a professional singer was out of the question.

Here's a memory piece I wrote about Rose when she left us.

Rose... silver-crowned head of la famiglia Cribari

On a visit to her apartment on Collins Avenue when she was in her 80's,

I was surprised to discover a unique photograph of her hanging on the wall in the shadowy bedroom. It was a Rose I'd never seen, never even imagined.

There she was, a sensual, dark-haired beauty with the same soulful eyes as her brother, Wolfe, my father.

Rose before she was a wife and mother.
before she was an aunt, a godmother, a grandmother.
before any of us who were comforted, warmed, fed and uplifted
by her were even in this world.

Rose as she wanted to see herself, as she remembered

Rose when she was no longer a wife,
but always mother, aunt, godmother, grandmother
to la famiglia Cribari,
an array of independent, worldly adults who still needed
her comforting, warming, feeding, uplifting,
but were sometimes too busy, too proud.

Rose was always that sensual dark-haired Rosa in the photograph!

That photograph spoke volumes for the young Italian woman,
born with the century in a foreign land,
born the oldest girl.
born to be comforter, provider, nurturer for others.

Rose notices how I am examining that unfamiliar Rose in
the photograph

She silently, carefully, mysteriously
slides a box out from under her bed,
sits on the bed, pats the bedspread for me to join her,
takes off the box cover,
unwraps its contents, a long chestnut color fall of luxurious human
hair. Hers.

Rose strokes it lovingly and makes a joke,
"A lot of good it did me to keep it all these years."

She smiles when I ask to touch it.

I stroke it admiringly, comparing it to my own baby fine.
"I wish I had such beautiful hair, Rose, it's like velvet!"

And it was.

Rose was always that sensual, dark-haired soulful young woman.
I see her natural beauty, no makeup in a time of Joan Crawford
red lips,
An earthy, homey smell: roast potatoes, one minute,
corn beef and cabbage, the next, clinging to her clothes.

A youthful, confident, sometimes raucous voice,
No one needed Rose to express her opinions twice.
Her voice, loud and clear, from the changing rooms at Lord and Taylor
Or demanding one more free cookie for us kids at the
Fleetwood Bakery.

Oh yes, you could hear her!
Rose projected.
That she did.

Her singing voice, a God-given talent, soaring from the choir loft
Up, up, up, joining the trails of perfumed incense ascending from the altar.
Down, down, down to fill the hearts and souls of the congregation below.
A congregation whose heads always turned to locate the inspiring source.

I know their heads used to turn to look up at her.
Rose let me sit up in the choir loft with her
even though I wasn't old enough.
I was her godchild.

And energy, we should have tried to bottle it.
Rose was always on the move, just like her brother Wolfe.
Whether it was in her beloved black Studebaker or on foot.

Rose was a woman of her century, always thinking and moving ahead.
At age ninety, she had the pace and energy of a 30 year old power walker.

This morning, two days after she was put to rest
beside her loving supportive husband, Jim,
My Rose re-emerges from her photograph.

This morning when I said, "Grandfather, to whom we come"
Rose was right up there with dad for the first time.
And I cried.
Not for a loved one's loss,
but because I know she has returned.

Here's one of my favorite pictures of dad in all his playful grandfather glory with Denise, age 4, holding Dana, almost 1, and Diane age 2.

— 71 —

NOW NONO

THE SIXTIES WAS 20TH century America's decade of change and depending on who you're talking to, the change could be called amazing or frightening. Sometimes both. Mention the phrase "The Sixties" to someone and notice the reaction. One thing's for sure, there'll be one. So too with Wolfgang E. Cribari, Wolfe, dad. Now nono.

Dad 's happy change? He was now nono to three adorable little girls. I'm slightly biased, but I should be. They're my daughters.

The swing, which dad bought for his second set of three girls, is in the backyard of our home, aka nana Cribari's house. A safe plaything, right?.

My daughter Diane reminded me about another playground toy dad bought for his "little dolls" called a "whirla-gig." I remember it. I'm sure our neighbors do too because I never let other children use it. I was afraid they would go flying off. Considering dad's lawyer-based horror stories about what happened to others when they did something 'dangerous', I was surprised at that gift. We have a movie of dad sliding down the girls' slide, a better, safer ride.

My family lived in nana's house for four years. For half of that time, I was a single parent; Warren and I separated in 1963. When I remember those days I wonder if there wasn't a seismic shift that caused such dramatic changes: first human in space; Freedom Riders, Cesar Chavez 's migrant workers, the Beatles, the Cuban Missile Crisis, Martin Luther King's "I Have a Dream" speech, President John F. Kennedy's assassination, and the Great Northeast Blackout.

November 9, 1965, the Great Northeast Blackout, is my clearest memory from those years. The blackout started while it was still light, at 5:00, rush hour. Warren called to let me know he was ok; he was living at the NY Athletic Club.

After the girls and I ate dinner, it was already dark. The full moon hadn't risen yet. I went upstairs to see how we might manage going to bed and Denise, Diane and Dana were right behind me. There was no way they were going to sleep upstairs when the house was pitch black. We had to sleep together. But where?

I said, "let's all sleep in the dining room!" The girls loved crawling under our big dining room table. So we crawled under the table. I started telling them a story. They didn't want me to tell a story, they wanted me to read them a book like I did every night. I only had two candles. I didn't want to waste one reading a book, so I said, "Let's call nono, he tells good stories."

Dad got on the phone. ***"Have a parade. March upstairs. Get a blanket and pillow, bring it downstairs into the dining room. Get marshmallows, have a camp-out under the table. I wish I could come, but Carola won't let me out tonight. See you tomorrow!"***

I'm sure of it, my father said so.

— 72 —

FATHER OF A MOTHER

ANOTHER OF DAD'S PATERNAL changes happened when his daughter Doni became "Mother Marie Regina *Cribari*" as he addressed the envelope in a 1962 letter.

It reveals his deepest feelings about her chosen profession, a religious in a semi-cloistered convent. These are excerpts that show dad's attempt at acceptance.

Dear sweetheart,

It was wonderful to hear your dear voice this morning after too many weeks. You sounded like your old ebullient self and this of course made me happy. I enclose a bank money order for $50. That can be cashed anywhere. Please tell your superior that I would be most happy if it could be used for little luxuries such as ice cream, cake, candy, pizza, spaghetti, champagne, etc. If you need more you have but to call or drop a line.

Don't think because I have not written that my sentiments have altered in the slightest. I love you with all my heart. I was going to say more as each day flits by. This would be silly. My love for you is incapable of increasing beyond the full measure it has attained. I miss you though, more each day.

However, I have reasonably reconciled myself to your wishes and I don't ever intend, if at all possible, to make you miserable again by harassing you with repeated requests that you come home. If you should decide to come home I will guarantee you a Madonna Del Arco feast (like on Fifth Avenue, downtown Mount Vernon, you know you were a devotee of them).

I pray for your continued happiness and good health, my darling. You are always in my thoughts and almost always in my conversations. If you return to Quebec I will plan a nice visit up there in the early fall.

All my love,

Daddy

A 1940's picture of the future Mother Marie Regina, my sister Doni, on her First Communion on May Day when we would sing "Oh, Mary we crown thee with blossoms today, queen of the angels, queen of the May."

I love that Doni took Marie Regina as her religious name, "Mary Queen" in English.

Here's proof of Doni's multifaceted dad-like persona as seen through the two photos below taken during her growing up years.

Above is a newspaper photo of the Mount Vernon Recreation "Kicking, Passing Contest" which 10 year old Donna Cribari won in her age category; the only girL Our friend Ralph Branca is fifth from right in the back row.

And below is debutante Donna at the first cotillion held at Westchester Country Club, 1956.

That all changed when Doni took her vows as a religious of the Sacred Heart of Mary at age 21.The most difficult part was distancing herself from her parents. Dad's powerful letters to her reveal exactly what he was feeling about her life choice. But her superiors withheld personal letters from their novices, so dad's voice was silenced. However, this picture of him, mom and Doni on visiting day shows what he was feeling. For dad that meant trying NOT to feel.

The torch was officially passed. Dad was the true ***pater familia.*** This included ownership of the house he originally bought for nana. We agreed it would be perfect for me and my growing family. Here we are in front of our 'new' home.

Our happy family on a 1960's Easter Sunday, a wonderful dream that didn't last long.

Those three little dolls as dad called them were always uppermost in dad's mind and heart.

Mom called them her little angels.

I can still hear their voices as I write these words.

Here's an incident Bill recalls involving my three little girls and racing to get to the beach…

> *You and I were racing over the bumps with the girls and I got caught by a nasty Rye cop and hit with reckless driving tickets (two tickets – one for speeding and the other for going through a stop sign). I went home and told dad and burst out crying thinking I'd lose my license at age 17.*
>
> *Dad said **"I'm not mad about getting the tickets, but don't ever come here crying about something that stupid again."** Then he proceeded to take on the city of Rye, he knew **"there must be a loophole."***
>
> *There was, he got the city to make a deal by accusing them of having improper signage. He said **he would make a case against them that would go back years and nullify all the traffic tickets based on their speed signs if they didn't let his daughter off the speeding ticket.** They did!*
>
> *I was charged with going through a stop sign and that was the end of it. He said **he'd be glad to do the research on the signs since his summer was slow with cases anyway**. I am sure he loved the challenge and of course, he won.*

I'm sure of it, my father said so.

— 73 —

WOLFE AND CAROLA's SECOND ACT

FREE OF HIS BIRTH-FAMILY responsibilities for the first time, dad made plans to take mom on a transcontinental train tour. He always insisted that every long trip we took was by rail, he found the sound of the train tracks calming.

Here is a letter he wrote in August 1962 aboard the California Zephyr. It was one of his dreams to take this trip. How wonderful that he made the time to do it when he did!

My dearest sweetheart

I started to write separate notes to each one of my dear children but after I got through with the first one mommy read it and insisted I send the same one to each of you. Nutty, but here goes.

As I write this at about 11 A.M. (2 P.M. your time) we are entering upon the last two hundred miles of our transcontinental tour. I can't go to Mass but I want to tell you that I have never been closer to my maker than I have the past two days.

It is inconceivable that what we have seen is explainable by reference to the usual and banal expression "freaks of nature" that nature itself is explained by "freakish" evolutionary changes and not by divine inspiration.

After two days of breathtaking and constantly changing panoramas that defy description, I am left with the unalterable conviction that what I have beheld (the wonder of it all) has, for me, brought into focus with dramatic clarity that the hand of the Creator was at the root of it all.

Yes, I have seen nature exposed in all her naked grandeur, beauty, majesty, austerity and even cruelty. But the nature I saw couldn't possibly have spontaneously and haphazardly evolved from the eruptive cooling of a fireball without plan or design.

Severe jagged and sheer rock cliffs rapidly changing into a wonderland of snow capped peaks, graceful pine-lined mountain slopes, deep pools of quiet waters, needle-like falls, foaming rapids, tumultuous rivers seeming to flow furiously and endlessly to nowhere or everywhere in their serpentine courses, plateaus of ruby colored stone so magically carved out by years of erosion as to give the appearance of ancient man made ruins, endless canyons and even an occasional desert at the top of a mountain.

Hundreds of miles on end with never a sign of civilization except for an occasional cow or sheep, their havens nowhere in sight. Beauty, ruggedness, grandeur every where as far as the eye can see alternately changing and interchanging.

God surely must have looked with special favor upon America at the Creation.

I hope I captured a bit of what we saw with my camera. How I regret now that we didn't all take this trip together.

No, I couldn't go to church this Palm Sunday, but I attended Mass in a very special way – in the Almighty's vast and inspiring outdoor Cathedral.

Happy Easter and all our love,

Daddy

This poetic praise of the Almighty is a powerful example of dad's ability to express all aspects of his personality, in this case his non-religious spirituality.

— 74 —

SHIELDING HIS LOVED ONES

WRITING AN ENDING FOR dad's journey made me realize that for the last two years of his life he tried to shield us all from knowing the state of his health. Even mom was probably only partially aware of what dad knew about its seriousness. This is what I know now.

In late 1964 dad underwent a difficult surgery at a prestigious N.Y. City hospital after which his doctors assured him they "got it all." He had to have a lung removed, a drastic solution to what had originally appeared to be a single cancerous growth on his back. He never talked to us about the fact that his lifelong addiction to smoking might have caused the cancer that had already invaded his lungs. I visited dad in the hospital after that awful operation as often as I could and watched him slowly recover. But I was blind to his prognosis until much later.

Dad's letters to Doni from March to October 1965 reveal more than I ever heard him speak of and show how dad put a positive spin on everything.

> ***March 1965***
> *I am now improving steadily it seems, regaining strength each day. It sure has been a slow convalescence but I feel the worst is behind me (again God willing). I am now working part time mostly out of the house. I have regained a few of the pounds I lost and my appetite now is normal. In fact, I'm eating things I haven't touched for years, cake, custard, puddings, etc. But you know me and weight, sweetheart, I never did have very much.*
>
> *Five more pounds and I'll be o.k."*
>
> ***April 1965***
> *I love you with all my heart and I don't want you to worry about me any more – not one bit. Remember I may look young, but I've lived a long time and it is the young that should be everyone's concern.*
>
> *If I've learned one lesson from my unfortunate illnesses, it is that worry just doesn't do any good at all as attest the more than seven years after my heart attack when that vital organ was my constant concern. So be happy, have fun and take care of your health which is much more important to me than mine.*
>
> ***October 1965***
> *First of all, let me reassure you as to the state of my health. I am very well (not quite the guy I used to be), but unfortunately again back on the treadmill and working a bit too hard. But there doesn't seem to be anything I can do about it. It is compulsive and probably a form of insanity. Too late in life to go to a head shrinker or I might try one. But then again if I had nothing to do or even a little to do, I probably would die on the vine.*
>
> ***January 1966***
> *Do me a big favor – try not to worry about anything and try to get a little pleasure and happiness out of life and don't be a damn fool like your father was. I give you this admonition because I unfortunately see*

myself mirrored in you (not in looks, thank heavens) when it comes to that most troublesome temperament of ours which seems to give us no surcease whatever from constant worry and anxiety about everything and everybody. So please, listen to me; stop worrying, have fun, and take good care of yourself.

Doni's concern for dad's health was assuaged by dad optimistic letters, Bill was living at home so she experienced his recovery first hand. I lived only a few blocks away and saw dad once or twice a week. He hadn't looked himself for several years so his decline was not as apparent to me as it should have been. He still looked youthful and a nurse once accused him of dying his hair black; he hadn't.

Probably no one but mom was completely aware of the seriousness of the battle he was going through. Remember, dad was an amazing actor.

Mom never talked to us about what she went through in those dark times. I recently discovered a journal entry I made October 12,1966 which sheds a light on how difficult it was; she knew dad didn't want us to know. What could she do but respect his wishes?

My mother keeps calling to see how things are. This I feel is due to a lack of someone to talk to. She probably doesn't get too much of a reaction from dad who thinks so much about his illness. So I think she needs a companion in conversation. I really don't mind, but unfortunately there are times when things get out of hand around here and I'm too busy. This is too bad really because I would love to give her the time.

My casual reference to dad thinking about his illness reveals my own denial.

I was surprised to see how many major events happened in my life in the months leading up to dad's passing. In April 1966 Bill and I directed the musical, "The Sound of Music" at Holy Child Academy. We cast my daughters Denise, 9, and Diane, 7, as the youngest von Trapp children and invited mom and dad to the performance. For the first time, dad wasn't up to attending a show we were involved in. Nevertheless, it was another full circle for their actor grandfather.

The Von Trapp children as played by Diane and Denise Voigt, Pat Sexton, Pat Sudbay, Cassie Collins, Greg Cunnion and Kathy Stutz.

At this writing there are five Wolfe Cribari generations who have been bitten by the acting bug. Or is it genetic?

Second: Camille, Doni and Bill.

Third: Denise, Diane, Dana, Carla.

Fourth: Denise's two daughters, dad's great granddaughters, Christina Colangelo Beadle and Julie Colangelo Dore who performed in high school and direct theatrical productions in Westchester high schools. I'm not sure about dad's great grandsons: Stephen and Scott Lucas and Giles Rutson yet, I know they inherited dad's quick wit and charm.

The fifth, Denise's granddaughter Samantha Beadle, an acting veteran at ten, shows her acting skill in this picture as U. S. Supreme Court justice Ruth Bader Ginsburg. Nono would be so proud of Sammie *and* Mrs. Ginsberg. One of dad's proudest professional moments was when he was admitted to practice in front of the Supreme Court.

— 75 —

A DREAM DEFERRED: DAD AS COLLEGE PROFESSOR

DAD USED TO DREAM of becoming a college professor when he retired from his law practice. He even had a scenario worked out: he would teach at Brown University in New England and become an expert on the specific subject he taught, language, the arts, theater, public speaking.

When I discovered dad's 1940's speech on Education, I was saddened by the fact that he never had the chance to live out his dream. Karma? All three of his daughters and two of his great granddaughters are teachers.

> **The real values of education are not how much arithmetic you learn but the following. If you can learn to activate these virtues, if you can take from education these splendid attributes you will have accomplished much toward ensuring for yourselves a bright, happy and successful future when your days of education are at an end.**

1. CULTIVATE AN OPEN MIND.

You should learn to keep your mind open on every question until the evidence is all in. Education really teaches you this and all the characteristics I am about to mention; in our haste for book learning we completely overlook them.

It doesn't matter greatly what a person knows or how much he knows, the thing that separates an educated person from an uneducated one is "how he learned what he knows." It has been correctly said that about half of what a man learns in school/ college is of no use and that he forgets most of the other half.

However, this is not at all serious provided he acquired right habits of learning. If a person learns better in school or in college to keep his or her mind open to new facts, even though some new fact might be against his personal opinion, if he has got over being afraid to change his mind, no matter what it may cost him, personal pride, if he has got so he is not afraid to think on all sides of a question, if he has learned to hold back his judgment and not come to any conclusion at all until the evidence is all in, then that person will likely wake up some fine morning and find he is one of the most trusted citizens in his community and may be one of the greater human beings of his generation.

Unless you achieve open-mindedness you can never hope to be assumed truly educated. For notwithstanding the motto

"Knowledge is power," knowledge is not power unless you are willing to surrender your mind and heart completely to examine the reasons for your opinions. It is very easy to learn everything in your books and still be unable to apply what you have learned to better your own ideas.

2. ALWAYS LISTEN TO THE MAN WHO KNOWS.

Old John Crosby was the farmer in Johnson County. He won prizes for his hogs, corn, pumpkins, etc. However John ploughed, fed his cows, planted his crops was correct because he did it. It was the Crosby way and that was the last word.

Old Crosby scorned the "scientific fellers." He said that you couldn't teach farming in college. But John's son had gained a different notion from his high school principal. The principal inspired young John Crosby to go to the State Agricultural College. Old Crosby pooh poohed the idea.

For all I know old John Crosby may have gone to college for the next 20 years and may now be a professor of agriculture, but the biggest day in his education was the day when he opened his mind to listen to the voice of those who knew.

There is an extremely important point about education in this story that we should not overlook and that is that old Crosby already knew a great deal. His long practical experience had taught him many things worth knowing. He was not altogether wrong.

In many respects he was right. He was right when he said, "You can't make a farmer in college." You can't. Neither can you make a doctor or lawyer or engineer.

The best educational systems will never be able to put forth a youth equipped with both experience and academic training. It is only when the schools and practical man get together that we shall have the best farmers, lawyers, doctors, etc. That is why there are teachers teaching you. They combine the school training with experience and give you the benefit of both. If everybody could be put through old John Crosby's experience and listen to the person who knows, all would be so much further advanced.

3. NEVER LAUGH AT NEW IDEAS.

Education is after all not an assembling of facts in your head as much as it is a matter of the attitude of your mind. It's not so much the facts a man has lodged in his cranium but what he can do with his facts and what his facts do to him that determine whether or not he is educated.

4. RESEARCH WAYS OF GETTING ALONG WITH OTHER PEOPLE.

I have seen, sadly, many young men and women getting out of school and starting upon their business or professional careers hurt themselves by lack of tact or social judgment. I often think how wonderful it would be to have a special course at school for young boys and girls to teach good manners.

The ability to control yourself and get along with others is probably one of the greatest steps toward success in business, professions, etc.

5. CULTIVATE HABITS OF SUCCESS.

Read stories of successful people from history; they can guide us. These stories are always about a person who became interested in a specific aspect of life, applied him/herself, talked about nothing but success to himself /herself and ultimately became that success.

6. HAVE AN AMBITION TO FIT YOUR ABILITY.

Most young persons who have started their college education would like ten years from now to be lawyers, doctors. They frequently have not given the slightest thought as to whether they would like the work that has to be done in that occupation.

A large number of them get the idea they would like to be doctors and lawyers because these men go around town well dressed and have offices with names on the doors, etc. Every young person thinks it would be fine and grand to be such a person picturing himself as an important person without the slightest idea of the kind of life that person really leads or of the work that has to be done to get there.

Young people who have a clear understanding of their own abilities, a definite knowledge of what they can and cannot do, of what they like and don't like, these are the ones who exhibit distinct marks of education.

7. IT'S NEVER TOO LATE TO LEARN.

There is a deep-seated notion that you "can't teach an old dog new tricks" which prevents many people from doing big, happy things which they can and should do. It has been stated that age is a handicap after 45 years to learning anything you want or need to learn. I disagree. It is never too late to begin and the time to begin is today.

8. NEVER LOSE FAITH IN YOURSELF.

Your whole life should be guided by a picture of what you want yourself to be and education is the constant effort to make yourself better.

9. WHATEVER YOU PUT INTO LIFE YOU GET OUT OF IT.

If you put in poetry and music, you get them back; poverty gets poverty; wealth gets wealth; hate gets hate; love gets love; beauty get beauty. Learn to see beauty in everything and you will reap a priceless reward.

I hope every educator who reads dad's heartfelt, insightful speech will feel uplifted as a member of his/her noble profession, I know I did.

I'm sure of it, my father said so.

— 76 —

THE MOST PAINFUL DAY

I'VE BEEN AVOIDING THIS part of dad's story for six months. It's time…

The day he left us was a Sunday, December 11, 1966. Of course it was a Sunday, that was Cribari family day. Dad couldn't have been aware of what day it was, but I was. Every Sunday meant nana's house. Nana was only five years gone. Was dad going to join her so soon? He's too young. He can't. Stop it.

Fragmented thoughts bombarded my brain as I stood by the window of dad's hospital room that Sunday. Bill and I had been sitting with him for most of the afternoon. Here's what I wrote about those painful days right after I lived them.

> *In the vestibule of the mourning room or whatever you call those rooms… My ideas on the whole ritual of dying would fill several pages; however Jessica Mitford and Evelyn Waugh did it already and pretty well too. But who listened?*
>
> *A former client, a Damon Runyon figure, shades of Nathan Detroit, vowed that the best he could do now would be jump in front of the nearest train. I dare say this was the closest to my feelings at the time. I've always believed in the wisdom of simple folk.*

But it's really all a blur. My mind kept returning to the lone figure in the hospital bed. It was over now – the anguished glaze in his eyes replaced with serenity. The fear, that which he tried to hide from the four of us, was no more. He knew. He didn't want us to know he knew. It all makes sense now. It was part of what I want to say now.

That last day! A beautiful man, physically relegated to a shell of his former exquisiteness, deprived of its physical life, oxygen, struggling, struggling to regain a foothold, without it unable to further his climb.

It was true, the doctor was right. That mind, the center of all humanistic appreciation, was not to be totally destroyed, even by its unrelenting ravages. Maybe he willed it, maybe he wanted to save us from it! It's all part of what so many of us feel, felt, no, feel for him.

Once I broke down, concealed, I thought, by the pretense of staring out the window. ***"It's not the wake yet"*** *was the surprisingly strong retort I heard coming from the still sheeted man who was my father. No, who is my father. Who was, is everything I am and will be. That's it, you know, that's what eternity means. Oh no, I thought, is it possible as sick as he is, he still sees things.*

We left the hospital that Sunday night. I don't really recall why. He seemed peaceful enough, no real danger we presumed anyway. Anyway, what a cold word.

Maybe this time it's the end that creates the beginning. Anyway (there it is again) I have to deal with the end, get it over with.

It was after it was all over. People were arriving in droves in spite of the typical December slush, snow. They were saying things, tributes, I guess, I don't remember. Oh, there were a few, a brother tearfully suggested that since dad had gotten there ahead of us, heaven would be well organized and we could all expect royal welcomes and places proper to our standing! Don't say such things.

There is no heaven. Or is there? Please!!

A beautiful young nun consoled us with the thought that he, (where is he?) could never have survived a similar ordeal for one of us, my two sisters, me or my mother. That it was better this way.

Better not at all!

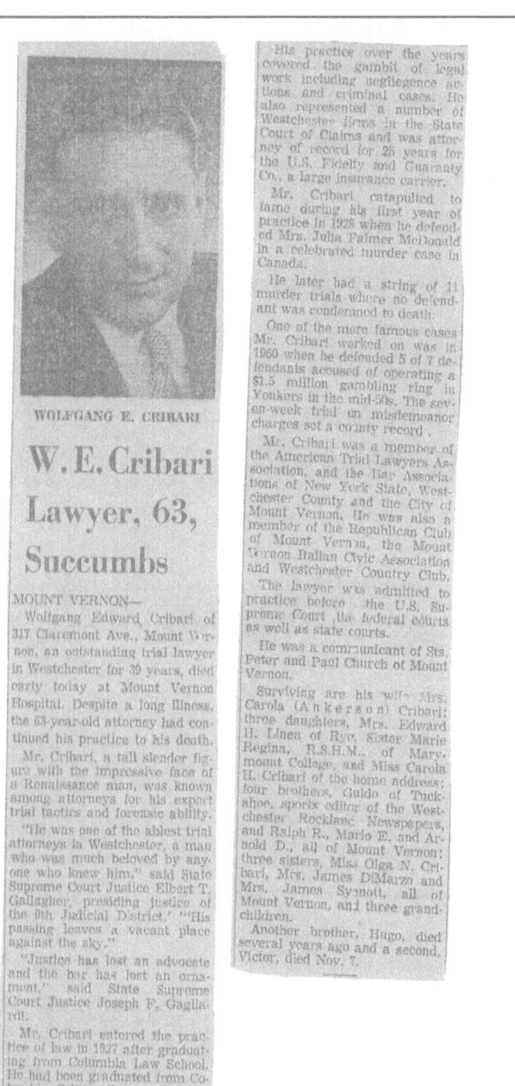

WOLFGANG E. CRIBARI

W. E. Cribari Lawyer, 63, Succumbs

MOUNT VERNON—

Wolfgang Edward Cribari of 317 Claremont Ave., Mount Vernon, an outstanding trial lawyer in Westchester for 39 years, died early today at Mount Vernon Hospital. Despite a long illness, the 63-year-old attorney had continued his practice to his death.

Mr. Cribari, a tall slender figure with the impressive face of a Renaissance man, was known among attorneys for his expert trial tactics and forensic ability.

"He was one of the ablest trial attorneys in Westchester, a man who was much beloved by anyone who knew him," said State Supreme Court Justice Elbert T. Gallagher, presiding justice of the 9th Judicial District.' "'His passing leaves a vacant place against the sky."

"Justice has lost an advocate and the bar has lost an ornament," said State Supreme Court Justice Joseph F. Gagliardi.

Mr. Cribari entered the practice of law in 1927 after graduating from Columbia Law School. He had been graduated from Columbia College three years earlier.

His practice over the years covered the gambit of legal work including negliegence actions and criminal cases. He also represented a number of Westchester firms in the State Court of Claims and was attorney of record for 25 years for the U.S. Fidelty and Guaranty Co., a large insurance carrier.

Mr. Cribari catapulted to fame during his first year of practice in 1928 when he defended Mrs. Julia Palmer McDonald in a celebrated murder case in Canada.

He later had a string of 11 murder trials where no defendant was condemned to death.

One of the more famous cases Mr. Cribari worked on was in 1960 when he defended 5 of 7 defendants accused of operating a $1.5 million gambling ring in Yonkers in the mid-50s. The seven-week trial on misdemeanor charges set a county record.

Mr. Cribari was a member of the American Trial Lawyers Association, and the Bar Associations of New York State, Westchester County and the City of Mount Vernon. He was also a member of the Republican Club of Mount Vernon, the Mount Vernon Italian Civic Association and Westchester Country Club.

The lawyer was admitted to practice before the U.S. Supreme Court, the federal courts as well as state courts.

He was a communicant of Sts. Peter and Paul Church of Mount Vernon.

Surviving are his wife Mrs. Carola (Ankerson) Cribari; three daughters, Mrs. Edward H. Linen of Rye, Sister Marie Regina, R.S.H.M., of Marymount College, and Miss Carola H. Cribari of the home address; four brothers, Guido of Tuckahoe, sports editor of the Westchester Rockland Newspapers, and Ralph R., Mario E. and Arnold D., all of Mount Vernon; three sisters, Miss Olga N. Cribari, Mrs. James DiMarzo and Mrs. James Synnott, all of Mount Vernon, and three grandchildren.

Another brother, Hugo, died several years ago and a second, Victor, died Nov. 7.

WESTCHESTER ROCKLAND NEWSPAPERS OBITUARY

MOUNT VERNON – December 12, 1966

Wolfgang Edward Cribari of 317 Claremont Avenue, an outstanding trial lawyer in Westchester for 39 years, died early today at Mount Vernon Hospital. Despite a long illness, the 63 year old attorney had continued his practice to his death.

Mr. Cribari, a tall, slender figure with the impressive face of a Renaissance man, was known among attorneys for his expert trial tactics and forensic ability.

"He was one of the ablest trial attorneys in Westchester, a man who was much beloved by anyone who knew him." Said State Supreme Coourt Justice Elbert T Gallagher, presiding justice of the 9th Judicial District. "His passing leaves a vacant place against the sky."

"Justice has lost an advocate and the bar has lost an ornament." Said State Supreme Court Justice Joseph F. Gagliardi.

Mr. Cribari entered the practice of law in 1927 after graduating from Columbia Law School. He had graduated from Columbia College three years earlier.

His practice over the years covered the gamut of legal work including negligence actions and criminal cases. He also represented a number of firms in the State Court of Claims and was attorney of record for 25 years for the U.S. Fidelity and Guaranty Company, a large insurance carrier.

Mr. Cribari catapulted to fame during his first year of practice when he defended Mrs. Julia Palmer McDonald in a celebrated murder case in Canada.

He later had a string of eleven murder trials where no defendant was condemned to death.

One of the more famous cases Mr. Cribari worked on was in 1960 when he defended 5 of 7 defendants accused of operating a $1.5 million gambling ring in Yonkers in the mid-50's The seven week trial on misdemeanor charges set a county record

Mr. Cribari was a member of the American Trial Lawyers Associatio and the Bar Associations of New York State, Westchester County and the City of Mount Vernon. He was also a member of the Republican Club of Mount Vernon, the Mount Vernon Italian Civic Association and Westchester Country Club.

The lawyer was admitted to practice before the U.S. Supreme Court, the federal courts as well as state courts.

He was a communicant of Sts. Peter and Paul Church of Mount Vernon.

Surviving are his wife Mrs. Carola (Ankerson) Cribari, three daughters Mrs. Edwin K. Linen of Rye, Sister Marie Regina, RSHM, of Marymount College, and Miss Carola H. Cribari of the home address; four brothers, Guido of Tuckahoe, sports editor of the Westchester Rockland Newspapers, and Ralph R., Mario E. and Arnold D., all of Mount Vernon, three sisters, Miss Olga N Cribari, Mrs James DiMarzo and Mrs James Synnott, all of Mount Vernon and three grandchildren.

Another brother, Hugo died several years ago and a second, Victor, died November 7.

WOLFGANG E. CRIBARI

Special to the New York Times
MOUNT VERNON, N.Y. Dec. 12.

Wolfgang E. Cribari, a lawyer in Westchester County since 1927, died of a heart ailment yesterday at Mount Vernon Hospital. He was 63 years old and lived at 317 Claremont Avenue.

Mr. Cribari, a graduate of the Columbia University Law School, had been counsel for several insurance companies. He was counsel for the defense in a dozen first-degree murder cases.

Surviving are his widow, the former Carola Ankerson; three daughters, Mrs. Edward K Linen, Sister Marie Regina of Marymount College and Miss Carola Cribari; four brothers, three sisters and three grandchildren.

— 77 —

TRIBUTES

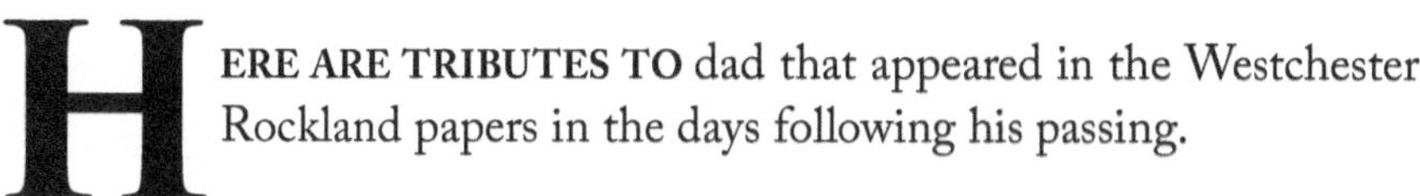

HERE ARE TRIBUTES TO dad that appeared in the Westchester Rockland papers in the days following his passing.

Tribute Paid To Cribari

December 16, 1966 Westchester Rockland Newspapers

Just days after dad's passing the Mount Vernon Common Council paid tribute to dad. Alderman Robert Cerchiara asked to read the Council's formal resolution which noted the sadness of the occasion.

These are Bob's words which were printed in the article:

> *A few days ago Wolfe Cribari, a lawyer who many jurists called one of the greatest trial lawyers this county has ever seen, a man whose dedication to the law was as big as his genius in the courtroom, an orator, envied by any man who has ever addressed a gathering of other men, a scholar intolerant only of those capable of more, a father, a husband, brother and friend with a tremendous capacity for love.*
>
> *He cradled me as an infant, advised me in my youth and counseled me as I began working toward my adult endeavors. I knew this man as I know few others. His dreams, illusions, victories, and defeats. I knew*

well this complex, humorous, fun-loving, intense giant.

The privileged intimacy, however, was not something earned for we were not contemporaries, but was something inherited from the man he is said to have loved most on earth, my father. My relationship prompted Wolfe to say upon my father's death, ***"I never again want a friend like that for fear of again suffering such a loss."***

I miss them both.

At the end of the meeting, one of the other alderman asked to read this column Guido had written for his weekly sports column. Dad would have loved Guido's word-pictures. His beloved younger brother had learned from the best.

Cribari Says...*My Hero*

He was only a utility infielder at Columbia University during baseball heyday.

But he was my hero.

He was of medium stature, but to me he was a physical and mental giant.

He was full of love, patience. humility and understanding.

He was the kind of son every mother should have, and the kind of brother every brother would like to be.

He had achieved greatness in his profession, and if his profession had honored its best through some sort of All-America recognition, he would have been a unanimous selection.

He was highly regarded and sincerely respected, but success never upset his equilibrium.

He always found time for the little man.

He was a composite of the old country doctor, the kindly judge, and the lovable man down the street quick to offer a helping hand, with recompense unthinkable.

He generated warmth from deep within his frail body and from a pair of warm friendly eyes that always seemed to say "Welcome!"

He loved all sports and he was a hero worshiper of the highest order.

Oh, how he loved to brag about the good ol' football days at Columbia and the gridiron exploits of such notables as Walter Koppisch, Ralph Hewitt, Cliff Montgomery and others.

He played tennis and golf during his younger days, and like everything he did, he played them well.

But his favorite was bocci, the Italian version of lawn bowling. He and a few of his friends built a bocci court some years ago, and every Saturday they gathered just for the sport of it. It was a happy talk-a-thon each Saturday. And, brother, could he talk.

Yes, he was only a utility infielder at Columbia. But to me he was the greatest hero of all.

He was my dear brother.

He died early yesterday and with him died a precious piece of a family which knew only the full measure of his love and devotion.

WESTCHESTER BAR HOLDS SERVICE FOR W.E. CRIBARI

This article appeared in the Westchester Gannett newspapers on January 4, 1967, two weeks after dad's passing. The photo was taken the same day.

Dad would have been so proud of mom.

The Westchester Bar Association held memorial services yesterday for the late Wolfgang E. Cribari, an outstanding Westchester trial lawyer who died last month.

Speaking at the services were Daniel Danziger of White Plains, Anthony J. Caputo of Bronxville, and George Scapolito of Mount Vernon, a law partner of Mr. Cribari.

Besides the three attorneys, State Supreme Court Justice Elbert T. Gallagher, who presided at the services, also spoke.

Andrew J. Barnes, former White Plains City Judge, conducted the services for the bar association at the courthouse.

About 250, including Mr. Cribari's family, attended.

— 78 —

CLOSURE A HALF CENTURY LATER

AFTER DAD'S FUNERAL AND burial we left him in a small temporary mausoleum at the cemetery because his permanent place wasn't ready. No lowering of the coffin, thank the lord. I had to face my three little girls every night and found myself using whatever emotional strength I had to protect them from my terrible angst. My daughters recently told me it was the first time they saw me cry. They also remember my trying to explain what had happened. One of the girls said she hid under a table in the living room the day I cried. A pure child instinct.

I do remember this. Our family was bombarded with hundreds of letters, mass cards, and notes. A primitive anger kicked in while I read through 20-30 religious plenary indulgence cards. Well-meaning friends and relatives had enrolled dad in a religious program that offered $100. Plenary indulgence cards guaranteeing the soul's release from purgatory. I pictured dad's soul being released from purgatory with the first $100. Indulgence then having to repeat the process until all the indulgences were used up. Really, I did.

On the other hand, I can understand why mom kept this sympathy note. Mrs. Tompkins had played a major part in dad's early love for acting and theater.

December fifteenth '66

Dear Carola,

We have just received a clipping from Claire (you remember our Claire?) telling of Wolf's untimely death. We were all so saddened by it. The Tompkins were so fond of Wolfe and so proud of him. We send you our deepest sympathy.

Not knowing Rose's address, would you be kind enough to give her the enclosed note? Thank you.

Very sincerely,

Florence Tompkins

DONI'S POEMS FOR DAD

Do you know that you hold
In the palm of your lovely hand
my heart
So that all the world can see the pieces
And do you know that spring will come again
because of you
And the stars will laugh again
And the sky will sing
Because you are … and always are
And that beats all death
all deaths and dying.

If ever there were eyes or smile
Like yours, my sweet dad
Then surely no land of silence or darkness
Could separate you
A whole so integral
So warm…unique
So always heart
Ah, forgive my weak continuation of you
Which aches so deeply to have the world
Remember.

I miss you, plain and simple, dad
Who left no monument or book behind
But only the imprint
of your once and gentle
Heart
So inseparable from all I love
Entwined in all my world which goes on
Now without you…but can't forget…
nor can ignore your noble life.

DECEMBER 15, 1966: Thoughts from my journal

This is one day removed from a day I had been dreading for the past two years – a day I fully expected to be the most painful day in my entire life – my father's funeral. How can such a thing have come about so completely opposite?

My mother is the answer.

I have never been a witness to such strength encased in such a frail seemingly helpless body. She was able to hold us all up. She was so admirable I could only suppose God allowed daddy to see such a sight – sufficient reward for a job well done. What a difference from the despairing, hopeless attitudes I had always been a party to at other such events.

I cannot express the sympathy and tenderness she provokes in us all, but I cannot help but marvel at such a person, a person I have never seen before even though she is my mother.

The merciful death of daddy has inspired beautiful words from relative strangers to deeply involved members of his family. He was such a man to all of us. It was, at the same time, wonderful and awesome to have such a man as a father.

There was a quality – that unknown appeal that people tried to express – that will never cease to exist for us all. Maybe that is why it is not as difficult as I expected at this point.

He will always be with us, always. There is no possibility that his existence will cease – there is a slight indication of eternity in the feeling I hold here. He has gone ahead to a place where we will all meet someday.

At dad's bedside, Father Scanlon's gentle words to dad who was surrounded by his daughters and nurses, "Blessed art thou amongst women. **It must be so.**

We can do nothing to bring him back to us – even though he loved all of us and would want nothing but to remain with us for many, many more years. None of us would wish him back to the life he had recently. We can not even imagine another day such as Sunday was for him – I know it would get nothing but worse. God did not allow him to suffer any more. God ***was*** *good.*

It seemed that I would sense a big part of me had been torn away, but it is instead a big part of him will remain with me forever.

It is important that the girls know when they are grown how people felt about him – how many people said he didn't have an enemy in the world. What an incredible thing to be able to say about someone.

The tribute to him at the wake Tuesday night was unbelievable. There were so many people that needed comforting from my mother. There were so many shocked faces. It was so comforting to know that our feelings about dad were repeated and repeated by others.

Adam P. telling my mother she was the best thing that happened to dad – a fitting tribute to the person he cared about most. Mario saying that in one way we could always think that heaven will be well organized by the time we all arrive.

The stunned expressions of people that could not believe something had finally defeated his indomitable will. They do not know that he was not defeated - he was willing and ready to go on to what I know is a more peaceful, more trouble-free existence. It is certain to me that all the trials and tribulations he endured through those he loved best are now just forgotten memories.

He was so unselfish – we were all so hard on him at times. Surely there is a compensation somewhere.

I shall have a picture of his meager face in profile as he rested in the hospital bed Sunday afternoon – in direct and perfect contrast to Bill as she sat by him in the chair. I shall see his sensitive, beautiful hands in repose in the most relaxed position on the sheets of the bed.

Hands…thank God, that were never ravaged by the disease that was so cruel to him. I shall try to forget the frustration of his last hours, the frustration of a keen and alert mind struggling against the blessed and slowly increasing loss of reality we prayed for.

In the weeks, months, years to come I want to remember the countless hours and days, the laughter we all shared. The way we really should remember him.

A dynamic, magnetic man that should never have died.

A kind, sensitive soul that only wanted happiness and the best for his family who can rightly feel the loss – a family who maybe never knew him until now.

How unworthy they were to share in his greatness.

We know that he would not have wanted us to grieve and grieve but I know he wants us to think of him often with faith in what he meant and will continue to mean.

I am not aware of what has come about to the fullest extent, but I know he is gone. (His body is gone.) I will continue in the belief that such a man's spirit, will, soul, will never be gone from us.

I could not even say goodbye. I will only admit his body, what he existed in, is apart from us. He will never, ever, be fully apart from us. It is not possible.

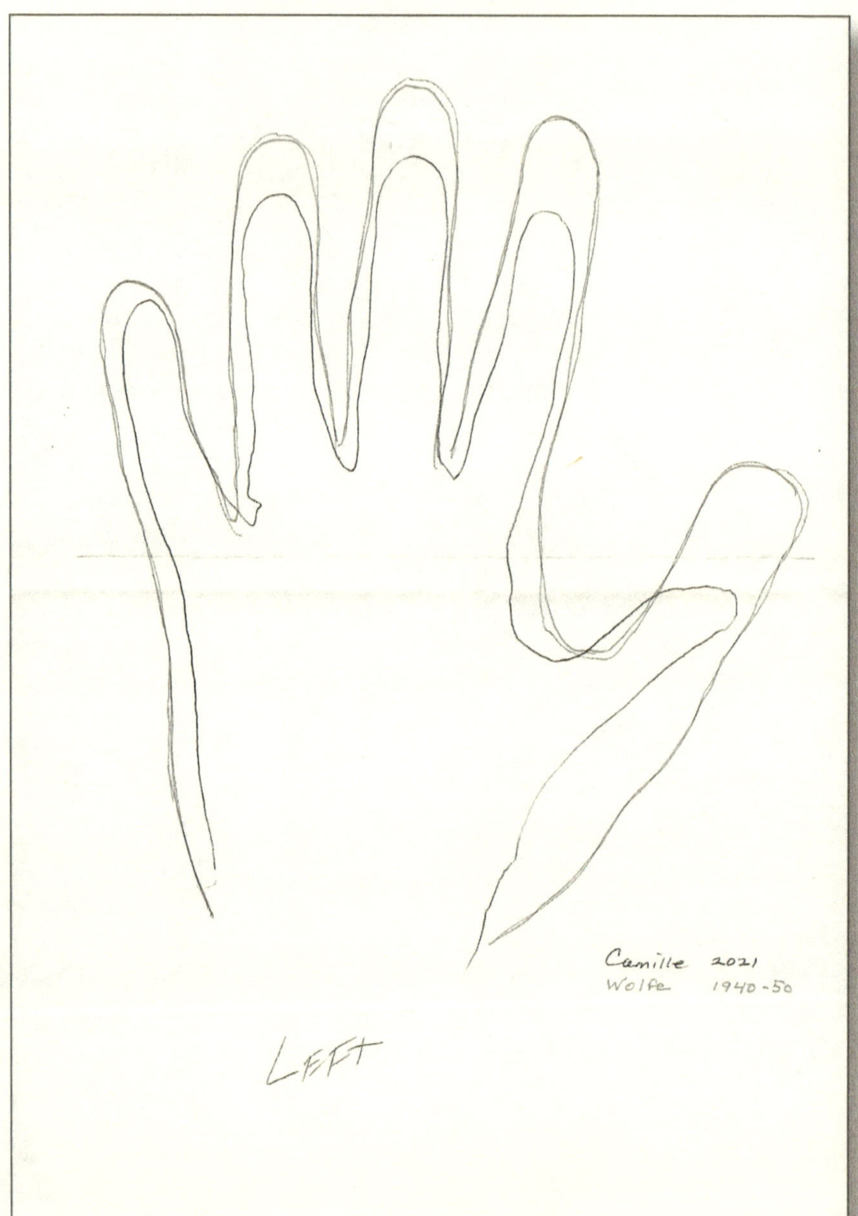
Camille 2021
Wolfe 1940-50
LEFT

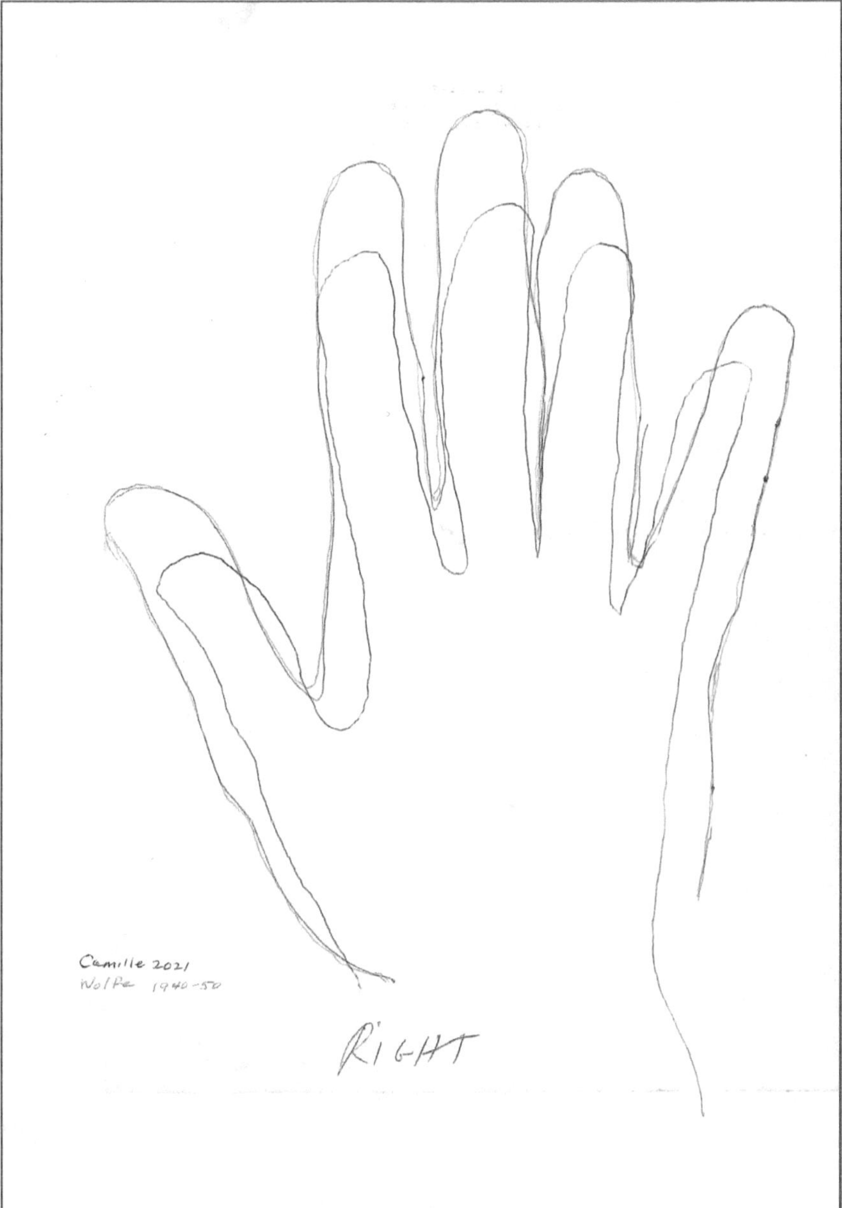
Camille 2021
Wolfe 1940-50
RIGHT

IN MY FATHER'S HANDS... PERSONALITY TRAITS

To distract myself from the inevitable ending of dad's story, I did research on how hands reveal personality traits. Dad's hands were not only the core of his dynamic self-expression, they were simply beautiful! Happily, he actually left tracings of both his hands. I compared them to mine and saw a clear similarity.

I made copies of his original tracings then I put my left hand over dad's and traced it in pencil. Then I asked Lou to help me repeat the process for the right.

Then I googled "*Shape of hand and fingers psychology*" and discovered the following dad-related traits. (Try doing it for yourself, it's fun!)

> *If the index finger is shorter than the ring finger, you have higher verbal and physical aggression, a better sense of direction and superb athletic ability.*
>
> *If the nails are almond shape, you are a gentle person and oozing with creativity.*
>
> *If thumb is at an obtuse angle you are a natural leader and like to control. But you are also calm, meditative and creative.*

If the pinky is slightly shorter than the uppermost joint of your ring finger,

(a) you don't hold a grudge
(b) you are uncomfortable with anything new
(c) you respect other's opinions
(d) you can be bossy
(e) you keep problems to yourself
(f) you want others to depend on you

If the tops of your fingers are round-shaped you wish to be at peace with others and fear disapproval.

If the gaps between your fingers are wide apart you are independent fond of experiments.

If the ring and middle finger are close to each other you tend to live up to social expectations and follow the rules.

By the way, most of the traits described are consistent with dad's personality.

— ACKNOWLEDGEMENTS —

MY GIFTED, LOVING HUSBAND, Lou Del Bianco, for inspiration, patience, and unequivocal support. You are a son-in-law dad would have embraced and cherished.

My sisters, Donna Cribari and Carola Cribari for priceless anecdotes, memories, and wonderful hours spent in heartfelt, artistic collaboration.

My children, Denise Colangelo, Diane Lucas and Dana Rutson, for inspiring me, listening, reading and supporting my "never-too-late" project.

My grandchildren, Christina Colangelo Beadle, Julie Colangelo Dore, Stephen Lucas, Scott Lucas, Giles Rutson who I hope will become storytellers and pay it forward.

Cribari cousins who happily contributed first hand accounts that reveal why dad deserves this long overdue tribute : Arnold Cribari, Stephen Cribari, Kathleen DePasquale, Maryann Di Marzo, James Wolfe DiMarzo, Virginia Ruth Cribari King.

Friends and colleagues who have taken time to read my first ever full length memoir/biography and provide honest, helpful feedback: Mary Edwards, Sue Covino, Janet Davis.

James Woosley of Free Agent Press, for editorial suggestions, formatting, and cover design.

Alex Fidelibus, Art of English Website update advice and expertise.

Art of English ESL students who remind me of the formidable challenges that faced my own immigrant family as they face theirs.

— ABOUT THE AUTHOR —

Camille Cribari Linen has been writing in one form or another since she had her first real job as a newspaper reporter for the Mount Vernon Daily Argus when she was just out of high school. She is a graduate of Marymount and Iona Colleges. The variety of her writings range from a full length musical, *Thomas J.*, for the Bicentennial to English language curricula for NYS Adult Literacy and Interact publishers. Camille was honored by the Westchester Arts Council as "one of 20 women making history in the arts."

Camille and her husband Lou Del Bianco, live in Port Chester, N.Y.

To learn more and for exclusive audio and video recordings of scenes from Wolfe's life, visit:

ArtofEnglish.net